Learning Julia

Build high-performance applications for scientific computing

Anshul Joshi
Rahul Lakhanpal

BIRMINGHAM - MUMBAI

Learning Julia

First published: November 2017

Production reference: 1221117

Published by Packt Publishing Ltd.
Livery Place
35 Livery Street
Birmingham
B3 2PB, UK.

ISBN 978-1-78588-327-9

www.packtpub.com

Credits

Authors
Anshul Joshi
Rahul Lakhanpal

Reviewer
Nicholas Paul

Commissioning Editor
Kunal Parikh

Acquisition Editor
Denim Pinto

Content Development Editor
Rohit Kumar Singh

Technical Editor
Ketan Kamble

Copy Editor
Safis Editing

Project Coordinator
Vaidehi Sawant

Proofreader
Safis Editing

Indexer
Francy Puthiry

Graphics
Jason Monteiro

Production Coordinator
Nilesh Mohite

About the Authors

Anshul Joshi is a data scientist with experience in recommendation systems, predictive modeling, neural networks, and high performance computing. His research interests encompass deep learning, artificial intelligence, and computational physics. Most of the time, he can be caught exploring GitHub or trying anything new he can get his hands on. He blogs at `https://anshuljoshi.com/`.

I'd like to thank my parents, who have been really supportive through this whole journey, and my professors and my friends, who were very understanding. A big thanks to the Julia community, especially, Dr. Viral Shah. These people are amazing and are the rock stars of our generation.
I would also like to thank Packt Publishing, the editors, coauthor, and my friend Rahul Lakhanpal, and the reviewer of the book, Nicholas Paul, who helped us throughout.

Rahul Lakhanpal is a technology and open source enthusiast. With diversified skills including systems engineering, web development, the cloud, and big data, he is language-agnostic and a firm believer in using the best tools and the right language for a particular job.

Rahul is an active contributor to various community portals and loves to solve challenging real-world problems in his leisure time. He is active on Twitter and blogs at `http://rahullakhanpal.in/`.

I 'd like to thank my parents whose blessings kept me motivated, my wife, who was very supportive during the time I was writing the book and made sure that I was consistent in my routine, and to my younger brother, who continues to inspire me.
I will also like to thank Anshul Joshi for introducing me to the language, the whole Julia community, and finally to everyone at Packt who made this contribution a reality.

About the Reviewer

Nicholas Paul is a computer science graduate student studying intelligent systems and machine learning. He is involved in the campus as a tutor, research assistant, math club president, and captain of the autonomous vehicle development team. He has several years of experience using Julia for projects ranging anywhere from large-scale social media data mining and analysis to command-line interfaces and text editors. He is currently writing an open source learning platform for RobotOS for the students of his university, writing research papers focused on computer vision and deep leaning, and developing open source esoteric programming languages.

www.PacktPub.com

For support files and downloads related to your book, please visit www.PacktPub.com. Did you know that Packt offers eBook versions of every book published, with PDF and ePub files available? You can upgrade to the eBook version at www.PacktPub.com and as a print book customer, you are entitled to a discount on the eBook copy. Get in touch with us at service@packtpub.com for more details. At www.PacktPub.com, you can also read a collection of free technical articles, sign up for a range of free newsletters and receive exclusive discounts and offers on Packt books and eBooks.

https://www.packtpub.com/mapt

Get the most in-demand software skills with Mapt. Mapt gives you full access to all Packt books and video courses, as well as industry-leading tools to help you plan your personal development and advance your career.

Why subscribe?

- Fully searchable across every book published by Packt
- Copy and paste, print, and bookmark content
- On demand and accessible via a web browser

Customer Feedback

Thanks for purchasing this Packt book. At Packt, quality is at the heart of our editorial process. To help us improve, please leave us an honest review on this book's Amazon page at `https://www.amazon.com/dp/1785883275`.

If you'd like to join our team of regular reviewers, you can e-mail us at `customerreviews@packtpub.com`. We award our regular reviewers with free eBooks and videos in exchange for their valuable feedback. Help us be relentless in improving our products!

Table of Contents

Preface

Julia is a high-level, high-performance, dynamic programming language for numerical computing. It offers a unique combination of performance and productivity that promises to change scientific computing and programming. Julia was created to solve the dilemma between high-level, slow code and fast but low-level code, and the necessity to use both to achieve high-performance. It also puts performance center stage, achieving C-like execution speed and excellent applications in multicore, GPU, and cloud computing.

This book demonstrates the basics of Julia along with some data structures and testing tools that will give you enough material to get started with the language from an application standpoint. You will learn and take advantage of Julia while building applications with complex numerical and scientific computations. Through the journey of this book, you will explore the technical aspects of Julia and its potential when it comes to speed and data processing. Also, you will learn to write efficient and high quality code in Julia.

What this book covers

Chapter 1, *Understanding Julia's Ecosystem*, describes the steps needed to set up the Julia ecosystem. It will also help to understand how the packages are downloaded, installed, updated, and removed. This chapter will also briefly introduce the features of Julia that we will be studying in detail in further chapters.

Chapter 2, *Programming Concepts with Julia*, gives an overview of the basic syntax of Julia and the programming concepts to get you up and running. This will explain concepts by giving examples of basic programming problems.

Chapter 3, *Functions in Julia*, takes you through creating functions in Julia. It will explain the importance of functions and best practices of function creation. Various types of functions will also be explained in this chapter.

Chapter 4, *Understanding Types and Dispatch*, explains in detail the type concept of Julia and how it is able to achieve the performance of statically typed languages. It will also explain powerful techniques to exploit the multiple dispatch provided by Julia.

Chapter 5, *Working with Control Flow*, explains how to structure the Julia program and different control structures to organize the execution of the code.

Chapter 6, *Interoperability and Metaprogramming*, explains how Julia provides different ways to interact with the operating system and other languages. Also, this chapter will explain expressions and macros.

Chapter 7, *Numerical and Scientific Computation with Julia*, explains what makes Julia suitable for numerical and scientific computing and the related features that Julia provides.

Chapter 8, *Data Visualization and Graphics*, explains with different examples the various sophisticated packages and methods to create beautiful visualizations in Julia.

Chapter 9, *Connecting with Databases*, deals with the interaction of Julia with databases. Most real-world applications use a database in the backend. It is important to understand how Julia interacts with different types of databases.

Chapter 10, *Julia's Internals*, provides details and explanations about the intricacies of Julia. It will also explain the standard packages available and networking with Julia. This chapter will also explain the process of creating a package in Julia and publishing it.

What you need for this book

To execute the instructions and code in this book, you need to have a system with Julia installed on it. Detailed steps are given at the relevant instances in the book.

Who this book is for

This book allows existing programmers, statisticians, and data scientists to learn Julia and benefit from it while building applications with complex numerical and scientific computations. Basic knowledge of mathematics is needed to understand the various methods that will be used or created in the book to exploit the capabilities for which Julia is made.

Conventions

In this book, you will find a number of text styles that distinguish between different kinds of information. Here are some examples of these styles and an explanation of their meaning.

All recipes codes are written inside a numbered bullet and follow the following style:

```
F(Stat_0) = Stat_n(Stat_n-1(...(Stat_1(Stat_0)))) = Stat_n
```

Code words in text, HTML tags, database table names, folder names, filenames, file extensions, and pathnames are shown as follows: "The Stat refers to a statement and Stat_0, Stat_1, Stat_2, ... Stat_n are the *n* number of statements."

Any command-line input or output is written as follows:

```
$ julia -e 'println("Hello World")'
Hello World
```

 Warnings or important notes appear like this.

 Tips and tricks appear like this.

Reader feedback

Feedback from our readers is always welcome. Let us know what you think about this book-what you liked or disliked. Reader feedback is important for us as it helps us develop titles that you will really get the most out of. To send us general feedback, simply e-mail feedback@packtpub.com, and mention the book's title in the subject of your message. If there is a topic that you have expertise in and you are interested in either writing or contributing to a book, see our author guide at www.packtpub.com/authors.

Downloading the example code

You can download the example code files for this book from your account at http://www.packtpub.com. If you purchased this book elsewhere, you can visit http://www.packtpub.com/support and register to have the files e-mailed directly to you. You can download the code files by following these steps:

1. Log in or register to our website using your e-mail address and password.
2. Hover the mouse pointer on the **SUPPORT** tab at the top.
3. Click on **Code Downloads & Errata**.
4. Enter the name of the book in the **Search** box.

5. Select the book for which you're looking to download the code files.
6. Choose from the drop-down menu where you purchased this book from.
7. Click on **Code Download**.

Once the file is downloaded, please make sure that you unzip or extract the folder using the latest version of:

- WinRAR / 7-Zip for Windows
- Zipeg / iZip / UnRarX for Mac
- 7-Zip / PeaZip for Linux

The code bundle for the book is also hosted on GitHub at https://github.com/ PacktPublishing/Learning-Julia. We also have other code bundles from our rich catalog of books and videos available at https://github.com/PacktPublishing/. Check them out!

Downloading the color images of this book

We also provide you with a PDF file that has color images of the screenshots/diagrams used in this book. The color images will help you better understand the changes in the output. You can download this file from https://www.packtpub.com/sites/default/files/ downloads/Learning-Julia_ColorImages.pdf.

Errata

Although we have taken every care to ensure the accuracy of our content, mistakes do happen. If you find a mistake in one of our books-maybe a mistake in the text or the code-we would be grateful if you could report this to us. By doing so, you can save other readers from frustration and help us improve subsequent versions of this book. If you find any errata, please report them by visiting http://www.packtpub.com/submit-errata, selecting your book, clicking on the **Errata Submission Form** link, and entering the details of your errata. Once your errata are verified, your submission will be accepted and the errata will be uploaded to our website or added to any list of existing errata under the Errata section of that title. To view the previously submitted errata, go to https://www.packtpub.com/ books/content/support and enter the name of the book in the search field. The required information will appear under the **Errata** section.

Piracy

Piracy of copyrighted material on the Internet is an ongoing problem across all media. At Packt, we take the protection of our copyright and licenses very seriously. If you come across any illegal copies of our works in any form on the Internet, please provide us with the location address or website name immediately so that we can pursue a remedy. Please contact us at `copyright@packtpub.com` with a link to the suspected pirated material. We appreciate your help in protecting our authors and our ability to bring you valuable content.

Questions

If you have a problem with any aspect of this book, you can contact us at `questions@packtpub.com`, and we will do our best to address the problem.

1
Understanding Julia's Ecosystem

Julia is a new programming language compared to other existing popular programming languages. Julia was presented publicly to the world and became open source in February of 2012. It all started in 2009, when three developers—Viral Shah, Stefan Karpinski, and Jeff Bezanson at the **Massachusetts Institute of Technology** (**MIT**), under the supervision of Professor Alan Edelman in the Applied Computing group—started working on a project. This lead to Julia. All of the principal developers are still actively involved with the **JuliaLang**. They are committed not just to the core language but to the different libraries that have evolved in its ecosystem. Julia is based on solid principles, which we will learn throughout the book. It is becoming more famous day by day, continuously gaining in the ranks of the TIOBE index (currently at 43), and gaining traction on Stack Overflow. Researchers are attracted to it, especially those from a scientific computing background.

Anyone can check the source code, which is available on GitHub (`https://github.com/JuliaLang/julia`). The current release at the time of writing this book is 0.6 with 633 contributors, 39,010 commits, and 9,398 stars on GitHub. Most of the core is written in Julia itself and there are a few chunks of code in C/C++, Lisp, and Scheme.

This chapter will take you through the installation and a basic understanding of all the necessary components of Julia. This chapter covers the following topics:

- What makes Julia unique?
- Installing Julia
- Julia's importance in data science
- Using REPL
- Using Jupyter Notebook

- What is Juno?
- Package management
- A brief about multiple dispatch
- Understanding LLVM and JIT

What makes Julia unique?

Scientific computing requires the highest computing requirements. Over the years, the scientific community has used dynamic languages, which are comparatively much slower, to build their applications. A major reason for this is that applications are generally developed by physicists, biologists, financial experts, and other domain experts who, despite having experience with programming, are not seasoned developers. These experts always prefer dynamic languages over statically typed languages, which could have given them better performance, simply because they ease development and readability. However, there are now special packages to improve the performance of the code, such as Numba for Python. As the compiler techniques and language design has advanced, it is now possible to eliminate the trade-off between performance and dynamic prototyping. The requirement was to build a language, that is easy to read and code in, like Python, which is a dynamic language and gives the performance of C, which is a statically typed language. In 2012, a new language emerged—Julia. It is a general purpose programming language highly suited for scientific and technical computing. Julia's performance is comparable to C/C++ measured on the different benchmarks available on the JuliaLang's homepage and simultaneously provides an environment that can be used effectively for prototyping, like Python. Julia is able to achieve such performance because of its design and **Low Level Virtual Machine** (**LLVM**)-based **just-in-time** (**JIT**) compiler. These enable it to approach the performance of C and Fortran. We will be reading more about LLVM and JIT at the end of the chapter. The following quote is from the development team of Julia—the gist of why Julia was created (source: `https://julialang.org/blog/2012/02/why-we-created-julia`):

> *We are greedy: we want more. We want a language that's open source, with a liberal license. We want the speed of C with the dynamism of Ruby. We want a language that's homoiconic, with true macros like Lisp, but with obvious, familiar mathematical notation like MATLAB. We want something as usable for general programming as Python, as easy for statistics as R, as natural for string processing as Perl, as powerful for linear algebra as MATLAB, as good at gluing programs together as the shell. Something that is dirt simple to learn, yet keeps the most serious hackers happy. We want it interactive and we want it compiled. (Did we mention it should be as fast as C?)*

Julia is highly influenced by Python because of its readability and rapid prototyping capabilities, by R because of the support it gives to mathematical and statistical operations, by MATLAB (also GNU Octave) because of the vectorized numerical functions, especially matrices, and by some other languages too. Some of these languages have been in existence for more than 20 years now. Julia borrows ideologies from many of these languages and tries to bring the best of all these worlds together, and quietly succeeds too!

Features and advantages of Julia

Julia is really good at scientific computing but is not restricted to just that, as it can also be used for web and general purpose programming. Julia's development team aims to create a remarkable and previously unseen combination of power and efficiency in one single language without compromising ease of use. Most of Julia's core is implemented in Julia. Julia's parser is written in Scheme. Julia's efficient and cross-platform I/O is provided by the `libuv` of Node.js.

Some of Julia's features are mentioned as follows:

- It is designed for distributed and parallel computation.
- Julia provides an extensive library of mathematical functions with great numerical accuracy.
- Julia gives the functionality of multiple dispatch. It will be explained in detail in coming chapters. Multiple dispatch refers to using many combinations of argument types to define function behaviors. Julia provides efficient, specialized, and automatic generation of code for different argument types.
- The `Pycall` package enables Julia to call Python functions in its code and MATLAB packages using the `MATLAB.jl` package. Functions and libraries written in C can also be called directly without any need for APIs or wrappers.
- Julia provides powerful shell-like capabilities for managing other processes in the system.
- Unlike other languages, user-defined types in Julia are compact and quite fast as built-ins.
- Scientific computations makes great use of vectorized code to gain performance benefits. Julia eliminates the need to vectorize code to gain performance. De-vectorized code written in Julia can be as fast as the vectorized code.
- It uses lightweight *green* threading, also known as tasks or coroutines, cooperative multitasking, or one-shot continuations.
- Julia has a powerful type system. The conversions provided are elegant and extensible.

- It has efficient support for Unicode.
- It has facilities for metaprogramming and Lisp-like macros.
- It has a built-in package manager (Pkg).
- It's free and open source with an MIT license.

Installing Julia

As mentioned earlier, Julia is open source and is available for free. It can be downloaded from the website at http://julialang.org/downloads/.

The website has links to documentation, tutorials, learning, videos, and examples. The documentation can be downloaded in popular formats, as shown in the following screenshot:

Julia (command line version)			
Windows Self-Extracting Archive (.exe)	32-bit		64-bit
macOS Package (.dmg)		10.7+ 64-bit	
Generic Linux binaries	32-bit (X86) (GPG)		64-bit (X86) (GPG)
Linux builds for other architectures	ARMv7 32-bit hard float (GPG)		PowerPC 64 little endian (GPG)
Source	Tarball (GPG)	Tarball with dependencies (GPG)	GitHub

It is highly recommended to use the generic binaries for Linux provided on the julialang.org website.

As Ubuntu and Fedora are widely used Linux distributions, a few developers were kind enough to make the installation on these distributions easier by providing it through package manager. We will go through them in the following sections.

Julia on Ubuntu (Linux)

Ubuntu and its derived distributions are one of the most famous Linux distributions. Julia's deb packages (self-extracting binaries) are available on the website of JuliaLang, mentioned earlier. These are available for both 32-bit and 64-bit distributions. One can also add **Personal Package Archive** (**PPA**), which is treated as an apt repository to build and publish Ubuntu source packages. In the Terminal, type the following commands:

```
$ sudo apt-get add-repository ppa:staticfloat/juliareleases
$ sudo apt-get update
```

This adds the PPA and updates the package index in the repository. Now install Julia using the following command:

```
$ sudo apt-get install Julia
```

The installation is complete. To check whether the installation is successful in the Terminal, type the following:

```
$ julia --version
```

This gives the installed Julia's version:

```
$ julia version 0.5.0
```

To uninstall Julia, simply use `apt` to remove it:

```
$ sudo apt-get remove julia
```

Julia on Fedora/CentOS/Red Hat (Linux)

For Fedora/RHEL/CentOS or distributions based on them, enable the EPEL repository for your distribution version. Then, click on the link provided. Enable Julia's repository using the following:

```
$ dnf copr enable nalimilan/julia
```

Or copy the relevant `.repo` file available at:

```
/etc/yum.repos.d/
```

Finally, in the Terminal type the following:

```
$ yum install julia
```

Julia on Windows

Go to the Julia download page (`https://julialang.org/downloads/`) and get the `.exe` file provided according to your system's architecture (32-bit/64-bit). The architecture can be found on the property settings of the computer. If it is amd64 or x86_64, then go for 64-bit binary (`.exe`), otherwise go for 32-bit binary. Julia is installed on Windows by running the downloaded `.exe` file, which will extract Julia into a folder. Inside this folder is a batch file called `julia.exe`, which can be used to start the Julia console.

Julia on Mac

Users with macOS need to click on the downloaded `.dmg` file to run the disk image. After that, drag the app icon into the `Applications` folder. It may prompt you to ask if you want to continue, as the source has been downloaded from the internet and so is not considered secure. Click on **Continue** if it was downloaded from the official Julia language website. Julia can also be installed using `Homebrew` on a Mac, as follows:

```
$ brew update
$ brew tap staticfloat/julia
$ brew install julia
```

The installation is complete. To check whether the installation is successful in the Terminal, type the following:

```
$ julia --version
```

This gives you the Julia version installed.

Building from source

Building from source could be challenging for beginners. We assume that you are on Linux (Ubuntu) right now and are building from source. This provides the latest build of Julia, which may not be completely stable. Perform the following steps to build Julia from source:

- On the downloads page of the Julia website, download the source. You can choose Tarball or GitHub. It is recommended to use GitHub. To clone the repo, GitHub must be installed on the machine. Otherwise, choose **Download as ZIP**. Here is the link: `https://github.com/JuliaLang/julia.git`.
- To build Julia, it requires various compilers: g++, gfortran, and m4. We need to install them first, if not installed already, using the `$ sudo apt-get install gfortran g++ m4` command.
- Traverse inside the Julia directory and start the make process, using the following command:

```
$ cd julia
$ make
```

- On a successful build, Julia can be started up with the `./julia` command.
- If you used GitHub to download the source, you can stay up to date by compiling the newest version using the following commands:

```
$ git pull
$ make clean
$ make
```

Understanding the directory structure of Julia's source

Building from source on Windows and macOS is also straightforward. It can be found at `https://github.com/juliaLang/julia/`.

Julia's source stack

Let's have a look at the directories and their content:

Directory	Contents
base/	Julia's standard library
contrib/	Miscellaneous set of scripts, configuration files
deps/	External dependencies
doc/src/manual	Source for user manual
doc/src/stdlib	Source for standard library function help text
examples/	Example Julia programs

`src/`	Source for Julia's language core
`test/`	Test suits
`test/perf`	Benchmark suits
`ui/`	Source for various frontends

A brief explanation about the directories mentioned earlier:

- The `base/` directory consists of most of the standard library.
- The `src/` directory contains the core of the language.
- There is also an `examples` directory containing some good code examples, which can be helpful when learning Julia. It is highly recommended to use these in parallel.

On the successful build on Linux, these directories can be found in the Julia's folder. These are usually present in the build directory.

Julia's importance in data science

In the last decade, data science has become a buzzword, with Harvard Business Review naming it the sexiest job of the 21st century. What is a data scientist? The answer was published in The Guardian (`https://www.theguardian.com/careers/2015/jun/30/whats-a-data-scientist-and-how-do-i-become-one`):

> *A data scientist takes raw data and marries it with analysis to make it accessible and more valuable for an organization. To do this, they need a unique blend of skills—a solid grounding in maths and algorithms and a good understanding of human behaviors, as well as knowledge of the industry they're working in, to put their findings into context. From here, they can unlock insights from the datasets and start to identify trends.*

The technical skills of a data scientist are varied but, generally, they are good at programming, and have a very strong background in mathematics—especially statistics, skills in machine learning, and knowledge of big data. A data scientist is required to have in-depth understanding of the domain he/she is working in. Julia was designed for scientific and numerical computation. And with the advent of big data, there is a requirement to have a language that can work on huge amounts of data. Although we have Spark and `MapReduce` (Hadoop) as processing engines that are generally used with Python, Scala, and Java, Julia with Intel's High Performance Analytics Toolkit can provide an alternative option. It may also be worth noting that Julia excels at parallel computing but is much easier to write and prototype than Spark/Hadoop.

One great feature of Julia is that it solves the 2-language problem. Generally, with Python and R, code that is doing most of the heavy workload is written in C/C++ and it is then called. This is not required with Julia, as it can perform comparably to C/C++. Therefore, complete code—including code that does heavy computations—can be written in Julia itself.

Benchmarks

We mentioned the speed of Julia above, and that's what sets this language apart from traditional dynamically typed languages. Speed is its specialty. So, how fast can Julia be? The following micro-benchmark results were obtained on a single core (serial execution) on an Intel(R) Xeon(R) CPU E7-8850 2.00 GHz CPU with 1 TB of 1067 MHz DDR3 RAM running Linux:

	Julia 0.4.0	Python 3.4.3	R 3.2.2	MATLAB R2015b	Go go1.5	Java 1.8.0_45
fib	2.11	77.76	533.52	26.89	1.86	1.21
parse_int	1.45	17.02	45.73	802.52	1.20	3.35
quicksort	1.15	32.89	264.54	4.92	1.29	2.60
mandel	0.79	15.32	53.16	7.58	1.11	1.35
pi_sum	1.00	21.99	9.56	1.00	1.00	1.00
rand_mat_stat	1.66	17.93	14.56	14.52	2.96	3.92
rand_mat_mul	1.02	1.14	1.57	1.12	1.42	2.36

These benchmark times are relative to C (smaller is better, C performance = 1.0). Benchmarks can be misleading and are not always true. Good coding practices need to be followed and exactly identical conditions are required to measure them side by side. Julia has been quite open about how it measured these benchmarks and the code is available at https://github.com/JuliaLang/julia/tree/master/test/perf/micro.

- Julia is significantly faster than Python. There is a huge difference in performance in the benchmarks. However, some libraries for numerical computation available to Python are written in C, and here it performs nearly equivalent to Julia.
- R was specifically designed for statisticians. It has a huge set of libraries for statistics and numerical computation and is available for free. It used to be the language of choice for data scientists (now Python is preferred). R is single-threaded and is a lot slower than Julia.

- MATLAB is not a free product. It comes with a paid license (students may get discounts). It is used by statisticians and academicians for some specific use cases. The above benchmarks run a lot slower on MATLAB.
- Go is designed from scratch for system programming. It was created by Google and the source code is available on GitHub, where it is actively developed. Go performs really well on these benchmarks, but it is not designed for numerical and scientific computing.
- Java performs well. It beats Julia in some benchmarks and Julia beats it in others. But we need to consider the development time associated with it. Julia is designed in a way that it can be used even for rapid prototyping. That makes it unique.

Julia is therefore well-suited to data science problems. Its ecosystem may not be as comprehensive as other languages right now, but it is growing at a great pace.

Using REPL

Read-Eval-Print-Loop (REPL) is an interactive shell or the language shell that provides the functionality to test out pieces of code. Julia provides an interactive shell with a JIT compiler (used by Julia) at the backend. We can give input in a line, it is compiled and evaluated, and the result is given in the next line:

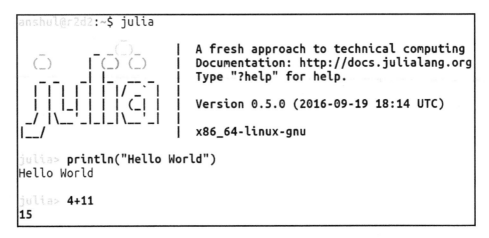

Julia's shell can be started easily, just by writing Julia in the Terminal. This brings up the logo and information about the version. This `julia>` is a Julia prompt and we can write expressions, statements, and functions, just as we could write them in a code file. The benefit of having the REPL is that we can test out our code for possible errors. Also, it is a good environment for beginners. We can type in the expressions and press *Enter* key to evaluate them. A Julia library, or custom-written Julia program, can be included in REPL using `include`.

For example, let's create a file with the name `hello.jl` and write a function with the name `helloworld()`, which just prints the line `Hello World from hello.jl`:

```
anshul@r2d2: ~/code/learningJulia
# a simple function to print hello world

function helloworld()
  println("Hello World from hello.jl")
end

~
~
"hello.jl" 6L, 108C
```

Now, use this function inside the REPL by writing an `include` statement for the specified file:

```
:~/code/learningJulia$ julia
               _       |  A fresh approach to technical computing
   (_)         | (_) (_)  |  Documentation: http://docs.julialang.org
    _ _   _| |_  __ _   |  Type "?help" for help.
   | | | | | | |/ _` |  |
   | | |_| | | | (_| |  |  Version 0.5.0 (2016-09-19 18:14 UTC)
  _/ |\__'_|_|_|\__'_|  |
 |__/                   |  x86_64-linux-gnu

julia> include("hello.jl")
helloworld (generic function with 1 method)

julia> helloworld()
Hello World from hello.jl
```

When we include the file inside the REPL, we see that it gave the information about the function present inside the file. We used the function and it printed the desired line. Julia also stores all the commands written in the REPL in the .julia_history folder. This file is located at C:\Users\%username% on Windows, or ~/.julia_history on Linux or macOS. Similar to Linux Terminal, we can reverse-search using *Ctrl* + *R* keys in Julia's shell. This helps us to find the previous commands or to debug the errors if necessary.

Using help in Julia

There is another nice feature provided in the REPL of Julia, which is help. One can use this by typing a question mark (?) and the prompt will change to:

```
help?>
```

It is used to give information about the functions, types, macros, and operators used in Julia:

```
        include
search: include include_string include_dependency

  include(path::AbstractString)

  Evaluate the contents of a source file in the current context.
  During including, a task-local include path is set to the directory
  containing the file. Nested calls to include will search relative to
  that path. All paths refer to files on node 1 when running in
  parallel, and files will be fetched from node 1. This function is
  typically used to load source interactively, or to combine files in
  packages that are broken into multiple source files.


        +
search: + .+

  +(x, y...)

  Addition operator. x+y+z+... calls this function with all arguments,
  i.e. +(x, y, z, ...).
```

In the preceding screenshot, we used help?> to give information about the include and "+" key (please read the information provided for "+" key).

Julia also provides the functionality to use regular shell commands from REPL. This can be used by writing ";" key inside the REPL, which will change the prompt to:

shell>

```
shell> ls
hello.jl

shell> ping 8.8.8.8
PING 8.8.8.8 (8.8.8.8) 56(84) bytes of data.
64 bytes from 8.8.8.8: icmp_seq=1 ttl=58 time=16.1 ms
^C
--- 8.8.8.8 ping statistics ---
1 packets transmitted, 1 received, 0% packet loss, time 0ms
rtt min/avg/max/mdev = 16.115/16.115/16.115/0.000 ms
```

In the preceding screenshot, we used the `ls` command (`dir` in Windows) to list the files in the current directory and did a ping to `8.8.8.8`. This is helpful, as we don't have to leave the REPL for tasks that we need to do on the Terminal. Tab-completion works fine in `shell>` mode too, as it does in `julia>` mode. There are some interactive functions and macros available, which increase the productivity from the REPL:

- `whos()`: This gives information about the global symbols currently present:

```
julia> whos()
                    Base    33971 KB    Module
                    Core    12397 KB    Module
                    Main    40587 KB    Module
                     ans        0 bytes Void
```

  We can see it also gives the size of the module.

- `@which`: It gives the information about the method that would be called for the particular function and arguments:

```
julia> @which sin(10)
sin(x::Real) at math.jl:204
```

- `versioninfo()`: Although when we start the Julia REPL, it gives some information about the version, if we want more detailed information, then `versioninfo()` is used:

```
julia> versioninfo()
Julia Version 0.5.0
Commit 3c9d753 (2016-09-19 18:14 UTC)
```

```
Platform Info:
  System: Linux (x86_64-linux-gnu)
  CPU: Intel(R) Core(TM) i7-6700HQ CPU @ 2.60GHz
  WORD_SIZE: 64
  BLAS: libopenblas (NO_LAPACKE DYNAMIC_ARCH NO_AFFINITY
  Haswell)
  LAPACK: liblapack.so.3
  LIBM: libopenlibm
  LLVM: libLLVM-3.7.1 (ORCJIT, broadwell)
```

- `edit("any_file_in_home_directory")`: This is used to edit a file in the home directory.

  Let's edit the same file that we used in the earlier examples:

  ```
  julia> edit("hello.jl")
  ```

  ```
   GNU nano 2.5.3          File: hello.jl

  # a simple function to print hello world

  function helloworld()
    println("Hello World from hello.jl")
  end
  ```

  This brings up a default editor based on the OS being used, like Vim.

- `@edit rand()`: If required, we can also edit the definition of the built-in functions. This will bring up a similar window as the preceding one, which is for the default editor.
- `less("any_file_in_same_directory")`: This is similar to the shell utility for showing the file.
- `clipboard("some_text")`: This is used to copy `some_text` to the system clipboard.
- `clipboard()`: This is used to paste the contents of the keyboard to the REPL. Useful when copying some commands from elsewhere to the REPL.
- `dump()`: This displays information about a Julia object on the screen.
- `names()`: This gets an array of the names exported by a module.
- `fieldnames()`: This is used to get the array of the data fields belonging to a particular symbol.
- `workspace()`: This brings out a clean workspace (all user defined variables are erased) and cleans up the top-level module (Main).

Plots in REPL

There is also the possibility to create plots in REPL. These are simple plots, but look quite nice and are very light on memory. To do this, we need to add a package. We will study package management later, but for now, we can directly add a package and start using it.

```
julia> Pkg.add("UnicodePlots")
```

This has been provided by a developer called Christof Stocker. Remember how to enter the symbol "π"? If yes, then please go through the previous sections. Let's use this to create a simple plot:

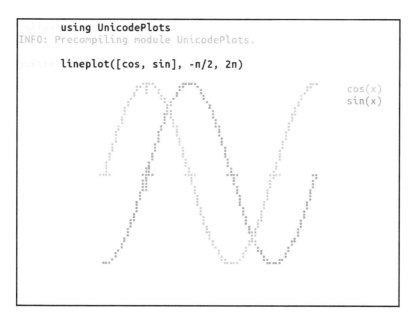

We can create many similar plots such as scatterplots, line plots, histograms, and so on using UnicodePlots.

Using Jupyter Notebook

Data science and scientific computing are privileged to have an amazing interactive tool called Jupyter Notebook. With Jupyter Notebook, you can write and run code in an interactive web environment that also has the capability to have visualizations, images, and videos. It makes the testing of equations and prototyping a lot easier, has the support of over 40 programming languages, and is completely open source.

GitHub supports Jupyter Notebooks (static). A Notebook with a record of computation can be shared through the Jupyter Notebook viewer or other cloud storage. Jupyter Notebooks are extensively used for coding machine-learning algorithms, statistical modeling and numerical simulation, and data munging. Jupyter Notebook is implemented in Python, but you can run the code in any of the 40 languages, provided you have their kernel. You can check whether Python is installed on your system or not by typing the following into the Terminal:

```
$ python --version
Python 2.7.12 :: Anaconda 4.1.1 (64-bit)
```

This will give the version of Python if it is on the system. It is best to have Python 2.7.x, 3.5.x, or a later version. If Python is not installed, then you can install it by downloading it from the official website for Windows.

It is highly recommended to install Anaconda if you are new to Python and data science. Commonly used packages for data science, numerical, and scientific computing—including Jupyter Notebook—come bundled with Anaconda, making it the preferred way to set up an environment. Instructions can be found at https://www.continuum.io/downloads.

Otherwise, for Linux (Ubuntu), typing the following should work:

```
$ sudo apt-get install python
```

Jupyter is present in the Anaconda package, but you can check whether the Jupyter package is up to date by typing in the following:

```
$ jupyter --version
```

If, for some reason, it is not present, it can be installed using:

```
$ conda install jupyter
```

Another way to install Jupyter is by using the `pip` command:

```
$ pip install jupyter
```

Now, to use Julia with Jupyter, we need the `IJulia` package. This can be installed using Julia's package manager. In the REPL, type the following commands:

```
julia> Pkg.update()
julia> Pkg.add("IJulia")
```

The first step updates the metadata and current packages and the second step installs the desired package. After installing IJulia, we can create a new Notebook by selecting Julia under the **Notebooks** section in Jupyter, as shown in the following screenshot:

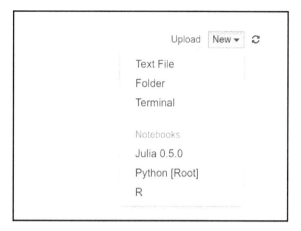

Here, we can create a new Julia Notebook. Notebooks are very easy to use. The following screenshot shows the menu bar and the options available with Jupyter Notebook:

The symbols are quite self-explanatory. It also supports adding markdown to the notebook. GitHub is also Jupyter Notebook-friendly. Just type a command and click the run icon or press *Shift + Enter* keys on the code block to run the code. The following screenshot shows that the command prints two lines and does an arithmetic operation:

```
In [1]: println("This is Jupyter notebook")
        This is Jupyter notebook

In [2]: println("This is also called as IJulia")
        This is also called as IJulia

In [3]: 1+3
Out[3]: 4
```

Jupyter is a great interactive environment when visualizations or graphs are involved. The following code creates a nice plot (we will learn about Gadfly and RDatasets in later chapters):

```
# Use Plotting library and RDatasets package for iris dataset
using Gadfly
using RDatasets
# Create a dataframe
# We will learn about dataframes in later chapters
iris = dataset("datasets", "iris")
# This will create an image
p = plot(iris, x=:SepalLength, y=:SepalWidth, color=:Species, Geom.point)
```

The following screenshot classifies different species of flowers by their color:

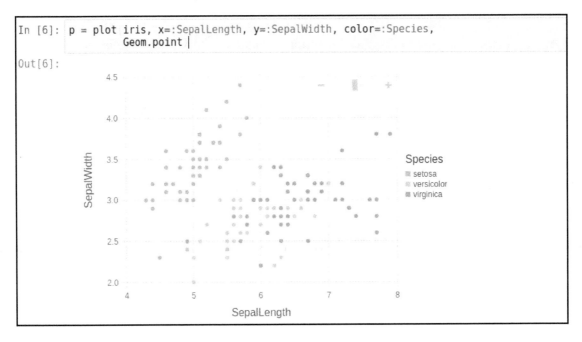

Juno IDE Atom is an open source text editor developed using Electron, a framework by GitHub. Electron is a framework designed to build cross-platform apps using HTML, JavaScript, CSS, and Node.js. It is completely configurable and can be modified according to your needs. Basic tutorials are available on their website at https://atom.io/. There are thousands of open source packages available for Atom. Most of them are there to add or improve functionality, and there are thousands of themes to change the look and feel of the editor.

There are many features of Atom:

- Split the editor in panes to work side by side
- Open complete projects to navigate easily
- Autocomplete
- Available for Linux, Mac, and Windows

In the following screenshot, we can see an open project, multiple panes, a stylized interface, and syntax highlighting. Atom is not just limited to this:

What is Juno?

Juno is built on Atom. It is a powerful and free environment for the Julia language. This contains many powerful features, such as:

- Multiple cursors
- Fuzzy file finding
- Vim key bindings

Juno provides an environment that combines the features of the Jupyter Notebook and the productivity of the IDE. It is very easy to use and is a completely live environment. With Atom, you can install new packages through the **Settings** panel or through the command line using the apm command. So, if we need to install a new package and we know its name (let's say xyz), we can just write:

```
$ apm install xyz
```

There are many apm commands, which can be read using --help command:

```
$ apm --help
```

The following screenshot shows the Juno IDE installing process through **Settings**. We just need to go to the **Settings** tab and install new packages:

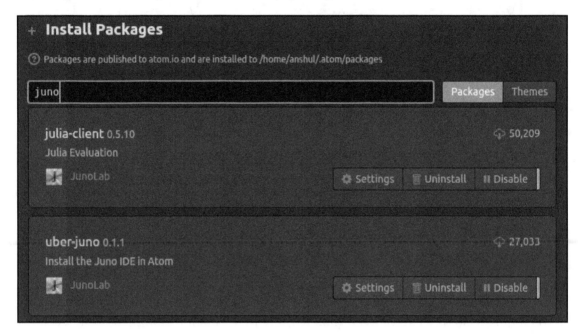

It is recommended to install Juno and go through it. It is an amazing development environment and should be used when you become a little more familiar with the language. Juno will look familiar to RStudio and Yhat's Rodeo users. The following screenshot from Juno's website shows us the coding panel, plots, console, and workspace:

We don't have to move to newer windows just to check the plot or don't need to manually find out the variables currently in the variable.

Package management

Julia provides a built-in package manager. Using `Pkg`, we can install libraries written in Julia. For unregistered packages, we can also compile them from their source or use the standard package manager of the operating system. A list of registered packages is maintained at `http://pkg.julialang.org`. The `Pkg` module is provided in the base installation. The `Pkg` module contains all the package manager commands.

Pkg.status() – package status

The `Pkg.status()` is a function that prints out a list of currently installed packages with a summary. This is handy when you need to know whether the package you want to use is installed or not. When the `Pkg` command is run for the first time, the package directory is automatically created. The command requires that the `Pkg.status()` function returns a valid list of the packages installed. The list of packages given by the `Pkg.status()` function are of registered versions, which are managed by `Pkg`. We currently have lots of packages installed, whose versions we can check, given as follows:

```
julia> Pkg.status()
7 required packages:
 - IJulia                1.3.2
 - PlotlyJS              0.5.1
 - Plots                 0.10.0
 - PyPlot                2.2.4
 - RDatasets             0.2.0
 - ScikitLearn           0.2.2
 - UnicodePlots          0.2.1
47 additional packages:
 - BinDeps               0.4.5
```

The `Pkg.installed()` function can also be used to return a dictionary of all the installed packages with their versions:

```
julia> Pkg.installed()
Dict{String,VersionNumber} with 54 entries:
  "Juno"               => v"0.2.5"
  "Lazy"               => v"0.11.4"
  "ZMQ"                => v"0.4.0"
  "DataStructures"     => v"0.4.6"
  "Compat"             => v"0.9.4"
  "RData"              => v"0.0.4"
  "GZip"               => v"0.2.20"
  ...
```

You can see that the number of packages is the same, but the way the information is presented is different. Packages can be incomplete or in more complicated states. These states are generally indicated by annotations to the right of the installed package version. `Pkg.status()` will print branch information to the right of the version.

Pkg.add() – adding packages

Julia's package manager is declarative and intelligent. You only have to tell it what you want and it will figure out which version to install and resolve dependencies if there are any.

We can use `Pkg.add(package_name)` to add packages and `Pkg.rm(package_name)` to remove packages. This is the recommended way.

Otherwise, we can add the list of requirements that we want and it resolves which packages and their versions to install. The `~/.julia/v0.5/REQUIRE` file contains the package requirements. We can open it using a text editor such as **vi** or **atom**, or use the `Pkg.edit()` function in Julia's shell to edit this file:

```
$ cat ~/.julia/v0.5/REQUIRE
IJulia
ScikitLearn
RDatasets
Plots
UnicodePlots
PyPlot
PlotlyJS
```

After editing the file, run `Pkg.resolve()` to install or remove the packages. This installation and removal will be based on the packages mentioned in the `REQUIRE` file.

Remember earlier we used `Pkg.add("IJulia")` to install the IJulia package? When we don't want to have a package installed on our system anymore, `Pkg.rm()` is used to remove the requirement from the `REQUIRE` file. Similar to `Pkg.add()`, `Pkg.rm()` first removes the requirement of the package from the `REQUIRE` file and then updates the list of installed packages by running `Pkg.resolve()` to match. `Pkg.add()` and `Pkg.rm()` are convenient and are generally used to add and remove requirements for a single package. But when there is a need to add or remove multiple packages, we can call `Pkg.edit()` to manually change the contents of `REQUIRE` and then update our packages accordingly. The `Pkg.edit()` function does not roll back the contents of `REQUIRE` if `Pkg.resolve()` fails. In that scenario, we have to run `Pkg.edit()` again to fix the file's contents ourselves.

Working with unregistered packages

Often, we would like to be able to use packages created by our team members or someone who has published them on GitHub but that are not in the registered packages of `Pkg`. Julia allows us to do that by using GitHub clones. Julia packages are hosted on GitHub repositories and can be cloned using mechanisms supported by Git. The index of registered packages is maintained at `METADATA.jl`. For unofficial packages, we can use the following:

```
julia> Pkg.clone("git://github.com/path/unofficialPackage/Package.jl.git")
```

Julia repository names end with `.jl` on GitHub (the additional `.git` indicates a *bare* GitHub repository). This prevents Julia and other languages from colliding with repositories with the same name. This also makes the search easy. Sometimes, unregistered packages have dependencies that require fulfilling before use. If that is the scenario, a `REQUIRE` file is needed at the top of the source tree of the unregistered package. The unregistered packages' dependencies on the registered packages are determined by this `REQUIRE` file. When we run `Pkg.clone(url)`, these dependencies are automatically installed.

Pkg.update() – package update

It's good to have updated packages. Julia, which is under active development, has its packages frequently updated and new functionalities are added. To update all of the packages, type the following:

```
Pkg.update()
```

Under the hood, new changes are pulled into the `METADATA` file in the directory located at `~/.julia/v0.5/`, and checks are run for any new registered package versions that may have been published since the last update. If there are new registered package versions, `Pkg.update()` attempts to update the packages that are not dirty and are checked out on a branch. This update process satisfies top-level requirements by computing the optimal set of package versions to be installed. The packages with specific versions that must be installed are defined in the `REQUIRE` file in Julia's directory (`~/.julia/v0.5/`).

METADATA repository

Registered packages are downloaded and installed using the official METADATA.jl repository. A different METADATA repository location can also be provided if required:

```
julia> Pkg.init("https://julia.customrepo.com/METADATA.jl.git", "branch")
```

Developing packages

Julia allows us to view the source code, and, as it is tracked by GitHub, the full development history of all the installed packages is available. We can also make changes and commit to our own repository, or do bug fixes and contribute enhancements upstream. You may also want to create your own packages and publish them at some point in time. Julia's package manager allows you to do that too. It is a requirement that GitHub is installed on the system and the developer needs an account with their hosting provider of choice (GitHub, Bitbucket, and so on). Having the ability to communicate over SSH is preferred—to enable that, upload your public ssh-key to your hosting provider.

Creating a new package

It is preferable to have the REQUIRE file in the package repository. This should have the bare minimum of a description of the Julia version. For example, if we would like to create a new Julia package called HelloWorld, we would have the following:

```
Pkg.generate("HelloWorld", "MIT")
```

Here, HelloWorld is the package that we want to create and MIT is the license that our package will have. The license should be known to the package generator. Pkg.generate currently knows about MIT, BSD, and ASL but a user can use any license they want by changing LICENCE.md.

The above process creates a directory at ~/.julia/v0.5/HelloWorld. The directory that is created is initialized as a GitHub repository. Also, all the files required by the package are kept in this directory. This directory is then committed to the repository and can then be pushed to the remote repository for the world to use.

A brief about multiple dispatch

A function is an object, mapping a tuple of arguments using an expression to return a value. When this function object is unable to return a value, it throws an exception. For different types of arguments, the same conceptual function can have different implementations.

For example, we could have a function to add two floating point numbers and another function to add two integers. But, conceptually, we are only adding two numbers. Julia provides a functionality through which different implementations of the same concept can be implemented easily.

The functions don't need to be defined all at once; they are defined in small abstracts. These small abstracts are different argument type combinations and have different behaviors associated with them. The definition of one of these behaviors is called a method. The types and the number of arguments that a method definition accepts is indicated by the annotation of its signatures. Therefore, the most suitable method is applied whenever a function is called with a certain set of arguments.

To apply a method when a function is invoked is known as dispatch. There are two types of dispatch:

- **dynamic**-based on type evaluated at the run-time type
- **multiple**-based on all arguments, not just the receiver

Julia chooses which method should be invoked based on all the arguments. This is known as multiple dispatch. Multiple dispatch is particularly useful for mathematical and scientific code. We shouldn't consider the operations as belonging to one argument any more than any of the others. All of the argument types are considered when implementing a mathematical operator. Multiple dispatch is not limited to mathematical expressions, as it can be used in numerous real-world scenarios and is a powerful paradigm for structuring programs. The code is given as follows:

```
type MyType
    prop::String
end
MyType(v::Real) = ...
function MyType{T}(v::Vector{T})   # parametric type
    ....
end
```

Methods in multiple dispatch

The "+" symbol is a function in Julia using multiple dispatch. Multiple dispatch is used by all of Julia's standard functions and operators. For the various possible combinations of argument types and counts, all of them have many methods defining their behavior. A method is restricted to taking certain types of arguments using the ::type-assertion operator:

```
julia> f(x::Float64, y::Float64) = x + y
f (generic function with 1 method)
```

The function definition will only be applied for calls where x and y are both values of the Float64 type:

```
julia> f(10.0, 14.0)
24.0
```

If we try to apply this definition to other types of arguments, it will give a method error:

```
julia> f(5,10.0)
ERROR: MethodError: no method matching f(::Int64, ::Float64)
Closest candidates are:
 f(::Float64, ::Float64) at REPL[4]:1
```

The arguments must be of precisely the same type as defined in the function definition. The function object is created in the first method definition. New method definitions add new behaviors to the existing function object. When a function is invoked, the number and types of the arguments are matched, and the most specific method definition matching will be executed. The following example creates a function with two methods. One method definition takes two arguments of the Float64 type and adds them. The second method definition takes two arguments of the Number type, multiplies them by two and adds them. When we invoke the function with Float64 arguments, the first method definition is applied, and when we invoke the function with integer arguments, the second method definition is applied, as the number can take any numeric values. In the following example, we are playing with floating point numbers and integers using multiple dispatch:

```
julia> f(x::Number, y::Number) = x + y
f (generic function with 2 methods)
julia> f(100,200)
300
```

In Julia, all values are instances of the abstract type `Any`. When the type declaration is not given with `::`, that means it is not specifically defined as the type of the argument, therefore `Any` is the default type of method parameter and it doesn't have the restriction of taking any type of value. Generally, one method definition is written in such a way that it will be applied to certain arguments to which no other method definition applies. This is one of the Julia language's most powerful features. Specialized code can be generated expressively and efficiently, and complex algorithms can be implemented, without paying much attention to low-level implementations, using Julia's multiple dispatch and flexible parametric type system. We will study multiple dispatch in detail in the coming chapters.

Understanding LLVM and JIT

The LLVM project was started as a research project at the University of Illinois. Its aim was to create modern, **Static Single Assignment** (**SSA**)-based compilation strategies and type safety, low-level operations, flexibility, and the capability of representing all high-level languages cleanly. It is actually a collection of modular and reusable compiler and toolchain technologies. LLVM doesn't have to do much with traditional virtual machines. Some of the objectives of LLVM are:

- The LLVM Core libraries were created to provide a modern source—and target-independent optimizer, along with code generation support for many popular CPUs. These libraries are built around a well-specified code representation known as the **LLVM intermediate representation** (**LLVM IR**).
- Clang is an *LLVM native* C/C++/Objective-C compiler, which aims to deliver amazingly fast compiles (for example, about 3x faster than GCC when compiling Objective-C code in a debug configuration), extremely useful error and warning messages and to provide a platform for building great source-level tools.
- **DragonEgg** integrates the LLVM optimizers and code generator with the GCC parsers. This allows LLVM to compile Ada, Fortran, and other languages supported by the GCC compiler frontends, and access to C features not supported by Clang.
- The LLDB project builds on libraries provided by LLVM and Clang to provide a great native debugger. It uses the Clang ASTs and expression parser, LLVM JIT, LLVM disassembler, and so on, so that it provides an experience that *just works*. It is also blazingly fast and much more memory-efficient than GDB at loading symbols.

- The **SAFECode** project is a memory safety compiler for C/C++ programs. It instruments code with runtime checks to detect memory safety errors (for example, buffer overflows) at runtime. It can be used to protect software from security attacks and can also be used as a memory safety error debugging tool, like Valgrind.

In computing, JIT compilation, also known as dynamic translation, is compilation done during the execution of a program--at runtime—rather than prior to execution. Most often, this consists of translation to machine code, which is then executed directly, but can also refer to translation to another format. A system implementing a JIT compiler typically continuously analyses the code being executed and identifies parts of the code where the speedup gained from compilation would outweigh the overhead of compiling that code. The LLVM JIT compiler can optimize unnecessary static branches out of a program at runtime, and thus is useful for partial evaluation in cases where a program has many options, most of which can easily be deemed unnecessary in a specific environment. This feature is used in the OpenGL pipeline of Mac OS X Leopard (v10.5) to provide support for missing hardware features. Graphics code within the OpenGL stack was left in intermediate representation and then compiled when run on the target machine. On systems with high-end **graphics processing units** (**GPUs**), the resulting code was quite thin, passing the instructions onto the GPU with minimal changes. On systems with low-end GPUs, LLVM would compile optional procedures that run on the local **central processing unit** (**CPU**) and emulate instructions that the GPU cannot run internally. LLVM improved performance on low-end machines using Intel GMA chipsets. A similar system was developed under the Gallium3D LLVMpipe and incorporated into the GNOME shell to allow it to run without a proper 3D hardware driver loaded.

Summary

In this chapter, we learned how Julia is different and looked at some of its features. We introduced you to how to download Julia and set up the environment on your system. We went through different environments popularly available for Julia, such as REPL, Jupyter notebook, and Juno (Atom). Then, we learned about multiple dispatch and why it is a special feature. In addition, we got a basic understanding of the LLVM and JIT.

References

- https://github.com/JuliaLang/julia
- https://docs.julialang.org/en/stable/#Manual-1
- https://julialang.org/blog/
- Sherrington, Malcolm (2015) *Mastering Julia*. ISBN: 9781783553310. Packt Publishing.
- http://llvm.org/

2
Programming Concepts with Julia

In the previous chapter, we discussed how Julia is great for prototyping and performs almost as well as C. Julia caters to seasoned programmers and novices equally. Julia is designed in a way that someone who has just started with programming will be able to be up and running in a day with the help of REPL or Jupyter Notebook. It provides lots of features that are useful to data scientists, statisticians, and those working in the field of scientific computing.

Knowledge of other languages would make the reading enjoyable, but is not required. The reader will find that Julia is quite similar to MATLAB, Python, and R.

Julia's version 1.0 is planned for release in a few months. Although there could be some changes by then, most of the concepts and code should be valid for that version.

In this chapter, the reader will go through the syntax, as well as one of the many ways to program in Julia. The following topics will be covered in this chapter:

- Revisiting programming paradigms
- Starting with Julia REPL
- Variables
- Integers, bits, bytes, and bools
- Floating point numbers in Julia
- Logical and arithmetic operations
- Arrays and matrices
- DataFrames and data arrays
- Dictionaries

Revisiting programming paradigms

Before solving a problem, we should always try to understand where it came from, then break the problem into the steps that we will perform to solve it. We should make sure that we consider all the scenarios and the agents that will be involved in solving the problem.

The programming paradigm refers to the breaking up of the programming activity into a structure of thoughts. It is an approach towards a problem and the orientation of sub-tasks. Although a problem can be approached using different paradigms, one paradigm may be more suited to solving it than another.

There are many programming paradigms, so we will only be discussing a few of them here:

- Imperative
- Logical
- Functional
- Object-oriented

Understanding the programming paradigm is recommended, as one programming language may be more suited to one particular paradigm. For example, C is suited to imperative programming, Haskell is suited to functional programming, and Smalltalk is for object-oriented programming. Let's understand these different paradigms in more detail.

Imperative programming paradigm

Imperative programming is a procedural way of programming. The primary focus is on the variables and the sequential execution of the tasks that may change the values of these variables. This paradigm is based on the Von Neumann computer, which has reusable memory, allowing us to change the state.

The imperative paradigm makes the assumption that the computer is capable of maintaining the different states of the variables that are generated during the computation process. The sequence at which these statements are executed is important because, at any given step, there could be different states if the order of these statements is changed.

At any point in time, the state of the computation is the current values of the variables defined in the program, the next task or statement that will be executed, and the data expected from any active subprogram calls. These are the factors that can change the state of the program, and therefore the imperative paradigm is actually the consecutive execution of statements.

The advantages of using the imperative paradigm:

- It is efficient in utilizing system resources
- It is based on how a computer functions, and therefore closely resembles the machine
- There are many popular languages that use this programming paradigm

There are some disadvantages to using this paradigm:

- Many problems cannot be solved by just following the order of statements.
- There is no referential transparency, which means the state of the variables can change. This makes the program difficult to comprehend.
- Debugging is not straightforward.
- A very limited abstraction can be achieved using the imperative programming paradigm.

Logical programming paradigm

The logical programming paradigm, also referred to as the rule-based paradigm, is based on predicate logic. It is a declarative approach to solving a problem and focuses on relations. Prolog is well suited to logical programming.

This paradigm is well suited to being applied to fields where we are dealing with different facts and the relationships among them. The program handles the data and creates a combination of rules, which gives us a valid logical expression.

Such a program can be divided into three sections:

- Definitions and declarations, which define the domain of the problem
- Facts that are relevant to the domain and the given problem
- Queries, which are actually the goals we want to achieve from these logical expressions

We don't have functions now. We only have relations.

Therefore, the `Y = f(X)` expression is now replaced by `r(X,Y)`, where `r` defines the relation between `X` and `Y`.

In rule-based programming, we only need to provide facts (rules and axioms), and the program finds the proof of the statement by assigning values to free variables.

The programs created can compute in either direction. For example:

- Y can be computed when X is known
- Similarly, X can be computed when Y is known

The following is an example of where we define a relation--brother--using other relations in the family, such as male, father, and mother:

```
male(X)    // X is a male
father(F,X) // F is father of X
father(F,Y) // F is father of Y
mother(M,X) // M is mother of X
mother(M,Y) // M is mother of Y
```

The preceding relationship implies:

```
brother(X,Y) // X is a brother of Y
```

There are some disadvantages to logical programming too:

- Functions that can compute either way do not perform well enough
- Rule-based programming is restricted to domains that can be expressed well using relations

Functional programming paradigm

The functional programming paradigm originates from a purely mathematical ideology--the theory of functions. It treats all subprograms as functions.

Functions (in a mathematical sense) take an argument list and return outputs after computations. The result is dependent on the computations, which are themselves dependent on the inputs we provide to the functions. The focus is on the values and how the expressions are evaluated, rather than statements, as in the imperative paradigm.

Consecutive states are not valid in the functional paradigm. The result from a function would be an input to another expression and would not be saved as a variable.

The functional paradigm is a cleaner and simpler programming paradigm than others because it follows the mathematical functional theory.

Functions are first-class objects in the functional paradigm. This means that functions can be treated as data and we make the assumption that a function will return a value. This allows us to pass a function as an argument to another function or return a function from any other function.

Let's try to understand how we can program the functional paradigm and compare it with the imperative paradigm.

To do this, we need to create a function that will map the input to the result that we would have got if we had executed *n* number of statements in the imperative paradigm.

The Stat refers to a statement and Stat_0, Stat_1, Stat_2, ... Stat_n are the *n* number of statements.

Now, according to the functional paradigm:

```
F(Stat_0)= Stat_n
```

This function maps the initial state to the final state.

Now, we can break this down to individual expressions, which will represent the result of each statement:

```
F(Stat_0) = Stat_n(Stat_n-1(...(Stat_1(Stat_0)))) = Stat_n
```

This can also be written as:

```
F = Stat_n 0 Stat_n-1 0 ... Stat_1
```

Therefore, we can transform a program to the functional paradigm from the imperative paradigm by constructing functions for each imperative statement and executing them in reverse order. Although this will not be applicable to every situation or problem, the basic idea will be the same.

The characteristics and advantages of the functional paradigm:

- Functions provide a high level of abstraction, which reduces the possibility of committing errors.
- Programs are independent of assignment operations and it is possible to write higher-order functions. This makes the functional programming paradigm good for parallel computations.

- It maintains referential transparency, unlike imperative programming. This makes it more suited to mathematical expressions.
- The values in functional programming are non-mutable.

There are also some disadvantages to the functional programming paradigm:

- It becomes complicated in some situations, usually when there is a need to handle lots of sequential activity, which would be handled better with the imperative or object-oriented paradigm
- The program may be less efficient than a program written in other paradigms

Object-oriented paradigm

The **object-oriented programming (OOP)** paradigm is a representation of real-world entities, where everything is an object and we modify the state of an object using a behavior or methods.

The OOP paradigm places the focus on objects. These objects belong to a particular class. Classes have specific methods that objects can use. As objects are real-world entities, they are encapsulated, containing data and the methods that can change the state of this data.

The object-oriented programming paradigm is based on four major principles:

1. **Encapsulation**, as the name suggests, restricts access from outside of the object's definition. The methods that have access to the objects can only manipulate their state. This prevents outside methods from changing the state of the object to perform an invalid operation.
2. **Abstraction** is a way of defining conceptual boundaries using classes in terms of interfaces and functionalities. This protects the internal properties of the object.
3. **Inheritance** enables code re-usability. Classes are allowed to inherit attributes and behavior from existing classes, thus eliminating the need to rewrite them. This also helps in consistency as, if there is a change, we are only required to make it in a single place. The derived classes can add their own attributes and behavior, and can therefore extend the functionalities provided by the base class.

2. **Polymorphism** refers to having many forms of the same name. This means we can have different methods with the same name:

   - **Overriding**: Is runtime polymorphism, where two methods have the same name and signature. The difference is that one of the methods is in the base class and the other is in the derived class. With overriding, the child class can have the specific implementation of the method.
   - **Overloading**: Is compile-time polymorphism, where there are two or more methods in the same class with the same names but different signatures. The decision of which method will be called is based on the values passed as the arguments to the method.

In this section, we learned about the programming paradigms required to understand the various concepts that we will be learning throughout this book.

Starting with Julia REPL

We have already learned how to start the Julia REPL and evaluate basic statements in it.

There are various options provided by Julia for running the program. We can directly run statements without even opening the REPL:

```
$ julia -e 'println("Hello World")'
Hello World
```

We can even run a loop without starting the REPL:

```
$ julia -e 'for i=1:5; println("Hello World"); end'
Hello World
Hello World
...
```

It is also possible to pass arguments:

```
$ julia -e 'for i in ARGS; println(i); end' k2so r2d2 c3po r4 bb8
k2so
r2d2
c3po
r4
bb8
```

ARGS is used to take command-line arguments to the script.

We can find the different options that Julia supports using the `--help` option:

```
$ julia --help

julia [switches] -- [programfile] [args...]
-v, --version           Display version information
-h, --help              Print this message
-H, --home <dir>        Set location of `julia` executable
-e, --eval <expr>       Evaluate <expr>
-E, --print <expr>      Evaluate and show <expr>
-L, --load <file>       Load <file> immediately on all processors
-p, --procs {N|auto}    Integer value N launches N additional local
worker processes

                        "auto" launches as many workers as the number of

local cores
--machinefile <file>    Run processes on hosts listed in <file>
-i                      Interactive mode; REPL runs and isinteractive()
is true
```

(In the preceding output we have shown only the most used options. There are many more options which can be accessed using `julia --help`.)

Variables in Julia

Just as in other programming languages, we use a variable to store a value that is obtained from a computation or external source.

Start the REPL by typing `julia` in the Terminal:

```
$ julia

# assign 100 to a variable x
julia> x = 100
100

# multiple the value in the variable by 5
julia> x*5
500
```

We can change the values stored in a variable or mutate the state:

```
# assign a different value to x
# this will replace the existing value in x
julia> x = 24
24

# create another variable y
julia> y = 10
10
```

Simple operations, such as swapping, are easy:

```
# swap values of x and y
julia> x,y = y,x
(10,24)

julia> x
10
julia> y
24
```

The names of variables can start with a character or a "_" (underscore). Julia also allows Unicode names (UTF-8), but not all Unicode names are accepted in the variable name:

```
julia> _ab = 40
40
julia> @ab = 10
ERROR: syntax: unexpected "="
julia> 1000
1000
```

Please note "!" (exclamation mark) shouldn't be used in the variable name as functions ending with exclamation marks are used to modify their arguments.

We can use any set of symbols from UTF-8 greater than 00A0 (although, many symbols are not accepted):

```
# assigning value to a Hindi word.
julia> अंशुल= 101
101
```

Julia provides some built-in constants and functions and we can assign values to them, although it is not recommended to do so, as it can create confusion:

```
julia> pi
π = 3.1415926535897...

julia> pi = 300
300
```

There are some reserved keywords, which are not allowed to be used as variable names:

```
julia> for  = 100
ERROR: syntax: unexpected "="
julia> if = 1000
ERROR: syntax: unexpected "="
```

Naming conventions

Although Julia doesn't have many restrictions on naming and most combinations are allowed, it is good to follow some conventions as good practices:

- Generally, variable names are written in lowercase.
- Underscores are used to separate different words in a variable name, but it is not advisable to use names that would require underscores.
- Function and macros names are in lowercase. Underscores are not used.
- The first character of types and modules is uppercase. The separation between words in names is done using upper camel case.
- The functions that modify or write to any of their arguments end with "!" symbol.

We mentioned earlier that Julia is a strongly-typed language. Therefore, it is necessary for a variable's type to be defined. If it is not defined explicitly, then Julia will try to infer it from the value assigned to the variable.

We can use the `typeof()` function provided by Julia to find the type of the variable.

Let's do this to the variables that we defined in the previous section:

```
julia> typeof(_ab)
Int64

julia> langname = "Julia"
"Julia"

julia> typeof(langname)
String
```

The `Int64` and `String` in the preceding examples are the types. The `64` in `Int64` is the bit-length of the variable. There are different sizes of `Int` and the default generally accords to the word length of the operating system.

It should also be noted that, in Julia, we can separate numbers using underscores:

```
julia> 1_0_0
100
```

This is helpful in many scenarios:

```
julia> 100_000_000
100000000
```

Integers, bits, bytes, and bools

Integers, bits, bytes, bools, and floating point numbers are used in arithmetic operations. Built-in representations of them are called as numeric primitives, and numeric literals are their representations as values in code.

Let's understand Julia's primitive numeric types. The following is a table of Integer types, which includes bits, bytes, and bool:

Type	Number of bits	Smallest value	Largest value
Int8	8	-2^7	$2^7 - 1$
UInt8	8	0	$2^8 - 1$
Int16	16	-2^{15}	$2^{15} - 1$
UInt16	16	0	$2^{16} - 1$
Int32	32	-2^{31}	$2^{31} - 1$

UInt32	32	0	2^32 - 1
Int64	64	-2^63	2^63 - 1
UInt64	64	0	2^64 - 1
Int128	128	-2^127	2^127 - 1
UInt128	128	0	2^128 - 1
Bool	8	false (0)	true (1)

The UInt type refers to unsigned integers. These are those integers whose values start from 0.

This table shows the smallest and the largest values that a particular type of integer can hold.

We can also find the smallest and the largest value of a type of integer using the typemin() and typemax() function:

```
julia> typemax(Int32)
2147483647

julia> typemin(Int32)
-2147483648
```

This is also from the preceding table: the smallest value -2^31 and the largest value 2^31 - 1.

Playing with integers in REPL

We can get a better understanding of integers using the REPL.

```
$ julia

julia> 24
24

julia> typeof(24)
Int64
```

Here, it is Int64 because we are on a 64-bit system. If we were on a 32-bit system, then the default integer type would have been Int32.

We can check what the default word size (architecture) of the system we are working on is:

```
julia> Sys.WORD_SIZE
64
```

The type of architecture is also mentioned on the Julia banner when we start the REPL.

The architecture is mentioned on the last line:

```
x86_64-linux-gnu
```

This means that we are using Linux and are on the x86_64 (64-bit) platform. If you are on a 32-bit platform, you might get i386.

In a scenario where we are dealing with large numbers that cannot be represented by a 32-bit integer (Int32), Julia itself creates the 64-bit integer (64-bit), rather than Int32, even if we are on a 32-bit machine:

```
julia> large_integer = 99999999999
julia> typeof(large_integer)
Int64
```

Understanding overflow behavior

In Julia, we don't have type declarations that are applicable on a global scope. But we can definitely use them in the scope local to a function.

In the following example, we will define a function that has an x variable of the Int16 type. We are assigning it a value of 10000 (we will learn about functions and types in detail in the coming chapters):

```
julia> x = Int16(10000)
10000

julia> x*x
-7936
```

This function is very straightforward. It assigns the value of 10000 to x of type Int16 and prints x*x.

Why do we get x*x, which is `10000*10000` as `-7936`?

This is because we exceeded the value that the type of the variable can handle. This resulted in a wraparound behavior. The wraparound behavior is part of the modular arithmetic, where numbers wrap around when they reach a certain value, also called the modulus.

Another example to understand this concept is overflowing the largest possible value of a type:

```
# largest possible value of 16-bit Int: 32767
julia> x = typemax(Int16)
32767

# Julia will maintain variable types even if the max value # is exceeding
julia> x + Int16(1)
-32768
```

Understanding the Boolean data type

Bool is a logical data type that is widely used. It is assigned and can be `true` or `false`:

```
julia> 1 > 2
false

julia> typeof(ans)
Bool
```

Unlike other languages, `0`, `NULL`, or empty strings are not treated as `false` in Julia.

Example:

```
julia> if 0
    println("hello")
end
```

The preceding command will throw an error:

```
TypeError: non-boolean (Int64) used in boolean context

Stacktrace:
 [1] include_string(::String, ::String) at ./loading.jl:515
```

Floating point numbers in Julia

It is easy to represent floating point numbers in Julia. They are represented in a similar fashion as they are in other languages:

```
# Add a decimal point
julia> 100.0
100.0

julia> 24.
24.0

# It is not required to precede a number from the decimal point
julia> .10
0.1

julia> typeof(ans)
Float64
```

There is a concept of positive zero and negative zero in Julia. They are equal but with different binary representations:

```
# equating two zeroes
julia> 0.0 == -0.0
true

julia> bits(0.0)
"0000000000000000000000000000000000000000000000000000000000000000"

# different first bit for negative zero
julia> bits(-0.0)
"1000000000000000000000000000000000000000000000000000000000000000"
```

Exponential notation can be very useful and convenient in various scenarios. It can be used in Julia using e:

```
julia> 2.99e8
2.99e8

julia> 2.99e8>999999
true
```

We have been using `Float64` in the preceding examples. We can also use `Float32` on 64-bit computers if required:

```
# Replace e by f to generate Float32
julia> 2.99f8
2.99f8

# Check the type of the preceding variable if it is Float32
julia> typeof(ans)
Float32

# Compare it with the same value
julia> 2.99f8==2.99e8
true
```

It is easy to convert values from `Float64` to `Float32`:

```
julia> Float32(2.99e8)
2.99f8
```

In some use cases, hexadecimal floating point literals are used. In Julia, they are valid only as `Float64` values:

```
julia> 0x4.1p1
8.125

julia> typeof(ans)
Float64
```

The following is the table of floating point types:

Type	Precision	Number of bits
`Float16`	half	16
`Float32`	single	32
`Float64`	double	64

Special functions on floating point numbers

There are some special floating point numbers that are worth mentioning:

- `Inf` and `-Inf`
- `NaN`

They are obtained when we write an expression that does not evaluate to a real number:

```
julia> 1/0
Inf

julia> -1/0
-Inf

julia> 0/0
NaN

julia> Inf/Inf
NaN
```

There are also some special functions that can prove to be useful in some scenarios. For example, if we need to find the next floating point number (that can be represented in Julia), there is a function provided by Julia that can help us to do so:

```
julia> nextfloat(0.0)
5.0e-324
```

In the preceding example, it shows that the next floating point number after 0.0 is 5.0e-324.

Similarly, there is a function to find the previous float:

```
julia> prevfloat(0.0)
-5.0e-324
```

Operations on floating point numbers

We regularly come across simple operations on floating point numbers in various programming languages not giving the expected value.

One common example is:

```
julia> x = 1.1; y = 0.1; x+y
1.2000000000000002
```

This happens when that particular number doesn't have the expected floating point representation.

We can use the `setrounding()` function provided by Julia to handle this:

```
julia> setrounding(Float64,RoundDown) do
x + y
end

1.2
```

Computations with arbitrary precision arithmetic

In the preceding sections, we studied the `Int` and `Float` types. There are two specific data types available for arbitrary precision arithmetic. They are:

- `BigInt`
- `BigFloat`

Arbitrary precision arithmetic refers to computations whose digits of precision are limited only by the available memory on the system they are executed on. Therefore, these can be useful in various scenarios requiring such computations.

```
julia> BigFloat("2.99123191231231414314134")
2.99123191231231414314133999999999999999999999999999999999999999999999999999999
99996


# example of BigInt
julia> factorial(BigInt(100))
93326215443944152681699238856266700490715968264381621468592963895217599993229
91560894146397615651828625369792082722375825118521091686400000000000000000000
00000000


# There are other ways too:
julia> big(0.2)
2.0000000000000001110223024625156540423631668090820312500000000000000000000000
00000e-01
```

Writing expressions with coefficients

It becomes extremely convenient to be able to write mathematical expressions without the need to explicitly write the multiplication operator:

```
# example of expression
julia> x = 4; y = 11;
julia> 3x + 4y + 93
149

julia> 23(x+1) + 12(y+1) + 15
274
```

This feature makes equations easy to read and understand.

Logical and arithmetic operations in Julia

Logical and arithmetic operations are very similar to in other programming languages. Julia has an exhaustive collection of all the operators required.

Let's start with the most common operators--arithmetic operators.

Performing arithmetic operations

Performing arithmetic operations, as discussed in the examples in previous sections, is straightforward. Julia provides a complete set of operators to work on.

Binary operators: $+$, $-$, $*$, $/$, $\wedge$, and $\%$. These are just the most used and small subset of the binary operators that are available.

```
julia> a = 10;   b = 20; a + b
30
```

Unary operators: $+$, and $-$.

These are the unary plus and unary minus. The former performs the identity operation and the latter maps the values to their additive inverses.

```
julia> -4
-4

julia> -(-4)
4
```

There is a special operator ! that can be used with bool types. It is used to perform negation:

```
julia> !(4>2)
false
```

Performing bitwise operations

These are not frequently used, except for it few. They are used to perform bitwise operations.

Expression	Name
~x	bitwise not
x & y	bitwise and
x | y	bitwise or
x ⊻ y	bitwise xor (exclusive or)
x >>> y	logical shift right
x >> y	arithmetic shift right
x << y	logical/arithmetic shift left

Here are a couple of examples of bitwise operations:

```
julia> 100 | 200
236

julia> ~100
-101
```

Operators for comparison and updating

Julia provides operators that can be used for easy comparison and updating:

```
# updating a variable by adding a value to it
julia> x = 4; x += 10
14

# similarly, division operation can also be done
julia> x = 4; x/=2
2.0
```

In the preceding example, the type of x changes from `Int` to `Float`. This happens because the updating operator binds the value to the variable on the left side.

The following is a small subset of the updating operators:

- +=
- -=
- *=

Similarly, there are operators for numerical comparisons. These operators are frequently used.

The following is a small subset of the comparison operators:

- ==
- !=
- <
- <=
- >
- >=

Examples of comparison operations:

```
julia> 100 > 99.9
true

julia> 24  == 24.0
true

julia> 24 === 24.0
false
```

```
julia> 24 !== 24.0
true
```

The NaN is not equal to anything, even itself:

```
julia> NaN == NaN
false
```

```
julia> NaN === NaN
true
```

```
# Inf is equal to itself and greater that every real number.
# It results to false when compared with NaN
julia> Inf == Inf
true
```

```
julia> Inf >= NaN
false
```

The preceding operations discussed can be chained together for ease of use:

```
julia> 10 > 20 < 30 >= 30.0 == 100 > 101
false
```

Precedence of operators

There is a specific order of priority for operators being called (also including their element-wise equivalents):

1. Syntax (. followed by : :)
2. Exponentiation (^)
3. Fractions (//)
4. Multiplication (*, /, %, &, and \)
5. Bitshifts (<<, >>, and >>>)
6. Addition (+, −, |, and $)
7. Syntax (:, .., and |>)
8. Comparisons (>, <, >=, <=, ==, ===, !=, !==, and <:)
9. Control flow (&& followed by || followed by ?)
10. Assignments (=, +=, −=, *=, /=, //=, \=, ^=, ÷=, %=, |=, &=, $=, <<=, >>=, and >>>=)

Type conversions (numerical)

We have used conversion in previous examples. Type conversion refers to changing the type of the variable, but keeping the value of the variable the same:

```
#creating a 8-bit Integer
julia> Int8(100)
100

#we will get an error here as we exceed the size of the Int8
julia> Int8(100*10)
ERROR: InexactError()
in Int8(::Int64) at ./sysimg.jl:53

#this is solved by using Int16
julia> Int16(100*10)
1000

#create a variable x of type Int32
julia> x = Int32(40); typeof(x)
Int32

#using type conversion, convert it to Int8
julia> x = Int8(x); typeof(x)
Int8
```

We were successful, as 40 is in the range of the signed Int8.

Understanding arrays, matrices, and multidimensional arrays

An array is an indexable collection of objects such as integers, floats, and Booleans, which are stored in a multidimensional grid. Arrays in Julia can contain values of the Any type. Arrays are implemented internally in Julia itself.

In most of the other languages, the indexing of arrays starts with 0. In Julia, it starts with 1:

```
# creating an array
julia> simple_array = [100,200,300,400,500]
5-element Array{Int64,1}:
100
200
300
400
```

```
500

# accessing elements in array
julia> simple_array[2]
200

julia> simple_array[2:4]
3-element Array{Int64,1}:
200
300
400
```

In the preceding example, we can see that, unlike other programming languages, indexes start from 1.

```
# creating an array using randomly generated values
julia> rand_array = rand(1:1000,6)
6-element Array{Int64,1}:
378
 57
 ...
```

We previously discussed that the types of values in an array are homogeneous:

```
# types of values in array are homogeneous
julia> another_simple_array = [100,250.20,500,672.42]
4-element Array{Float64,1}:
100.0
250.2
500.0
672.42
```

In the preceding example, we provided two Int type values and 2 Float type values to create an array. Julia converted the Int type values to Float to create the array.

If possible, Julia tries to use promote() to promote the values of the same type. If not possible, the array will be of the type Any.

```
julia> [1,2,"foobar"]
3-element Array{Any,1}:
 1
 2
 "foobar"
```

List comprehension in Julia

List comprehensions are frequently used and make populating arrays easier. Let's create an array using list comprehension, where we will populate it with the power of 2:

```
# create an array of size 10
julia> pow2 = Array(Int64,10)
10-element Array{Int64,1}:
...
# assign 2 to the first element
julia> pow2[1] = 2
2
# using list comprehension populate it with powers of 2
julia> [pow2[i] = 2^i for i = 2:length(pow2)]; pow2
10-element Array{Int64,1}:
    2
    4
    8
   16
   32
   64
  128
  256
  512
 1024
```

List comprehension can prove to be very powerful and convenient in various scenarios.

Creating an empty array

Although the size of the array is fixed, Julia provides certain functions that can be utilized to alter the length of the array. Let's create an empty array and add values to it:

```
# this creates an empty array
julia> empty_array = Float64[]
0-element Array{Float64,1}

# the function push!() adds values to the array
julia> push!(empty_array,1.1)
1-element Array{Float64,1}:
 1.1
```

We can keep on adding values:

```
julia> push!(empty_array,2.2,3.3)
3-element Array{Float64,1}:
1.1
2.2
3.3
```

Adding values one by one may not suit the purpose. There is another way to add values to the array using the append!() function. Using append!(), we can add all the items of another collection to our collection:

```
julia> append!(empty_array, [101.1,202.2,303.3])
6-element Array{Float64,1}:
  1.1
  2.2
  3.3
101.1
202.2
303.3
```

In the preceding examples, we created an empty array and added values to it. We can also create an array with specific dimensions:

```
julia> X = Array{Int64}(4,1)
4x1 Array{Int64,2}:
140114385365424
140114336334352
140114336432272
0
```

This is not a typical array like in other languages. More specifically, it is 4 arrays with size 1 (or a 4x1 column matrix).

Now, we can add values to this array using the index of the array, or simply by using the fill!() function if we want to fill the array with the same values:

```
# using fill function to copy the same values to the array
julia> fill!(X,4)
4x1 Array{Int64,2}:
4
4
4
4

# changing value using index of the array
julia> X[2] = 10; X
4x1 Array{Int64,2}:
```

```
 4
10
 4
 4
```

Operations on arrays

Various operators and functions that are valid for integers and arrays are also valid for arrays. Following are the most used operators:

- Unary arithmetic (−, +, !)
- Binary arithmetic (+, −, * , .* , /, ./, \, .\, ^, .^, div, mod)
- Comparison (.==, .!=, .<, .<=, .>, .>=)
- Unary Boolean or bitwise (~)
- Binary Boolean or bitwise (&, |, $)

Working with matrices

In the preceding section, we worked with arrays and operations on them. It is also possible to create two-dimensional arrays or matrices. There is a small difference in the syntax that helps to create these matrices:

```
# this will create an array
julia> X = [1, 1, 2, 3, 5, 8, 13, 21, 34]
9-element Array{Int64,1}:
 1
 1
...

# constructing a matrix
julia> X = [1 1 2; 3 5 8; 13 21 34]
3×3 Array{Int64,2}:
  1   1   2
  3   5   8
 13  21  34
```

The difference is that we didn't provide "," (comma) between the elements and separated the rows of the matrix using a ";" (semicolon). This type of indexing is called column order.

Different operation on matrices

Just like arrays, there are different operations that can be performed on matrices:

```
# a 3x2 matrix
julia> A = [2 4; 8 16; 32 64]
3×2 Array{Int64,2}:
  2   4
  8  16
 32  64
```

We can change the shape of a matrix using the `reshape()` function:

```
julia> reshape(A,2,3)
2×3 Array{Int64,2}:
2  32  16
8   4  64
```

This converts a 3x2 matrix to a 2x3 matrix:

```
# same could be achieved using the transpose function
julia> transpose(A)
2×3 Array{Int64,2}:
2  32  16
8   4  64
```

Operations such as addition and multiplication are also valid, with some restrictions:

```
julia> B = [1 1 2; 3 5 8]
2×3 Array{Int64,2}:
1  1  2
3  5  8
```

```
# adding both the matrices
julia> transpose(A)+B
2×3 Array{Int64,2}:
 3   9 34
 7  21 72
```

This operation is performed successfully. Now, let's try the multiplication operation on the same matrices:

```
julia> transpose(A)*B
ERROR: DimensionMismatch("matrix A has dimensions (2,3), matrix B has
dimensions (2,3)")
...
```

As anticipated, it didn't work because matrix B should have had the dimensions (3,2). Let's transpose matrix B and perform the operation again:

```
# multiplying after transposing the matrix B
julia> transpose(A)*transpose(B)
2x2 Array{Int64,2}:
   74 302
  148 604
```

There is another special operator provided by Julia, which helps us to do element-wise multiplications. These operators are traditional operators preceded by "." key:

```
# the following performs elemental operations on two (2x3) matrices.
julia> A.*B
2x3 Array{Int64,2}:
   2   8  64
  12  80 512
```

There are other elemental operations supported by matrices:

```
# Define 2 matrices of dimensions (2x3)
julia> A = [1 2 2 ; 4 5 6]
2×3 Array{Int64,2}:
1  2  2
4  5  6

julia> B = [0 2 3 ; 4 4 6]
2×3 Array{Int64,2}:
0  2  3
4  4  6

# perform elemental operation to check if values are equal
# return a matrix of booleans of the same dimension (2x3)
julia> A .== B
2×3 BitArray{2}:
false   true  false
 true  false   true
```

Working with multidimensional arrays (matrices)

In the previous section, we studied arrays, matrices, and operations on them. In this section, we will study multidimensional arrays in Julia.

We will start by constructing a 3x3x3 multidimensional array using the `rand()` function, which generates random values:

```
# multidimensional array
julia> multiA = rand(3,3,3)
3×3×3 Array{Float64,3}:
[:, :, 1] =
0.330416  0.927464  0.767308
0.637868  0.17889   0.274145
0.506475  0.790026  0.634805

[:, :, 2] =
0.850958  0.869152  0.912493
0.125413  0.82839   0.0164393
0.039429  0.494712  0.891798

[:, :, 3] =
0.310575  0.679891  0.639199
0.900038  0.475569  0.954107
0.576849  0.261151  0.252355
```

We can access the values just as we accessed values in arrays and matrices, using the index:

```
julia> multiA[1,3,2]
0.9124929764541214
```

The preceding number is actually represented as `0.912493` in the array.

We can also reshape the array into a two-dimensional array using the `reshape()` function:

```
julia> reshape(multiA,9,3)
9×3 Array{Float64,2}:
0.330416  0.850958   0.310575
0.637868  0.125413   0.900038
0.506475  0.039429   0.576849
0.927464  0.869152   0.679891
0.17889   0.82839    0.475569
0.790026  0.494712   0.261151
0.767308  0.912493   0.639199
0.274145  0.0164393  0.954107
0.634805  0.891798   0.252355
```

Understanding sparse matrices

In the preceding sections, we worked with matrices and multidimensional arrays. In our examples, the arrays and matrices are filled with values. In many scenarios, there could be lots of zeroes.

When there are more zeroes than cells with values, it is recommended to store them in an efficient and specially designed data structure for sparse matrices:

```
julia> sm = spzeros(5,5)
5×5 sparse matrix with 0 Float64 nonzero entries

# assigning a value
julia> sm[1,1] = 10
10

julia> sm
5×5 sparse matrix with 1 Float64 nonzero entries:
 [1, 1]  =   10.0
```

In this section, we studied and worked on arrays, matrices, multidimensional arrays, and sparse matrices. In the next section, we will study a special data structure called DataFrames.

Understanding DataFrames

A DataFrame is a data structure that has labeled columns, which may individually have different data types. Like a SQL table or a spreadsheet, it has two dimensions. It can also be thought of as a list of dictionaries, but fundamentally, it is different.

DataFrames are the recommended data structure for statistical analysis. Julia provides a package called DataFrames.Jl, which has all the necessary functions to work with DataFrames.

Julia's package, DataFrames, provides three data types:

- NA: A missing value in Julia is represented by a specific data type, NA.
- DataArray: The array type defined in the standard Julia library, though it has many features, doesn't provide any specific functionalities for data analysis. The DataArray type provided in DataFrames.jl provides such features (for example if we needed to store some missing values in the array).

- `DataFrame`: This is a two-dimensional data structure, such as spreadsheets. It is much like R or Pandas DataFrames and provides many functionalities to represent and analyze data.

NA data type in DataArray

In the real world, we come across data with missing values. This functionality is provided in the `DataFrames.jl` package.

The `DataFrames` package brings with it `DataArray` packages, which provide the NA data type. Multiple dispatches is one of the most powerful features of Julia and NA is one such example.

Julia has the NA type, which provides the singleton object NA that we are using to represent missing values.

The requirement of the NA data type

Suppose, for example, we have a dataset with floating-point numbers:

```
julia> x = [1.1, 2.2, 3.3, 4.4, 5.5, 6.6]
```

This will create a six-element array {Float64,1}.

Now, suppose this dataset has a missing value at position [1]. That means instead of 1.1, there is no value. This cannot be represented by the array type in Julia. When we try to assign an NA value, we get this error:

```
julia> x[1] = NA
Error: UndefVarError: NA not defined
while loading In[2], in expression starting on line 1
```

Therefore, right now, we cannot add NA values to the array that we have created.

So, to load the data into an array that does have NA values, we use `DataArray`. This enables us to have NA values in our dataset:

```
julia> using DataArrays
julia> x = DataArray([1.1, 2.2, 3.3, 4.4, 5.5, 6.6])
```

This will create a six-element array `DataArrays.DataArray{Float64,1}`.

So, when we try to have an NA value, it gives us:

```
julia> x[1] = NA
NA

julia> x
6-element DataArrays.DataArray{Float64,1}:
 NA
2.2
3.3
4.4
5.5
6.6
```

Therefore, by using `DataArrays`, we can handle missing data. One more feature provided is that NA doesn't always affect functions applied on the particular dataset. So, a method that doesn't involve an NA value or is not affected by it can be applied to the dataset. If it does involve the NA value, then it will give NA as the result.

In the following example, we are applying the mean function and `true || x`. The mean function doesn't work, as it involves an NA value, but `true || x` works as expected:

```
julia> true || x
true

julia> true && x[1]
NA

julia> mean(x)
NA

julia> mean(x[2:6])
4.4
```

DataArray – a series-like data structure

In the previous section, we discussed how `DataArray` types are used to store datasets containing missing (NA) values, as Julia's standard `Array` type cannot do so.

There are other features similar to Julia's `Array` type. Type aliases of `Vector` (a one-dimensional `Array` type) and `Matrix` (a two-dimensional `Array` type) are `DataVector` and `DataMatrix`, provided by `DataArray`.

Creating a one-dimensional `DataArray` is similar to creating an `Array` type:

```
julia> using DataArrays

julia> dvector = data([10,20,30,40,50])
5-element DataArrays.DataArray{Int64,1}:
10
20
30
40
50
```

Here, we have `NA` values, unlike in arrays. Similarly, we can create a two-dimensional `DataArray`, which will be a `DataMatrix`:

```
julia> dmatrix = data([10 20 30; 40 50 60])
2x3 DataArrays.DataArray{Int64,2}:
10 20 30
40 50 60

julia> dmatrix[2,3]
60
```

In the previous example, to calculate the mean, we used slicing. This is not a convenient method to remove or not consider the `NA` values when applying a function. A much better way is to use `dropna`:

```
julia> dropna(x)
5-element Array{Float64,1}:
2.2
3.3
4.4
5.5
6.6
```

DataFrames – tabular data structures

Arguably, this is the most important and commonly used data type in statistical computing, whether it is in R (`data.frame`) or Python (`Pandas`). This is due to the fact that all the real-world data is mostly in a tabular or spreadsheet-like format. This cannot be represented by a simple `DataArray`.

To use `DataFrames`, add the `DataFrames` package from the registered packages of Julia:

```
julia> Pkg.update()
julia> Pkg.add("DataFrames")
julia> using DataFrame
```

Let's start by creating a simple data frame:

```
julia> df = DataFrame(Name = ["Julia", "Python"], Version = [0.5, 3.6])
2×2 DataFrames.DataFrame
```

Row	Name	Version
1	"Julia"	0.5
2	"Python"	3.6

This dataset, for example, can't be represented using `DataArray`. The given dataset has the following features because it cannot be represented by `DataArray`:

- This dataset has different types of data in different columns. These different data types in different columns cannot be represented using a matrix. A matrix can only contain values of one type.

- It is a tabular data structure and records have relations with other records in the same row of different columns. Therefore, it is a must that all the columns are of the same length. Vectors cannot be used because same-length columns cannot be enforced using them. Therefore, a column in a `DataFrame` is represented by `DataArray`.

- In the preceding example, we can see that the columns are labeled. This labeling helps us to easily become familiar with the data and access it without the need to remember its exact positions. So, the columns are accessible using numerical indices and also by their label. Therefore, due to these reasons, the `DataFrame` package is used. So, `DataFrame` packages are used to represent tabular data, and have `DataArrays` as columns.

We will be studying DataFrames in detail in `Chapter 7`, *Numerical and Scientific Computation with Julia*.

Summary

In this chapter, we revisited programming paradigms to understand the best approach to the problem. We then explored Julia using the REPL and found out that it is quite easy to get started with Julia. In subsequent sections, we went through the concepts and how primitive data types are used and operated in Julia. After studying integers and floating point operations, we went through important and widely used data structures, arrays, and matrices. Multidimensional arrays used in numerical computing were explained in the section that followed. After arrays, we explored `DataArray` and `DataFrame` packages, which are more suited to representing real-world data and are widely used in statistical computing. In the next chapter, we will study functions in Julia.

3
Functions in Julia

Functions form an integral part of any programming language because they increase code modularity, as well as making the code much more readable than unorganized non-function code. Julia is no different, as it also provides functions as part of the built-in library, along with the ability to add in user-defined functions.

This chapter is divided into different sections, with each section talking in detail about itself and providing you with a good stronghold. A list of the things covered in this chapter is provided as follows, which acts as a quick reference for you to go through:

- Creating functions
- Function arguments
- Anonymous functions
- Multiple dispatch
- Recursion
- Built-in functions

After going through this chapter, you will be able to:

- Create and define functions inside Julia REPL as well as independent Julia scripts
- Clearly understand and differentiate between various argument passing methods and their usage
- Create recursive functions, along with having a good understanding of what recursion is and how it is performed in Julia
- Define anonymous functions
- Use the most commonly used built-in Julia functions in your own code

Creating functions

Functions in Julia are declared with the `function` keyword, which is then followed by the body of the function. Another keyword, `end`, puts or marks a logical end to the function in general. The syntax of defining a function can be summarized as:

```
function name()
        ...
    body
        ...
end
```

The function's name has to be followed by a bracket `()`. Failing to do so will result in an error. People coming from languages such as Python may find it a little different, but it becomes easy as you start coding in Julia. Let's just have a look at how a function is defined and used inside Julia's REPL:

```
julia> function greet()
           println("hello world")
       end
greet (generic function with 1 method)

julia> greet()
hello world
```

Here is what the official documentation says about functions:

> *"A function is an object that maps a tuple of argument values to a return value."*

To present a better example of how we can make useful functions and how to call them, we have created a function named `calculator()`, which computes the four basic operations of a calculator. For now, just focus on the results and how the function is created, as we will be discussing parameter passing later on in this chapter, and we will be taking up conditionals such as `if...then...else` statements in another chapter:

```julia
julia> function calculator(x, y, operation)
           if operation == "+"
               x+y
           elseif operation == "-"
               x-y
           elseif operation == "*"
               x*y
           elseif operation == "/"
               x/y
           else
               println("Incorrect operation")
               return 0
           end
       end
calculator (generic function with 1 method)

julia> calculator(10,20, "+")
30

julia> calculator(10,20, "-")
-10

julia> calculator(10,20, "*")
200

julia> calculator(10,20, "/")
0.5
```

Functions in Julia can also be defined using a compact form. A simple implementation could be:

```julia
f(x,y) = x^2 + y^2
```

The usage of this form is very convenient for those working very closely with mathematical functions, as it turns out to be very handy and saves a significant amount of development time.

An important thing to keep in mind is that although Julia's functions closely resemble mathematical functions, they aren't purely mathematical, as they can change with or be affected by the global state of the program.

The special !

Sometimes, when defining a function in Julia, we may also include a ! (not to be confused with the Boolean operator ! for not in Julia) just after the function name. For example, in Julia, we have a function named push! whose job is to insert one or more items at the end of a collection. Representing that in code, we have:

```
push!(collection of items, the item you want to push to the end of
collection)
julia> push!([1, 2, 3], 4)
  4-element Array{Int64,1}:
   1
   2
   3
   4
```

But what does the ! really stand for here? It is a convention which says that the function can actually mutate its input or, in other words, a function can modify its arguments. An important condition for that to happen is that inputs are mutable and should have the ability to be changed once created.

 Any function regardless of the name, may mutate the argument. Likewise, a function with declared with ! may not mutate the argument.
A function defined with ! is merely a convention to explicitly state that the function will mutate the argument.

All types, including String, Tuples, Int64, and float64, and so on are immutable, as well as all the types defined using the immutable keyword.

Function arguments

So far, we have been discussing the syntax of functions in Julia and how to create one when required. One very important aspect when we talk about functions are arguments. Undoubtedly, we have been using them freely in almost every other language, knowing that they may be either passed by a value or a reference.

But Julia is different. Julia follows a convention knows as **pass by sharing**! Wait, now what does *pass by sharing* mean? For this, let's first go back to the two most commonly used conventions.

Pass by values versus pass by reference

When we say *pass by value*, it means that the value of whatever is passed to a function as an argument will be copied into that function, meaning that two copies of the same variable will be passed.

On the other hand, when we say *pass by reference*, the reference or location of whatever is passed to the function is also passed into that function, meaning that only one copy of the variable will be passed.

Pass by sharing

In *pass by sharing*, we see that variables passed as arguments are not copied. Instead, the function arguments themselves act as new bindings, which refer to the same values as those passed.

Before we move on to discuss more about functions, let's spend some time talking about the return statement in Julia.

The return keyword

A `return` statement terminates the execution of a function and returns control to the calling function. A function in Julia may or may not use the `return` statement explicitly to return a value. This may be a little different for people coming from other languages, such as Python, but will become relatively easier to follow later.

In the absence of the `return` statement, the last expression is evaluated and returned. For instance, the underlying pieces of code are equal in terms of the value they return:

```
# function returns the value computed in the last statement
julia> function add_without_return(x,y)
            x+y
       end
add_without_return (generic function with 1 method)

julia> add_without_return(20,30)
```

```
50

# function with return statement
julia> function add_using_return(x,y)
          return x+y
       end
add_using_return (generic function with 1 method)

julia> add_using_return(20,30)
50

julia> add_without_return(20,30) == add_using_return(20,30)
true
```

Arguments

A `function` argument is a variable passed to a function in the form of an input so that it returns a specific output. A very simple example of a function taking an argument is stated as follows:

```
julia> function say_hello(name)
          println("hello $name")
       end
say_hello (generic function with 1 method)

julia> say_hello("rahul")
hello rahul
```

Here, the `say_hello` function takes an argument called `name`, which is a string. Upon calling the function with the name `rahul`, the `hello` string becomes `hello rahul`. Simple!

One thing to keep in mind is that, although Julia is dynamically typed, it supports the use of statically-typed variables. Modifying the preceding code, we have:

```
julia> function say_hello(name::String)
          println("hello $name")
       end
say_hello (generic function with 1 method)

julia> say_hello("rahul")
hello rahul
```

As you may have noticed, there is no change to the way the function behaves. However, there is one huge benefit of declaring the type of the arguments passed, which is **speed**. We will talk about speed later on in the book, when we explicitly cover the performance-related enhancements of Julia.

There are multiple ways in which arguments can be passed to a function. Let's discuss those one by one.

No arguments

Sometimes, we may not want to define a function with any arguments. Some functions are defined like this:

```
julia> function does_nothing
          end
does_nothing (generic function with 0 methods)
```

Although this function isn't doing anything here, there will be specific use cases wherein we just want to have the function definition present in the form of an interface.

Varargs

Varargs stands for *variable arguments*. These come in handy when we are not sure about the total number of arguments to be passed to a function in advance. Hence, we want to have an arbitrary number of arguments.

The way we achieve this in Julia is by using three dots or . . . . Let's use an example to explain this further:

```
julia> function letsplay(x,y...)
            println(x)
            println(y)
        end
letsplay (generic function with 1 method)

julia> letsplay("cricket","hockey","tennis")
cricket
("hockey","tennis")
```

Here, we have defined a letsplay() function that prints the names of the games we pass. Here, Julia interprets these arguments as positional and maps them accordingly.

The first argument, x, is mapped to cricket on a function call and is displayed as it is with the help of the `println()` function. So, x=`"cricket"`.

On the other hand, y is interpreted as a tuple being passed because it was originally followed by . . . at the time the function was declared. Hence, y is mapped to hockey and tennis. So, y=`("hockey","tennis")`.

For those familiar with Python, this will sound very similar to the concept of `*args` being passed as a function argument.

On the flip side, the arguments to be passed to the function can be declared in advance in more than one way. For instance, let's have a function that takes in a variable number of arguments in the following fashion:

```julia
julia> x = (1,2,3,4,5)
(1,2,3,4,5)

julia> function numbers(a...)
           println("the arguments are -> ",x)
       end
numbers (generic function with 1 method)

julia> numbers(x)
the arguments are -> (1,2,3,4,5)
```

As you can see here, we have passed the function numbers a tuple of values:

```julia
julia> typeof(x)
Tuple{Int64,Int64,Int64,Int64,Int64}
```

We can also pass x as a list of values and the end result still won't be affected. To prove the point, we initialized x as an array and reran the code. The result was something we expected:

```julia
julia> x = [1, 2, 3, 4, 5]
5-element Array{Int64,1}:
 1
 2
 3
 4
 5

julia> typeof(x)
Array{Int64,1}

julia> numbers(x)
the arguments are -> [1,2,3,4,5]
```

Optional arguments

Sometimes, during the implementation of a specific use case, you may want to have some arguments fixed (that is, having a value) or set to a default. For example, you want to convert a number to another number with `base 8` or perhaps `base 16`. The approach best suited to this would be to have a generic function that takes up a parameter base, which is then set to the number as per the requirement.

Hence, instead of having functions like `convert_to_octal()` or `convert_to_hex()`, you just have `convert_to_base(base = 8)` or `convert_to_base(base = 16)`.

A simpler example for optional arguments:

```
# function f takes 1 mandatory argument and
# 2 optional arguments

julia> function f(x, y=4, z=10)
    x+y+z
end
f (generic function with 1 method)

julia> f(10)
24

julia> f(110)
124
```

We leave the exercise of creating the function `convert_to_base` with the reader.

Understanding scope with respect to functions

When we define functions in Julia, we may also define variables inside the function body. This way, that variable is said to be inside a function's local scope, hence, is called a local variable. On the other hand, any variable that isn't declared inside a function's body is said to be in a global scope, hence, is called a global variable.

Different blocks of code can use the same name without referring to the same entity. This is defined by the scope rules.

Julia has two main types of scopes, *global scope* and *local scope*. The *local* scope can be nested. Variables at module or in REPL are generally in global scope unless stated otherwise. Variables in loops, functions, macros, try-catch-finally blocks are of local scope.

The following example is to explain local scope:

```julia
julia> for i=1:5
    hello = i
end

julia> hello
ERROR: UndefVarError: hello not defined
```

`hello` is only available in the scope of the for loop and not outside of it.

We can modify the previous function, to have the `hello` available outside of the loop:

```julia
julia> for i=1:5
    global hello
    hello = i
end

julia> hello
5
```

Julia makes use of something called **lexical scoping**, which basically means that a function's scope does not inherit from its caller's scope, but from the scope in which the function was defined!

To understand this more clearly, let's use an example (we will go through modules in detail in next few sections and chapters):

```julia
julia> module Utility
    name = "Julia"
    tell_name() = name
end
Utility

julia> name = "Python"
"Python"

julia> Utility.tell_name()
"Julia"
```

Here, we have created a module with the name `Utility`, which holds a variable named as `name` and a function called `tell_name()`. The value of the name inside the `Utility` module is set to "Julia". Also, we declared yet another value for the `name` variable outside the `Utility` module and set it to "Python".

Now, when we call `Utility.tell_name()`, we get the "Julia" value. This shows that this function took the value of the `name` variable, which was inside the `Utility` module, where the function `tell_me()` was declared! Hence, the other name that was declared outside the `Utility` module did not impact the result.

Julia also provides further classification of the local scope, calling it either a **soft local scope** or a **hard local scope**. It's the hard local scope that is introduced by functions. We will come back to scope in upcoming chapters, but for now, we will keep our focus on function scope.

Suppose that we have a function named `alpha()`, which simply assigns a local variable named x to the variable passed and returns it. Yes, that simple! Also, we have defined a global variable as x, which is already set to a value:

```
julia> x = 23
23

julia> function alpha(n::Int64)
           x = n
           return x
       end
alpha (generic function with 1 method)

julia> alpha(25)
25

# global x is unchanged
julia> x
23
```

So, if you look closely, we set the value of x to 23, but when we call the `alpha()` function with the value 25 passed, we get back 25 and not 23! This is because the variable declared inside the function (that is, x) was locally assigned to the number (that is, n) passed as an argument.

But what if we wanted to use the same x declared globally? We would then use a special keyword, called `global`, which will do the trick for us! See the following code:

```
julia> x = 23
23

julia> function alpha(n::Int64)
                global x = n
            end
alpha (generic function with 1 method)

julia> alpha(25)
```

```
25

# global x is now changed
julia> x
25
```

The step where we assigned x to the number has now been removed and instead, we added code in order to make the function assign a value of number n to the globally available x. The results are evident, as the global variable x got changed to the value 25 instead of its originally set value of 23.

Nested functions

Or, in simpler words, functions defined within functions. For those coming from other language backgrounds, such as Python, the concept of closures should be very easily applicable to Julia. A Closure is a function object that remembers values in enclosing scopes even if they are not present in memory.

Nesting helps in places where you want to mask the real implementation of the function from the end user.

Let's just define a function with the name outer and another function inside it with the name inner:

```
julia> function outer(value_a)
                function inner(value_b)
                        return value_a * value_b
                end
        end
outer (generic function with 1 method)
```

If you look closely, we are passing two different arguments to both functions and then utilizing them to return a value that concatenates a string (* is used for string concatenation in Julia) OR multiplies two integers, depending upon the data type of the arguments being passed. Also, for the time being, let's also assume that we either pass two strings or two integers and don't intermix these values because with the current function defined, it will throw an error.

Firing the same function in Julia REPL, given that both inputs that we pass are of the `Int64` type:

```
julia> result = outer(10)
(::inner) (generic function with 1 method)

julia> typeof(result)
Function

julia> result(10)
100
```

Similarly, passing both the arguments inside the functions of the data type `String`, we have:

```
julia> result = outer("learning ")
(::inner) (generic function with 1 method)

julia> typeof(result)
Function

julia> result("Julia")
"learning Julia"
```

In both cases, we first assign the value of the function to a variable named result and then pass the second argument to the result callable. Once done, we get the desired results as expected.

Anonymous functions

Anonymous functions are shorthand notations for regular functions. These are the choice of code when a function has to be used only a limited number of times, hence, it may be slightly easier and quicker to have them rather than using named functions. In popular terms, they are also sometimes referred to as **lambda** functions.

To relate to the preceding sentence, just think of a scenario wherein you want to apply a functionality over a list of values using a `map()` function. Instead of writing down a full-fledged function, we can just define them in an easy way without even bothering about giving them a name!

In Julia, we define an anonymous function using the following syntax:

```
f -> 2f
```

The syntax uses **->** to notify that we are defining an anonymous function here. However, it should be kept in mind that anonymous functions themselves have no use, as they don't have a name, hence cannot be called from anywhere in the code:

```
julia> f ->2f
(::#1) (generic function with 1 method)
```

Let's consider an example using the Julia REPL:

```
julia> map(f -> 2f, [2,3])
2-element Array{Int64,1}:
 4
 6

julia> map(f -> 2f, [2 3])
1×2 Array{Int64,2}:
 4  6
```

Here, we have a map() function, which takes in two parameters, the first being a function and the latter being a collection of values that can easily be iterated upon. To keep things simple, we have used a list comprehension here.

The first argument here, f->2f, is an anonymous function that takes in a value from the list and doubles it.

The preceding example purely talks about anonymous functions that take in only one argument. *But what if we have more than one?* We may then be forced to use opening and closing parenthesis, that is, a tuple of variables inside our function body:

```
(f,g) -> 2f + 2g
```

Let's fire up a Julia REPL session again to dive deeper:

```
julia> map((f,g) -> 2f + 2g, [2,3], [3,4])
2-element Array{Int64,1}:
 10
 14
```

So, if you see here, we have used a map() function that takes in more than one list comprehension. When this map() function is executed, the results comes out to be 2f+2g that is 2(2)+2(3) = 10 and 2(3)+2(4)=14.

Multiple dispatch

Before we dive deep into the topic, let's just ask ourselves a quick question. What does dispatch mean? To come up with an answer in the easiest of terms, we can say that dispatch means to send!

In programming terms, dispatch means to send a message to a listener or a call to a function. Basically, to send a piece of data (or packet of information) to code that is ready to handle it.

Dispatch can be of many different types. Starting off with a few of them we have:

- **Static dispatch**: The dispatch order can be defined at compile time. Essentially, in static dispatch, all types are already known before the execution of the program. Compiler is able to generate specific code for every possible combination of datatypes and know in advance when and where they will be used. This is one of the most common in most languages. To break it down, if we have a place in the code where the function or a method is called using `funct()` or perhaps `x.funct()`, then that very same function will be invoked each and every time; there will not be any changes to it.

- **Dynamic dispatch**: The dispatch order can be defined at runtime. This simply means that the compiler has to make up a lookup table of all the functions defined and then determine which ones to actually call and which not to at runtime. In terms of code, let's say we have a few classes such as `classA` and `classB`, and both have the implementation of a function called `foo()`, then at runtime, both the classes will be examined, and finally, either of them (`classA.foo()` or `classB.foo()`) may be called.

- **Multiple dispatch**: The dispatch order is dependent on the function name as well as the argument types being passed, that is, the signature of the function and also the actual implementation that gets called is determined directly at runtime. In terms of code, let's suppose we have `classA`, which implements a method called `foo(int)` for integers and `foo(char)` for character types. Then, we have a call in the program that calls this function with `classA.foo(x)`. At runtime, we have both `classA` and `x` examined for the actual function to be called.

Julia supports multiple dispatch. We will now go step by step into the topic and explore how Julia implements this technique.

Understanding methods

Methods are a very important part of Julia's ecosystem. To better understand what multiple dispatch is and why Julia uses it, we need to get familiar with methods first.

Suppose we have a function that adds two numbers:

```
julia> function add_numbers(num1::Int64, num2::Int64)
           return num1 + num2
       end
add_numbers (generic function with 1 method)
```

If you closely observe the function definition, we have defined the add_numbers() to take in two arguments. Both of them being integer values (Int64, as I am currently on a 64-bit machine). What happens when we call the function add_numbers(10,20)? We get the following result:

```
julia> add_numbers(10,20)
30

julia> typeof(ans)
Int64
```

No surprises here, as 10+20 =30. Also, notice the type of ans that we get, that is, Int64, which is expected.

But what if we accidentally pass float values to the function?

```
julia> add_numbers(10.0,20.0)
ERROR: MethodError: no method matching add_numbers(::Float64, ::Float64)
```

Julia throws an error! But, wait... WHY?

The answer is very simple. We explicitly defined that the two arguments in the functions body we will be passing to the add_numbers() function will have to be of the type Int64. Had we not expressed the integer types explicitly, we wouldn't have landed in errors. Just see this function in action here:

```
julia> function add_without_types(num1,num2)
           return num1+num2
       end
add_without_types (generic function with 1 method)

julia> add_without_types(10.0,20)
30.0

julia> add_without_types(10,20.0)
```

```
30.0

julia> add_without_types(10,20)
30
```

This seems very close to what we do in Python. There, we just define the function, as we have done here, and leave the type inference part to Python's interpreter, which does the same job as Julia does here.

But, would this mean that we made a mistake by explicitly defining the types of arguments we intend to take? Absolutely NOT!

Defining the data type of arguments expected by the function makes them faster, as the compiler does not have to infer the types of arguments supplied to the function, hence, that prevents the compiler from wasting time. Instead, we get a good speed boost! We will discuss more about improving speed when we discuss how to have more performant Julia code.

Coming back to the function `add_numbers(num1::Int64, num2::Int64)`, imagine a situation wherein we wanted to have a float type output, even if we supplied `Int64` type arguments. A way to do this is to use `convert`, which does the typecasting of the arguments supplied:

```
julia> function add_numbers(num1::Int64, num2::Int64)
           float_num1 = convert(AbstractFloat, num1)
           float_num2 = convert(AbstractFloat, num2)
           return float_num1+float_num2
       end
add_numbers (generic function with 1 method)

julia> add_numbers(10,20)
30.0
```

Okay, but that is NOT what we want. Right? Instead, we want to make our function `add_numbers()` functional even when float arguments are supplied. The answer is defining another method that handles the `Float64` type numbers:

```
julia> function add_numbers(num1::Float64, num2::Float64)
           return num1+num2
       end
add_numbers (generic function with 2 methods)

julia> add_numbers(10.0,20.0)
30.0
```

Yes, you need to create another function that can accept the `Float64` type arguments. This is what we call creating another method for a function. To have a look at all the methods that a function has for itself, we can run `methods()` over our `add_numbers()` function here:

```
julia> methods(add_numbers)
# 2 methods for generic function "add_numbers":
add_numbers(num1::Float64, num2::Float64) at REPL[2]:2
add_numbers(num1::Int64, num2::Int64) at REPL[1]:2
```

Look closely at the output. It lists all the methods that we have defined for our function so far.

Hence, this way, each and every function can be assigned different methods depending upon the use cases. Julia then selects any one of these methods accordingly at runtime given the types of arguments you pass. This method of selecting methods at runtime is what we call multiple dispatch.

Recursion

Recursion is a technique in computer science that allows for a bigger problem to be broken down into smaller similar sub-problems that makes it easier to solve and debug.

Speaking about functions, we call a function recursive if it makes repeated calls to itself. This would typically involve the function having a `base` condition and being small enough to magnify itself easily enough to solve the overall problem.

Julia functions can also make recursive calls, just like any other language. Let's take the case of the Fibonacci series, wherein every number in the sequence is the sum of the previous two:

```
# fibonacci series
1,1,2,3,5,8,13....
```

So, if you look closely, the number 2 is the sum of its previous two digits 1+1, and then the next number, 3, is the sum of its previous two, 1+2, and so on. This problem makes a genuine case of recursion.

WHY? Simply because each and every step involves the usage of the same logic being applied, thus the overall sequence can be said to have been created by these smaller tasks.

Let's code it in Julia now to see how we can implement a Fibonacci series of any number n, where n is the total number of elements in the sequence:

```julia
julia> function generate_fibonacci(n::Int64)
           if n < 2
               return 1
           else
               return generate_fibonacci(n-1) + generate_fibonacci(n-2)
           end
       end
generate_fibonacci (generic function with 1 method)
```

In this function, first off, we define the base case, that is, the condition that prevents the function from calling itself over and over again, which could result in an error.

Once that is done, we move on to the else case, wherein the real function calls are done, hence, we have the summation of the previous two numbers, resulting in the formation of the current number in the sequence.

Now, if we just make some calls to this function to generate the Fibonacci series, we have:

```julia
julia> generate_fibonacci(1)
1

julia> generate_fibonacci(2)
2

julia> generate_fibonacci(3)
3

julia> generate_fibonacci(4)
5

julia> generate_fibonacci(5)
8

julia> generate_fibonacci(6)
13
```

Which is again 1, 1, 2, 3, 5, 8, 13.

Coming back to the original `genrate_fibonacci` function, we could have also done it in a much shorter way. This alternative syntax, which Julia uses, is much more simple and easy to read:

```
julia> generate_fibonacci(n) = n < 2 ? n : generate_fibonacci(n - 1) +
generate_fibonacci(n - 2)
generate_fibonacci (generic function with 2 methods)

julia> generate_fibonacci(5)
21
```

However, we will read more about this syntax when we jump to conditionals later on in this book.

Built-in functions

Julia provides a number of built-in functions, which are very helpful once you fully understand the richness of the Julia `base` library. Like every other language, Julia has functions for most common tasks performed by users, as well as some surprises as we go through this topic.

We will now walk through some of the most common built-in functions one by one, along with detailed examples:

- `workspace()`: This is a function specifically for Julia REPL and isn't available outside of it. The work of this function is actually to clear out the current workspace in the Julia REPL, deleting all the functions, variables, constants, or types defined by the user without needing to exit the REPL and restart it once again.

- `typeof()`: This function is used mainly to know the data type of an argument passed to it. This is similar to the `type()` function for those familiar with Python:

```
julia> typeof("Julia")
String

julia> typeof(1.0)
Float64

julia> typeof(1)
Int64

julia> typeof(0x23)
```

```
UInt8

julia> typeof(0b101)
UInt8

julia> typeof(typeof('julia'))
DataType
```

- `methods()`: This function is very useful and is frequently used when the user wants to know the methods available corresponding to a user-defined function. In other words, when you use multiple dispatch and want to inquire about the implementations we have for that particular function, then we use this method:

```
julia> methods(+)
# 163 methods for generic function "+":
+(x::Bool, z::Complex{Bool}) at complex.jl:136
+(x::Bool, y::Bool) at bool.jl:48
+(x::Bool) at bool.jl:45
+{T<:AbstractFloat}(x::Bool, y::T) at bool.jl:55
+(x::Bool, z::Complex) at complex.jl:143
+(x::Bool, A::AbstractArray{Bool,N<:Any}) at arraymath.jl:126
+(x::Float32, y::Float32) at float.jl:239
+(x::Float64, y::Float64) at float.jl:240
+(z::Complex{Bool}, x::Bool) at complex.jl:137
...
...
```

- `readline()` and `readlines()`: This function is used to take in input from the user. There are many ways to use this function. Like, for example, if we want to ask the user to enter his/her name in the Julia REPL, then we may use this as follows:

```
julia> name = readline()
"Julia"
"\"Julia\"\n"

julia> println(name)
"Julia"
```

You might notice here that it takes the input as a string. Sometimes, you may also encounter STDIN being supplied to this function, which does not affect the output and signifies the standard input being fed to the function.

We can also read from a file using the same function with a slight modification. Here, we just need to pass in the name of the file from which the user might want to read the data:

```julia
julia> readline("testfile.csv")
"1.10\n"
```

But, there is a problem. The function will just read the first line from the file and ignore the rest. You may be thinking, *well, that's completely obvious, as the name suggests that it can read only a single line*. So, what do we use instead then? We use the `readlines()` function to read in all the lines from the file:

```julia
julia> readlines("testfile.csv")
5-element Array{String,1}:
 "1.10\n"
 "2.35\n"
 "5.56\n"
 "7.89\n"
 "4.67"
```

- `enumerate()`: This is one of the most commonly known functions for people coming from a different language background. The `enumerate()` function must be used when we need to iterate over a collection of items and at the same time keep track of the index position of that particular item. One simple example is shown as follows:

```julia
julia> fruits
4-element Array{String,1}:
 "apples"
 "oranges"
 "bananas"
 "watermelon"

julia> for (index,fruit) in enumerate(fruits)
           println("$index -> $fruit")
       end
1 -> apples
2 -> oranges
3 -> bananas
4 -> watermelon
```

- `parse()`: This function is basically used to parse down a given string and return an expression. It can basically infer the data type of the argument passed as a string to itself. To understand what is meant by this, just have a look at the following example:

```
julia> parse("2")
2

julia> parse("2.22")
2.22

julia> parse("Julia")
:Julia
```

Do you see the difference? `parse()` was able to infer the data type of the input values passed. But how do we know? Let's confirm it using the `typeof()` function, which tells us the correct data type of the values returned:

```
julia> typeof(parse("2"))
Int64

julia> typeof(parse("2.22"))
Float64

julia> typeof(parse("Julia"))
Symbol
```

The `2` value was correctly inferred as `Int64` and `2.22` as `Float64`. But what about the value `Julia`? The `return` type shows the `Symbol` value, which is a data type. Now, what is `Symbol` and what does it signify? We might learn this in the next chapter when we read more about types.

An example using simple built-in functions

Let's walk through a practical example, wherein we will talk more about how functions can prove to be helpful in the real world when using Julia. We all, at some point in our software development careers, must have worked with CSV files. For those who haven't, there's nothing to worry about--CSV indicates a file format wherein the data is **comma (,)** separated.

Just imagine that we have a CSV file with the name `sample.csv` in our home location, and this file contains the day and night temperature values (in degrees Celsius) of a town in the summer for seven continuous days of a random week.

Here is the actual file:

```
mac-rahul:~$ cat sample.csv
"43.4","32.0"
"44.6","31.4"
"40.1","27.6"
"41.1","28.9"
"44.0","30.0"
"45.6","31.2"
"42.0","27.5"
```

We have values given in the form of strings and separated by a comma. The first value denotes the daytime temperature and the second value denotes the temperature at night for the same day.

Now, the task for us is to find the maximum temperature, minimum temperature, average day temperature, and average night temperature for this seven-day period, and finally, write the complete values in a file in the form of a CSV.

To start with, the first thing that strikes us should be the way to read this file using Julia. Julia, as usual, provides a function named `readcsv(your_file_name_here)`, which takes in a CSV file as input. Firing it on the Julia REPL in interactive mode, we have:

```
julia> readcsv("sample.csv")
7x2 Array{Float64,2}:
 43.4  32.0
 44.6  31.4
 40.1  27.6
 41.1  28.9
 44.0  30.0
 45.6  31.2
 42.0  27.5
```

Closely examining the output, we see that we get a `7x2` array of the `Float64` type. But did you see how Julia was able to understand that the values were `Float64` and not the `String` type because we had originally passed in the CSV file? This was because the `readcsv()` method internally uses the `parse()` function, which helps to infer the data type of the value passed.

Once the CSV file is successfully read in, we want to assign it to a variable named `data`, which we will use for further computation:

```
julia> data = readcsv("sample.csv")
```

Next, we find the maximum, minimum, and averages, as follows:

- **Maximum temperature**: This is pretty straightforward, as Julia provides a function named `maximum`, which operates over a collection of items and returns the maximum values from it:

```
julia> max_temp = maximum(data)
45.6
```

- **Minimum temperature**: Again, we have a function provided by Julia specifically for this, called `minimum`:

```
julia> min_temp = minimum(data)
27.5
```

- **Average daytime temperatures**: We compute the average daytime temperatures by first looking up the data we have, getting only the daytime temperatures and then calculating the average by dividing the sum of temperatures by the size of the week.

```
# First we need to grab all the day time temperature values
# over a period of 7 days
# we can do this as under, notice the index, which starts from
# value 1 and NOT 0
julia> data[1:7]
7-element Array{Float64,1}:
 43.4
 44.6
 40.1
 41.1
 44.0
 45.6
 42.0

# next, we need to get the sum of all the values, we do it by
# using the sum() function
julia> total_daytime_temperatures = sum(data[1:7])
300.8

# the we quickly find the size of the array, which is easily
# computed by the size() function
julia> total_size = size(data)[1]
```

```
7
```

```
# finally, we compute avarage as
julia> day_average = total_daytime_temperatures/total_size
42.971428571428575
```

```
# rounding off to 1 decimal places, we have
julia> round(day_average, 1)
43.0
```

- **Average nighttime temperatures**: This, again, will be almost similar to the previous part, the only exception being the index range of the data variable, which will start from 8 and go to 14:

```
julia> data[8:14]
7-element Array{Float64,1}:
 32.0
 31.4
 27.6
 28.9
 30.0
 31.2
 27.5
```

```
julia> total_nighttime_temperatures = sum(data[8:14])
208.6
```

```
julia> night_average = total_nighttime_temperatures/total_size
29.8
```

At the end, we need to write all of this data to a CSV file. We do this using the `writecsv()` function. But before we write data to the CSV file, we may want to organize the variables created so far into a single collection of items or as an array. A very simple and straightforward method is to create an empty array named `list` with all four values inside it:

```
julia> list = [max_temp, min_temp, day_average, night_average]
4-element Array{Any,1}:
 45.6
 27.5
 43.0
 29.8
```

Once we have the `list` ready, we can now use the `writecsv()` function. We write the data into the file with the name `output.csv`:

```
julia> writecsv("output.csv",list)

Press a semicolon to change to shell mode
shell> cat output.csv
45.6
27.5
43
29.8
```

 'max' and 'min' functions are not same as 'maximum' and 'minimum'.

Summary

In this chapter, we saw how functions are defined in Julia and how to play around with function arguments. We covered different types of argument passing methods, such as variable arguments, single arguments, and even no arguments. Later on in the chapter, we discussed how multiple dispatch makes Julia one of the best languages available in the programming world because of the speed boost it provides. Interestingly, we focused on a topic named recursion, which, although not specific to functions, was covered just to give a brief overview of what recursive functions are and how recursion is done in Julia. And, lastly, we covered some of the most commonly used built-in functions provided by Julia's rich library.

Now that we have a solid foundation of what functions are and how they empower a fellow Julia programmer, we shall head over to types, a very interesting and important topic, wherein we will talk in detail about types to help us understand what they are and how to create one when needed.

4
Understanding Types and Dispatch

Every programming language needs to understand the kind of data it is being supplied with. **Types**, often referred to as **data types**, are simply a classification of data that lets the computer know the differences between the kinds of input being provided by the user. Julia also uses a **type system** that uniquely identifies integers, strings, floats, Booleans, and other data types.

In this chapter, we will closely walk you through the extensive type system of Julia, and how just supplying the data type greatly enhances the overall speed of execution. Here is the list of topics that we will be covering in this chapter:

- Julia's type system
- Type annotations
- More on types
- Subtypes and supertypes
- User-defined and composite data types
- Inner constructors
- Modules and interfaces
- Module file paths
- Multiple dispatch explained

After going through this chapter, you will be able to:

- Understand the various types in Julia and be able to supply them
- Create new data types using the existing ones
- Clearly, understand the difference between a module and an interface
- Have a solid understanding of what multiple dispatch is, and how it is used in Julia.

Julia's type system

Before we go any further and start exploring Julia's types system in detail, we need to know what types are, and why they are even required.

What are types?

To answer this question, consider the following four lines:

```
1
1.10
'j'
"julia"
```

What do we see here? For sure, it's very plain and simple for us to understand that all four lines have different kinds of data. Starting from the first line: we have 1, which is an integer; 1.10, which is a float (or decimal); 'j', which represents a single character; and lastly, "Julia", which is a simple string made from a collection of characters used together.

But, even though we have prior knowledge about the data types in use, how do we let the machine know the same? How will the computer know that 1 is an integer, and not a float or a string? Well, the answer to this question is types!

Statically-typed versus dynamically-typed languages

In the modern programming world, we simply have two different ways of telling the compiler or the interpreter about the type of data being supplied.

In the first method, we have **statically-typed** languages, such as C, C++, or Java, wherein we need to explicitly define the type of the data beforehand. This lets the compiler know about the incoming data before the program is actually executed. In the second method, we have **dynamically-typed** languages such as Perl, Python, and Ruby, in which the user need not declare the type of data beforehand and the interpreter will automatically infer the type of data at runtime.

 Note, even though in dynamically-typed languages you are not required to declare the type of the variable before assigning it to a value, the language still assigns a type to the data internally, so that it is easily recognized as a string, or an integer, or any other data type.

So, is Julia a dynamically-typed or statically-typed language?

The answer to this question is both (yes!). However, it inclines towards being a dynamically-typed language, because of its ability to infer the type of data at runtime. Having said that, it doesn't mean that Julia does not have a rich type system. You will be surprised to know that a Julia code that has types already declared is a lot faster in terms of execution speed!

Quoting from the official Julia documentation:

> *Julia's type system is dynamic but gains some of the advantages of static type systems by making it possible to indicate that certain values are of specific types. This can be of great assistance in generating efficient code, but even more significantly, it allows method dispatch on the types of function arguments to be deeply integrated with the language. (More on* https://docs.julialang.org/en/stable/manual/types/.)

Type annotations

In the previous chapter, we read about functions in Julia and how to statically declare the data type of the argument in a function definition. In this section, we will be focusing on type **declarations** and **conversions**, while at the same time using our newly acquired knowledge about functions in order to complement each section with examples.

Let's have a look at the following example, where we declare a simple mathematical function to find the cube of a number:

```
# declare the function
julia> function cube(number::Int64)
         return number ^ 3
         end
cube (generic function with 1 method)

# function call
julia> cube(10)
1000
```

If you follow along closely, you will notice the use of an operator, : :, along with Int64 being used while declaring this function cube. The : : is nothing but a simple operator available in Julia that lets you attach type annotations to an expression or a variable in a program. The Int64 is a type that is used to denote that the argument number is of the Integer data type. We shall study further the Int64 integer data type, and many others, at a later point. But first, let's first have a look at what : : has to do with types in Julia.

One of the main reasons for the usage of : : is to confirm that the function or the program that we have in place works for the desired value as expected. Going back to the function cube, we wanted to run it over integer values only, so we declared the argument number to be an integer using the : : operator.

If that was a bit too overwhelming, let's just see what would happen if we passed a String argument to the function cube:

```
julia> cube("10")
MethodError: no method matching cube(::String)
Closest candidates are:
  cube(::Int64) at In[3]:2
```

We got an error because we passed a String argument instead of an Int64 value! Hence, the : : operator makes sure that the result of the program does not stray from what we intend to achieve.

The second and very important reason for using the : : operator is to make sure that the Julia LLVM compiler does not have to infer the type on its own and waste time. Rather, it gets to know the type of the arguments, and hence, performance improves drastically.

For those of you who have come from a Python background, you will be very familiar with the `isinstance()` function. The `::` operator works on similar lines in Julia. Here is an example:

```
julia> 2::Int64
2

julia> 2::Float64
TypeError: typeassert: expected Float64, got Int64
```

Notice the error we got. In the first line, we had no errors, as 2 is an integer. But when we try to run the second line, we run into `typeassert` errors, which basically means that the value supplied on the left side of the `::` operator does not match with the type supplied on the right side of `::`. That is, 2 is not a `Float` type, but an `Integer` type.

More on types

Abstract data types are the ones that cannot be instantiated. They serve as the basic pillars of the type system in Julia. Or, in other words, other types inside Julia can inherit any one of these base types. Examples of abstract data types are `Number`, `Integer`, and `Signed`.

Julia supports all the basic data types, along with the ability to add in new user-defined data types as well as composite types. The way they are prioritized is something that we will learn about in the next section when we read about subtypes and supertypes.

Before we begin talking about the different data types in detail, I want to share three simple functions that we will be using to know more about types:

- `typeof()`: This is used to tell the **type of data** being supplied to it
- `typemax()`: This is used to know the **maximum value** supported by the specific type
- `typemin()`: This is used to know the **minimum value** supported by the specific type

As we are now moving into a territory wherein our machine bits would start to matter a lot, we need to have a better understanding of the kind of machine we are working on. Advantageously, Julia provides us with a function that can represent any number in the number of bits supported by the machine!

The function is called `bits`:

```
julia> bits(1)
"0000000000000000000000000000000000000000000000000000000000000001"

julia> sizeof(bits(1))
64
```

As we can see, we represented the 1 integer in bits, along with the count of 64, which is exactly the number of bits my laptop uses!

The Integer type

The `Integer` type is used to tell the Julia LLVM compiler about an incoming integer-type object. It's called `Int8`, `Int16`, `Int32`, `Int64`, or `Int128`, depending upon the machine you are using. For instance, if you are working on a 64-bit machine, the `Integer` type would be `Int64`:

```
# Knowing the type of the data type passed
julia> typeof(16)
Int64

# Highest value represented by the In64 type
julia> typemax(Int64)
9223372036854775807

# Lowest value resprented by the Int64 type
julia> typemin(Int64)
-9223372036854775808
```

We can also have unsigned integers, and the way Julia represents them is by using the types `Uint8`, `Uint16`, `Uint32`, `Uint64`, and `Uint128`.

The Float type

This one is used to denote the `Float` type; in other words, integers with decimals. We use the `Float64` type here. Notice that from now on, I will be using the 64-bit type for all my examples and code, as I will be working on a 64-bit machine:

```
julia> typeof(1.10)
Float64

julia> typemax(Float64)
```

```
Inf

julia> typemin(Float64)
-Inf
```

Here, `Inf` denotes infinity, which is Julia's unique way to denote the value infinity.

The Char type

The `Char` type is used to denote a single character:

```
julia> typeof('c')
Char
```

The String type

The `String` type is used to denote string data, which is a collection of characters. Notice that we have double quotes around a `String` type, unlike the single quotes around character type data:

```
julia> typeof("Julia")
String
```

The Bool type

The `Bool` type is used to denote the values of the Boolean type `true` and `false`:

```
julia> typeof(true)
Bool
```

A quick way to find out the data type we are working with is the `isa()` function. On checking the original documentation, we see the following:

```
isa(x, type) -> Bool

    Determine whether x is of the given type.
```

This is almost the same functionality provided by the `isinstance()` function in Python, which also checks for data type and returns a Boolean value. Practically, it's as simple as the following command:

```
julia> isa(5, Int64)
true

julia> isa(5.5, Float64)
true

julia> isa(5.5, UInt64)
false
```

Type conversions

So far in this chapter, we have been discussing various data types in Julia, mostly which specific type they are and how we declare them. Now, what if we wanted to have a value of a specific data type converted to another data type?

For instance, we have a function with the name `distance_covered` (speed::Int64, time_taken::Int64), which returns the distance covered by a moving vehicle's speed and time taken. Now, as we know, distance is calculated as the product of speed with the time taken. Or, in other words, we have the function definition like this:

```
julia> function distance_covered( speed::Int64, time_taken::Int64)
           return speed * time_taken
       end
distance_covered (generic function with 1 method)
```

Now, whatever the result of this product, we only want to have an integer output. But there is a catch! The product of an integer and an integer is always an integer. This means that the result of the `distance_covered()` function is always going to be an integer. Hence, to have a float value, we need to use type conversion here, so that we can get a float solution:

```
# Distance covered by vehicle having a speed of 64 kmph and traveling for 2
hours.
julia> distance_covered(64, 2)
128

# testifying that the result was a integer!
julia> typeof(ans)
Int64
```

To help us solve this issue, Julia has provided us with a function by the name of convert(). Before we learn more about the convert() function, let's first use it to get our desired result from the distance_covered() function in float.

The function convert() takes two arguments. The first argument is the data type, which you want to have in the final result, or to which you want to convert the existing value; while the second argument is the value you want to convert.

```
#converting 128kms in float value
julia> convert(Float64, 128)
128.0

julia> typeof(128.0)
Float64
```

So now, we get the result of the function distance in Float64, which is what we wanted.

In the preceding function, you will see we converted 128 to 128.0 (that is, from Int64 to Float64). But what if we wanted to convert a float value to an integer value? Take a look at the following code:

```
# easily done
julia> convert(Int64, 128.0)
128

# breaks! but why???
julia> convert(Int64, 128.5)
ERROR: InexactError()
 in convert(::Type{Int64}, ::Float64) at ./int.jl:239
 in convert(::Type{Int64}, ::Float64) at
/Applications/Julia-0.5.app/Contents/Resources/julia/lib/julia/sys.dylib:?
```

The first time, it's able to convert 128.0 to 128 easily, but what happens the second time? The function fails to convert a float with a non-zero value after the decimal! The error called InexactError() was raised due to Julia's inability to convert the value into a float.

As a technical language, Julia works hard to maintain accuracy in numerical computations. Since floating point numbers cannot be accurately represented as an integer, Julia raises an error.

How can we *force* Julia to do the conversion? We can give Julia specific instructions for converting from Float to Int via rounding.

```
julia> ceil(Int, 3.4)
4

julia> floor(Int, 3.4)
3

julia> round(Int, 3.4)
3
```

The official document has a statement regarding this behavior:

> *"If T is an Integer type, an InexactError will be raised if x is not representable by T, for example, if x is not integer-valued, or is outside the range supported by T."*

The subtypes and supertypes

Julia's type system is organized into a clean hierarchy of data types. Some of the data types sit above other data types, and vice versa. This, however, should not be confused with the precedence of types, as we are not talking about that here. Rather, our focus is mainly to understand how Julia's type system organized itself into a tree structure.

To start with, the starting point of all data types in Julia is the `Any` datatype. The `Any` type is like the parent node of the tree, and all the other possible data types are directly or indirectly its child nodes.

Following is Julia's type hierarchy (sample):

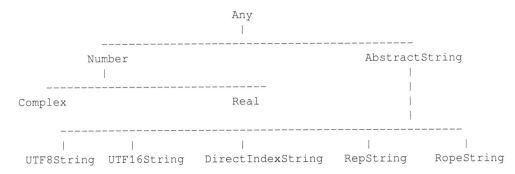

Looking at the tree structure clearly, in the simplest of terms you may get to understand that the `Number` type is a subtype of the `Any` type, which is acting as a child of the parent type `Any`. So what do we call the parent type with respect to the `Number` type? It is called a **Supertype**. If that was a bit difficult to follow, let's introduce two functions that are meant to demonstrate and showcase the exact explanation.

The supertype() function

This function is used to return the `supertype` function of a type passed as its argument. Opening the Julia REPL, we can now check for the supertype of the `Number` type:

```
julia> supertype(Number)
Any
```

What about the `supertype` of the type `Any`? Let's try that out too!

```
julia> supertype(Any)
Any

julia> typeof(Any)
DataType
```

No surprises there, as `Any` is the starting point of all the other data types.

The subtype() function

This function is used to return the `subtype` function of a type passed as its argument. Let's check the subtypes of the `Number` type:

```
julia> subtypes(Number)
2-element Array{Any,1}:
 Complex{T<:Real}
 Real
```

This is exactly what we were discussing in Julia's type hierarchy. An important relation to keep in mind is that now, for the types `Complex` and `Real`, the `Number` type will be seen as a `supertype` function. So, it depends upon the type hierarchy whether a specific data type becomes a `subtype` function and/or a `supertype` function.

Checking for subtypes of `Any`, we have a lot of them:

```
julia> subtypes(Any)
269-element Array{Any,1}:
```

```
AbstractArray{T,N}
AbstractChannel
AbstractRNG
AbstractSerializer
AbstractString
Any
Associative
Base.AbstractCartesianIndex
Base.AbstractCmd
Base.AsyncCollector
Base.AsyncCollectorState
Base.AsyncCondition
Base.AsyncGenerator
Base.AsyncGeneratorState
Base.BaseDocs.Keyword
Base.Cartesian.LReplace
Base.ChannelIterState
Base.CodegenHooks
Base.CodegenParams
Base.DFT.FFTW.fftw_plan_struct
Base.DFT.Plan
Base.DataFmt.DLMHandler
. . .
```

Let's play around with the types a little bit, and point our attention to learning all the subtypes of a given abstract type. Hence, let us create a function using the existing subtypes, to allow us to learn about all the subtypes of Number, or maybe an AbstractString type:

```julia
# function to check and print all the subtypes of a given abstract type
julia> function check_all_subtypes(T, space = 0)
         println("\t" ^ space, T)
         for t in subtypes(T)
           if t != Any
           check_all_subtypes(t, space+1)
         end
       end
     end
check_all_subtypes (generic function with 2 methods)
```

Calling this function over the Number type, we have:

```julia
julia> check_all_subtypes(Number)
Number
        Complex{T<:Real}
        Real
                AbstractFloat
                        BigFloat
```

```
                    Float16
                    Float32
                    Float64
          Integer
                    BigInt
                    Bool
                    Signed
                              Int128
                              Int16
                              Int32
                              Int64
                              Int8
                    Unsigned
                              UInt128
                              UInt16
                              UInt32
                              UInt64
                              UInt8
          Irrational{sym}
          Rational{T<:Integer}
```

Similarly, executing the same function over the abstract type `AbstractString`, we have:

```
julia> check_all_subtypes(AbstractString)
AbstractString
        Base.SubstitutionString{T<:AbstractString}
        Base.Test.GenericString
        DirectIndexString
        RepString
        RevString{T<:AbstractString}
        String
        SubString{T<:AbstractString}
```

User-defined and composite data types

Until now, we have been dealing with the data types that were available to a user and provided by Julia. Now we will be exploring ways to use types that are not made available to us by Julia, and we need to create them in order to address the problems we are dealing or intend to deal with.

The most important keyword that we need to create a user-defined data type is called an type. The following is an example of how to create a simple data type in Julia:

```
julia> type Person
                name::String
```

```
                           age::Int64
                 end

julia> rahul = Person("rahul",27)
Person("rahul",27)

julia> typeof(rahul)
Person

julia> rahul.name
"rahul"

julia> rahul.age
27
```

This example is one of the simplest examples of what we can consider a user-defined type in Julia. Observing closely, the Person type has two fields, namely name and age. The fields can easily be accessed by using a period (.) notation.

Interestingly, if you try to get the supertype or subtype function of this Person type, this is what you get:

```
julia> supertype(Person)
Any

julia> subtypes(Person)
0-element Array{Any,1}
```

This shows that the Person type is placed directly below the Any type in the tree hierarchy of Julia's type system. At this point in time, it will also be interesting to introduce a new function called fieldnames(), which is used to list down all the field names for any defined type:

```
julia> fieldnames(Person)
2-element Array{Symbol,1}:
 :name
 :age
```

The function `fieldnames(T)` takes in the datatype `T` and outputs all the field names declared in that data type. Fieldnames are of the Symbol type, which is yet again a different data type of the DataType type:

```
julia> typeof(:name)
Symbol

julia> typeof(Symbol)
DataType
```

Unlike traditional object-oriented languages like Java, Python, or C++, Julia doesn't have classes! Yes, that's correct. Julia separates the types along with their methods and prefers to use multiple dispatch instead.

Composite types

A **composite type** is a collection of named fields, which can be treated as a single value. We can quickly define a composite type as:

```
julia> type Points
          x :: Int64
          y :: Int64
          z :: Int64
          end
```

We have already covered the usage in the previous section. By mutable, we mean that the `fieldnames` type, once assigned, can be changed and reassigned to some new value, other than the one used while creating the object. This can be understood by the example given as follows:

```
julia> struct Point
             x::Int
             y::Int
             z::Int
          end

julia> p = Point(1,2,3)
Point(1, 2, 3)

julia> p.x = 10
ERROR: type Point is immutable
```

We see that we were not able to change the values of x, y, and z once they were assigned at the time of object creation. The `ERROR: type Point is immutable` error sums up the issue in simpler words.

We need to use the keyword mutable to make the type mutable.

```
julia> mutable struct MutPoint
  x::Int
  y::Int
  z::Int
  end

julia> p = MutPoint(1,2,3)
```

```
MutPoint(1, 2, 3)

julia> p.x = 10
10

julia> p
MutPoint(10, 2, 3)
```

Hence, we are able to assign the values of x, y, and z, which are the fields to different values than those declared or assigned at the time of creation of the object sample.

Inner constructors

Till now, we have seen how to use Julia's predefined types as well as user-defined composite types. Now, we are going to delve a little deeper into learning what happens when a user-defined type gets created, and the applications of making this feature more useful to the end user.

As we have already discussed, when we create a new type, we may or may not include field names in the body. Functions, on the other hand, remain distant, and unlike other object-oriented languages, the methods aren't present.

So when we create a new type's object, the default constructor comes into action:

```
julia> type Family
         num_members :: Int64
         members :: Array{String, 1}
       end

julia> f1 = Family(2, ["husband", "wife"])
Family(2, String["husband", "wife"])
```

We have declared a composite type, Family, and it has two fields, num_members and members. The first field name is for declaring the number of family members, and the second field name explicitly calls out all family members in an array.

But what if we wanted to validate the fields of the Family type? One way is to create another function that can validate the same, and apply it over the object being created for the same type:

```
julia> f2 = Family(1, ["husband", "wife"])
Family(1, String["husband", "wife"])

julia> function validate(obj :: Family)
               if obj.num_members != length(obj.members)
```

```
                              println("ERROR! Not all members listed!! ")
                    end
            end
    validate (generic function with 1 method)

    julia> validate(f2)
    ERROR! Not all members listed!!
```

So, as you can see, we created a function called `validate`, which will take an object of the `Family` type and then validate if the number of members mentioned are exactly equal to the members listed in the array!

Alternatively, we can do the same thing with a much simpler method, by declaring inner constructors. They can be used to validate the fields even before the object gets created, and hence, can provide a better control over the object creation process, along with saving us useful time.

We will create the object using `new`, which like in Java and other languages, is for the purpose of creating an object for a given specific type.

Here is what we could have done instead:

```
    julia> type Family
            num_members :: Int64
            members :: Array{String, 1}
            Family(num_members, members) = num_members != length(members) ?
    error("Not equal") : new(num_members, members)
            end

    julia> f1 = Family(1, ["husband", "wife"])
```

On running the preceding line of code, we get the result in which the first line of the error prints out what we wanted:

```
    ERROR: LoadError: Not equal
     in Family(::Int64, ::Array{String,1}) at ../sample.jl:4
     in include_from_node1(::String) at ./loading.jl:488
     in include_from_node1(::String) at ../julia/lib/julia/sys.dylib:?
     in process_options(::Base.JLOptions) at ./client.jl:265
     in _start() at ./client.jl:321
     in _start() at ../julia/lib/julia/sys.dylib:?
    while loading /../sample.jl, in expression starting on line 7
```

Declaring internal constructors can be time-saving, and also make the code more efficient by stopping the creation of unwanted objects if they don't fulfill a certain criterion.

Consider the following example:

```julia
julia> type A
           x
           y
       end

julia> type B
           x
           y
           B(x, y) = new(x, y)
       end

julia> a = A(1,1)
A(1,1)

julia> b = B(1,1)
B(1,1)
```

Interestingly, both the forms are equal, although we have declared the inner constructor form in `type B`. Julia automatically generates constructors for types. Users can declare additional constructors or override the default one using inner constructors.

Use of inner constructors is discouraged. From the manual: "It is considered good form to provide as few inner constructor methods as possible: only those taking all arguments explicitly and enforcing essential error checking and transformation."

Modules and interfaces

Like many other languages, Julia also has a way to group similar logical sets of code together into workspaces, or also called as namespaces. They help us in creating top-level definitions - that is, global variables, without taking on the risk of code conflicts, as the names and variables used inside a module remain unique.

In Julia, we create a module as follows:

```
module SampleModule
..
..
end
```

Modules help us to indicate code that can be imported into other parts of the program, as well as the set of code meant to be used (or visible) to the world outside.

Here is one small example of a functional module:

```
# marks the start of the module named Utilities
julia> module Utilities
        # marks the type, variable or functions to be made
          available
          export Stype, volume_of_cube
          type Stype
          name::Int64
          end
          function area_of_square(number)
          return number ^ 2
          end
          function volume_of_cube(number)
          return area_of_square(number) * number
          end
        # marks the end of the module
          end
```

Here, we have a module named `Utilities`, which has two functions named `volume_of_cube` and `area_of_square`, along with a user-defined type called `Stype`.

Out of these three, we have `volume_of_cube` and `Stype` exported, which are made available to the world outside. The `area_of_square` function is kept private.

Once a module is made, it is ready to be used by other parts of the program. To do so, Julia provides a number of reserved keywords that facilitate the usage. The two most used of them are `using` and `import`.

We will be focusing on the usage of these two, using a very simple example:

```
julia> module MyModule
          foo = 10
          bar = 20
          function baz()
            return "baz"
          end
```

```
        function qux()
          return "qux"
        end
        export foo, baz
        end
MyModule
```

We will attempt to use `foo` by importing MyModule.

```
# No public variables are brought into scope
julia> import MyModule

julia> foo
ERROR: UndefVarError: foo not defined

julia> baz()
ERROR: UndefVarError: baz not defined
```

We will attempt to do it now with `using`.

```
julia> using MyModule

julia> foo
10

julia> bar
ERROR: UndefVarError: bar not defined

julia> MyModule.bar
20

julia> baz()
"baz"
```

When we run the command:

- **using** MyModule, then all the exported functions, as well as other functions, are brought into the scope. We could also have chosen to individually call the functions declared in the MyModule module using MyModule.foo. A second form of the same can be to use MyModule:foo. In both these cases, we only get what we call - that is, only those functions enter the current scope that have been called explicitly.
- **import** MyModule, all functions from the MyModule module will populate the current scope. There is another keyword called importall, which is slightly different from import in a way that it just gets the functions or variables exported by the module.

However, the biggest difference between using and import is that, with using, none of the functions from the module are available for method extension, while with import, there is flexibility for method extension.

Including files in modules

We have seen how we can create a module using the `module` keyword. However, what if our package, or module, is spread up into different files? The way Julia addresses this issue is by introducing `include`, which can be used to include any Julia file (with the `.jl` extension) in a module.

Here is an example that will make things clear. Suppose that we have a module with the `PointTypes` name, and our code for it is written in the `transformations.jl`. It contains:

```
function move(p::Point, x, y)
  slidex(p, x)
  slidey(p, y)
end

function slidex(p::Point, dist)
  p.x += dist
end

function slidey(p::Point, dist)
  p.y += dist
end
```

Once we are done with module creation, the next step would be to test the same. This can be done as follows:

```
julia> module PointTypes
          mutable struct Point
             x::Int
             y::Int
          end

          # defines point transformations
          include("transformations.jl")

          export Point, move

       end
PointTypes

julia> using PointTypes
```

```
julia> p = Point(0,0)
PointTypes.Point(0, 0)

julia> move(p, 1, -2)
-2

julia> p
PointTypes.Point(1, -2)

julia> slidex(p, 1)
ERROR: UndefVarError: slidex not defined
```

Module file paths

In general, when you write a file path using `SomeSampleModule`, Julia looks for that package in the main (it acts as Julia's top-level module):

```
julia> using SomeSampleModule
ERROR: ArgumentError: Module SomeSampleModule not found in current path.
Run `Pkg.add("SomeSampleModule")` to install the SomeSampleModule package.
 in require(::Symbol) at ./loading.jl:365
 in require(::Symbol) at
/Applications/Julia-0.5.app/Contents/Resources/julia/lib/julia/sys.dylib:?
```

If not shown as in the preceding error, then it may try to look internally for a package installed from an outside source, typically calling the `require` function (`SomeSampleModule`).

Conversely, let's suppose you are working on a big project that has many modules in it. Now, a situation may come up wherein you are required to call one module's function into some other module's code. The first and foremost requirement for that to work is the presence of those two modules in the same path!

However, what happens in a situation where you have a module and then have many submodules, each being a part of that main module? The answer to this problem is the usage of what we call **relative imports**. Just have a look at this example:

```
julia> module shape
        # the submodule areas
          module areas
            # names of the exported functions
            export area_of_square
            # the function
            function area_of_square(num)
              return num ^ 2
```

```
        end
    end

    # the relative calling of the submodule areas
    using .areas

    # calling the function from the submodule
    println(areas.area_of_square(2))
  end
4
shape
```

Important note!

How do you set your default file path in Julia?

- Use `push!` to actually set the parameter called `LOAD_PATH`. This can be done as `push!(LOAD_PATH, "/module_path/")`.
- The load path can also be set by defining an environment variable, `JULIA_LOAD_PATH`.

What is module precompilation?

Whenever you create a complete module and try to load it in, it may take up to several seconds before the module is completely loaded for usage.

Whenever Julia loads a module, it starts reading code from the top-level statements one at a time. Then these top-level statements are further lowered down, and then possibly interpreted or compiled and executed.

Let's first look at a simple module, where we try to calculate a huge sum that will mimic the loading of a heavy module in the system. In order for pre-compilation to work, the module must be saved in a module format and added to Julia's load path.

```
julia> module SampleCode
        export sum_of_numbers
        sum_of_numbers = 0
        for num in 1:1000000000
        sum_of_numbers += num
        end
    end
```

Here, we have a module that simply exports a variable called `sum_of_numbers`, and computes the sum of the first 1,000,000,000 (or 10^9) numbers! Quite huge. Now let's try to load it for the first time on my machine:

```
julia> @time using SampleCode
  45.078140 seconds (2.00 G allocations: 29.802 GB, 2.08% gc time)
```

It took a good amount of time. Now, what could have been done better to reduce the time? To address this issue, Julia provides us with a directive or function called `__precompile__()`.

What this does is compile everything at first import! By doing so, Julia takes all the information that can be serialized (such as type inferences, ASTs from parsing, and so on), and saves them into a cache! This cache can then act as the source of the module to be used or referenced the next time it is called.

Let's just modify the code we had initially to calculate the sum of 1,000,000,000 numbers:

```
__precompile__()

module SampleCode

export sum_of_numbers

sum_of_numbers = 0
for num in 1:1000000000
    sum_of_numbers += num
end

end
```

So, as you can see, there is only one change made to the original code by adding a `__precompile__()` directive. Let's try to load this module on the machine again:

```
julia> @time using SampleCode
INFO: Precompiling module SampleCode.
  48.474224 seconds (312.21 k allocations: 13.075 MB)

julia> workspace()

julia> @time using SampleCode
  0.001261 seconds (606 allocations: 32.992 KB)
```

The difference in loading time is much, much better. We will be coming back to this topic in detail when we explore Julia's performance tips and tricks later on in this book.

Multiple dispatch explained

In Chapter 2, *Defining Functions*, we introduced the concept of multiple dispatch in Julia, which is deeply integrated into the language. Here, we will extend the same topic to cover types.

To have a quick look at what multiple dispatch means in functions, here is the same code for a function that prints out the cube of a number:

```
julia> function calculate_cube(num::Int64)
           return num ^ 3
       end
calculate_cube (generic function with 1 method)

julia> function calculate_cube(num::Float64)
           return num ^ 3
       end
calculate_cube (generic function with 2 methods)

# 2 methods for generic function "calculate_cube":
calculate_cube(num::Float64) at REPL[1]:2
calculate_cube(num::Int64) at REPL[1]:2

julia> calculate_cube(10)
1000

julia> calculate_cube(10.10)
1030.301
```

Here, the function supported both kinds of concrete types (which are Int64 and Float64) values. One gave an integer output and the other gave Float type output.

But how can the same technique be applied to user types? For that, we first have to equip ourselves with what we call **parametric types**. Let us first see an example:

```
julia> type Coordinate{T}
           x::T
           y::T
           z::T
       end
```

Here, we have a user-defined type named Coordinate, which represents a point in a 3D space that has x, y, and z axes. On closely watching the syntax, we see {T}, which is enclosed within curly braces. Here, T acts as an arbitrary type, which can be passed on this Coordinate user-defined type as a Parameter.

The body of the Coordinate type has the values x, y, and z, which are all annotated using
: : to the same type T. Moving ahead, we now create an object of this new type - let's see
how it works:

```
# when T is of Int64 type
julia> point = Coordinate{Int64}(1,2,3)
Coordinate{Int64}(1,2,3)

julia> point.x
1

julia> point.y
2

julia> point.z
3

# when T is of Float64 type
julia> point = Coordinate{Float64}(1.0,2.0,3.0)
Coordinate{Float64}(1.0,2.0,3.0)

julia> point.x
1.0

julia> point.y
2.0

julia> point.z
3.0
```

Here, the variable point holds values for an Int64 type, and then holds the Float64 type
values.

Let's get back to multiple dispatch. After clearly understanding how parametric composite
types are made or instantiated, let's implement multiple dispatch using parametric types:

```
# Creating a parametric type
julia> type Coordinate{T}
            x::T
            y::T
            z::T
       end

# Method that works on Int64
julia> function calc_sum(value::Coordinate{Int64})
           value.x + value.y +value.z
       end
```

```
calc_sum (generic function with 1 method)


# Method that works on Float64
julia> function calc_sum(value::Coordinate{Float64})
                   value.x + value.y +value.z
            end
calc_sum (generic function with 1 method)


# Multiple Dispatch
julia> methods(calc_sum)
# 2 methods for generic function "calc_sum":
calc_sum(value::Coordinate{Int64}) at REPL[61]:2
calc_sum(value::Coordinate{Float64}) at REPL[60]:2


# Calling the method on Int64
julia> calc_sum(Coordinate(1,2,3))
6
julia> typeof(ans)
Int64


# Calling the method on Float64
julia> calc_sum(Coordinate(1.0,2.0,3.0))
6.0
julia> typeof(ans)
Float64
```

Summary

In this chapter, we read about types and how they are implemented in Julia. We saw how vast and diverse Julia's type system is, and also how those types can then further be classified in a hierarchy using subtypes and supertypes. We spent time understanding how types can be defined by the user, and then dug deep into constructor methods, exploring inner and outer constructors. Towards the end, we revisited multiple dispatch and introduced parametric types, which finally helped us in implementing the dispatch technique.

In the next chapter, we will see how control flow works in Julia, and you will be reading in detail about the various looping techniques used by the language.

5
Working with Control Flow

Julia, like any other language, provides features to control the flow of the code. The control flow techniques follow a familiar pattern for the most part; however, there are subtle changes in a few of them.

In this chapter, we will be explaining in detail how to structure Julia programs using various control flow techniques to provide an efficient execution of the code. Here is the list of topics we will be covering in the chapter:

- Conditional and repeated evaluation
- Exception handling
- Tasks in Julia

Conditional and repeated evaluation

Conditional evaluation helps break the code into smaller chunks, with each chunk being evaluated based on a certain condition. There are many ways in which such conditions can be imposed and the code can be handled accordingly.

We will be walking you through various methods of conditional code evaluation. But before we go further, we need to familiarize ourselves with **compound expressions**.

Compound expressions are ways in which we can make sure that a sequence of code gets evaluated in an orderly fashion. Let's have a look at some code:

```julia
julia> volume = begin
        len = 10
        breadth = 20
        height = 30
        len * breadth * height
    end
6000

julia> volume
6000
```

Here, we have a simple logic implemented in the form of a compound expression. As you can see, the volume is being calculated as the product of all three dimensions, and then assigned back to the variable itself. The syntax being followed is begin ... end. The begin keyword, however, is not necessary to include, given that you use an alternate method to declare compound expressions using ";" key. This is shown in the following example:

```julia
# Correct method of using ";" key
julia> volume = (length = 10; breadth = 20; height = 30; length * breadth * height)

julia> volume
6000


# Wrong method of using ";" key
julia> volume = length = 10; breadth = 20; height = 30; length * breadth * height

julia> volume
10
```

It is, however, important to remember that we should include "(" and ")" (as opening and closing brackets) while using ";" key, as this might end up assigning the wrong result, as shown in the preceding code (volume gets assigned to the value of length). The semicolon has the lowest precedence of all other operators.

Conditional evaluation in detail

While writing any code, we are often confronted with situations where we need to make some decisions based on a set of rules or predefined business logic. In such cases, we would generally expect the code to be intelligent enough that it can take the right path accordingly. Here is when conditional evaluation comes into the picture.

Let's have a look at the example of FizzBuzz. Here, we will be implementing the famous FizzBuzz program which states that, for any given range of numbers (let's say 1 to 30), print `Fuzz` instead of the number for multiples of 3 and `Buzz` for multiples of 5. For numbers which are both divisible by 3 and 5, the program should print `FizzBuzz`.

```julia
julia> for i in 1:30
           if i % 3 == 0 && i % 5 == 0
             println("FizzBuzz")
           elseif i % 3 == 0
             println("Fizz")
           elseif i % 5 == 0
             println("Buzz")
           else
             println(i)
           end
       end

1
2
Fizz
4
Buzz
Fizz
7
8
Fizz
Buzz
11
Fizz
13
14
FizzBuzz
16
17
Fizz
19
Buzz
Fizz
22
23
```

```
Fizz
Buzz
26
Fizz
28
29
FizzBuzz
```

So, as expected, the `FizzBuzz` string got printed twice in positions 15 and 30, the `Fizz` string got printed eight times, and the `Buzz` string got printed four times.

The code also contains some unknown keywords such as `for` and `in`, which we will be discussing in detail later in the chapter. However, the keywords `if`, `elseif`, and `else` makeup what we collectively call **conditionals**.

This structure is present in almost every programming language of the modern era, with just the slight difference of using `end` as the logical ending of any functional conditional block of code.

The keywords `if`, `else`, and `elseif` basically evaluates the expressions in Boolean terms. So, given any condition, `if` will try to check whether that expression evaluates to `true` or `false`. If the condition comes out to be Boolean `true`, then the code in `if` block gets evaluated; otherwise, we have an `else` or an `elseif` block.

There are, however, no restrictions on the number of `else` or `elseif` blocks that may be used within a program (as we have already seen in the **FizzBuzz** algorithm coding solution previously discussed).

Let's walk through yet another example, this time using functions:

```
#Check whether a number is prime or not!

julia> function factors(num)
          factors = []
          for i in 1:num
              if rem(num, i) == 0
                  push!(factors, i)
              end
          end
          return factors
       end

# Main logic
julia> function is_prime(num)
          factors_array = factors(num)
          if length(factors_array) == 2
```

```
                return true
        else
                return false
        end
    end


julia> is_prime(10)
false

julia> is_prime(11)
true
```

So, as you must have noticed, we have used `if` block in the function factors to get the factors of any number. The biggest thing to notice is that an `if` block is not necessarily followed by an `else` block! While on the other hand, we have the `is_prime` function, which uses the `if...else` block to its advantage of returning Boolean `true` or `false` values.

Coming back to the usage of `if` blocks, we have a few surprises for the readers coming from other programming languages:

- The `if` blocks are leaky! This would mean that variables inside an `if` block can still be used, even if they were not introduced before. As mentioned in the official Julia documentation, *if blocks do not introduce a local scope*:

```
julia> function f(n)
            if n % 2 == 0
                parity = "even"
            else
                parity = "odd"
            end
            println("The number is $parity")
        end
f (generic function with 1 method)

julia> f(2)
The number is even

julia> f(1)
The number is odd
```

- The if blocks return a value! This is a surprise element for people coming from different languages, although a very helpful feature:

```
# if statements return values
julia> x = if true
           2
       end
2

julia> x
2

# println is a Void function
julia> x = if true
           println("test")
       end
test

julia> x

julia> x == nothing
true

julia> nothing == println("test")
test
true
```

The if block will not be able to evaluate the expression if the result is other than true or false. For instance, if we were to write this:

```
julia> if 1
           println(true)
       end
ERROR: TypeError: non-boolean (Int64) used in boolean context
```

The preceding code immediately throws an error, saying it cannot evaluate an expression returning a non-Boolean result. So, for people coming from languages such as Python, where it may be okay to write if 1; it is not a valid operation in Julia.

After having a good look at the if-elseif-else block, let us now focus on another kind of conditional expression called **ternary operators**. They work in almost the same fashion as if blocks, but are different in the way the syntax is written, along with a condition that the operators can just run over a single expression!

The syntax of a ternary operator can be summed up as follows:

```
condition ? do this, if true : do this, if false
```

Let's see an example using the same syntax:

```
julia> name = "Julia"
"Julia"

julia> isa(name, String) ? "Its a string" : "Not a string"
"Its a string"

julia> name = 'j'
'j'

julia> isa(name, String) ? "Its a string" : "Not a string"
"Not a string"
```

At the start, we defined `name` as equal to `Julia`. Using the ternary operator syntax and the `isa()` function, we check whether the given name is a `String` type or not. As expected, for the first call, it prints that the first condition, as the variable name is of `String` type, while in the latter case, the variable name is equal to `j`, which is a character type, hence making the condition `false`.

Short-circuit evaluation

In Julia, apart from the regular Boolean operators, such as `true` and `false`, we also have `&&` and `||`.

The idea behind them is fairly simple:

- Looking at the `var1 && var2` expression, `var2` only gets executed if `var1` evaluates to `true`

- Looking at the `var1 || var2` expression, `var2` only gets evaluated if `var1` evaluates to `false`

To get a better understanding of the two, let's have a look at some code:

```
julia> isdigit("10") && println("Reached me!")
Reached me!

julia> isdigit("Ten") && println("Reached me!")
false

julia> isdigit("Ten") || println("Reached me!")
Reached me!
```

```
julia> isdigit("Ten") && println("Reached me!")
false
```

In the first line of code, the isdigit("10") function takes in a string value and checks whether it's a digit or not. In this case, as the value is true, the second expression, println("Reached me!"), got successfully executed.

On the other hand, in the third line of code, the isdigit("Ten") expression evaluates to false, and hence the println("Reached me!") expression gets executed.

Repeated evaluation

After taking a closer look at how conditional evaluation works in Julia, let's shift our focus to one more important topic, **repeated evaluation**.

In Julia, we are provided with two constructs, namely while and for. These two are used for evaluating the code in loops. The following is an example, for both while and for loops:

```
julia> collection = [1,2,3,4,5,6,7,8,9]
9-element Array{Int64,1}:
  1
  2
  3
  4
  5
  6
  7
  8
  9

julia> while length(collection) > 1
            pop!(collection)
            println(collection)
       end
[1,2,3,4,5,6,7,8]
[1,2,3,4,5,6,7]
[1,2,3,4,5,6]
[1,2,3,4,5]
[1,2,3,4]
[1,2,3]
[1,2]
[1]
```

In this example, we have an array of integers from 1 to 9. We named it `collection`, and then we used a `while` construct to loop over the array of items till the length of `collection` was greater than 1. However, code written using `while` loops can easily become an infinite loop if our `end` condition is not correctly mentioned. For instance, in the preceding code, we have used a function provided by Julia called `pop!`, which takes in a collection of items and removes (or pops) the last item from it, this way modifying the original collection to be shorter and shorter.

Had we not controlled the end point of the `while` loop, this is what it would have resulted in:

```
julia> collection = [1,2,3,4,5,6,7,8,9]
9-element Array{Int64,1}:
 1
 2
 3
 4
 5
 6
 7
 8
 9

julia> while length(collection) > 1
           println(collection)
       end
[1,2,3,4,5,6,7,8]
[1,2,3,4,5,6,7,8]
[1,2,3,4,5,6,7,8]
[1,2,3,4,5,6,7,8]
[1,2,3,4,5,6,7,8]
[1,2,3,4,5,6,7,8]
[1,2,3,4,5,6,7,8]
....
.
.
```

We will eventually have to manually interrupt the program to stop the loop. So it must be kept in mind that, before using `while` loops, we must be very sure that we have an end point that must be reached.

After having a look over `while`, let's move on to a another construct called the `for` construct. It works in the following fashion:

```julia
julia> statement = "This is a great example!"
"This is a great example!"

julia> for words in split(statement)
            println(words)
        end
This
is
a
great
example!
```

So as you can see, `for` does a similar job by looping over each item of the collection it gets and executes the desired operation. The `split()` function *splits* a string into sections using a given character. By default, the space (" ") character is used.

```julia
# using the value of statement from the above example
julia> split(statement)
5-element Array{SubString{String},1}:
 "This"
 "is"
 "a"
 "great"
 "example!"
```

Had we not used `split()`, this is what we would have got:

```julia
julia> statement = "This is a great example!"
"This is a great example!"

julia> for words in statement
            println(words)
        end
T
h
i
s

i
s

a

g
r
```

```
e
a
t

e
x
a
m
p
l
e
!
```

This effectively showcases the difference. One important aspect that comes to mind while looping over an item is how we control the range of objects to be looped upon. This should be very familiar with people coming from a Python background, as it resembles the slicing techniques used in Python.

Again, with a closer look at an example, we can manipulate the collection of strings as shown here:

```
julia> statement = "Yet another awesome example!"
"Yet another awesome example!"
julia> for word in split(statement)[2:4]
            println(word)
        end
another
awesome
example!

julia> for word in split(statement)[2:3:2]
            println(word)
        end
another
```

Focusing on the `split(statement)[2:4]` code, we can break it down into two parts: the first part of the `split(statement)` code splits the String-type value and converts it to an array, `["Yet","another","awesome","example!"]`; while the second part of the code operates on this resultant array, and loops from `[2:4]`, that is, the second element to the fourth element, resulting in the ``` ` `` `["another","awesome","example!"]` value.

An important point not to be forgotten with regard to Julia is that the index of an array ALWAYS starts from 1! This is unlike many other languages, where the starting index is 0.

Defining range

While coding, we are often confronted with code that has something to do with the range of items to loop upon. For instance, how does someone know whether any number between 1 and 10 is either even or odd? This is very simple, but how do we start?

The following code shows how easily we can do this:

```julia
julia> numbers = [1,2,3,4,5,6,7,8,9,10]
10-element Array{Int64,1}:
  1
  2
  3
  4
  5
  6
  7
  8
  9
 10

julia> for n in numbers
           if rem(n,2) == 0
               println("$n is even")
           end
       end
2 is even
4 is even
6 is even
8 is even
10 is even
```

Simple! But wait - what if we had 100 numbers? Will we go on by first creating an array of 100 numbers? No. We will then use **range expression**. Let's see that in action:

```julia
julia> for n in 1:10
           if rem(n,2) == 0
               println("$n is even")
           end
       end
2 is even
4 is even
6 is even
8 is even
10 is even
```

Elegant, isn't it? Focus on how we used `1:10` to define a range of numbers starting from 1 to 10. It is easy to use, and comes in handy when you just have to loop over a given range of numbers.

Some more examples of the for loop

Imagine that we have been given a task to create patterns. This is very simple, yet it makes use of all our knowledge gained so far about the `for` construct.

- **The right-angled triangle**: A very simple looping exercise that involves mimicking the dimensions of a right-angled triangle:

```
julia> for i in 1:5
           for j in 1:i
               print("*")
           end
       println("")
       end
*
**
***
****
*****
```

Notice how we have carefully used the `print()` and `println()` functions to our advantage. The difference is that `print` does not changes the line, while `println` will use up a complete line.

- **The inverted triangle**: This is just the reverse of the initial triangle in the previous example:

```
julia> for i in 5:-1:1
           for j in 1:i
               print("*")
           end
       println("")
       end
*****
****
***
**
*
```

Focus on how we have used `5:-1:1` to reverse the range of numbers. Should we go further and try a quick string reversal? Why not!

- **Reverse a string**: Using slicing techniques in Julia to reverse a given string. The syntax is fairly simple, and closely resembles Python:

```julia
julia> my_string = "This is a great thing to do!"

julia> my_string[length(my_string):-1:1]
"!od ot gniht taerg a si sihT"
```

Here, we have used the length of the string to indicate the number of elements to be reversed. The `-1` number actually tells Julia to read/parse the string starting from the end.

The break and continue

We have, so far, read and experimented a great deal about the `for` and `while` constructs. However, as also provided by many different languages, we have `continue` as well as `break` statements.

The `break` block is used in places when we want the control to be shifted to an outer block of code. This means that we do not want to go further into evaluation, and want to immediately break and come out from that loop cycle. To understand this, let's look at the following example:

```julia
julia> word = "julia"
"julia"
julia> for letter in word
            println(letter)
            if letter == 'l'
                break
            end
        end
j
u
l
```

Here, we have a `word` with the `"julia"` value. We want a solution to come out of the `for` loop as soon as we encounter the `l` letter in the name. This is where `break` comes into action, and is able to cut off or break away from the loop as soon as the condition is met.

The `continue` statement is used in places where we want the evaluation to go on, if the given condition is met. Here is the code, modified to showcase the operation of a `continue` block:

```julia
julia> for letter in "julia"
           if letter == 'l'
              continue
           end
           println(letter)
       end
j
u
i
a
```

Exception handling

While writing any code, what do we do if something breaks? One possible answer is to write fully correct code in one go, but that doesn't happen so often in the real world. Many a time, a developer ends up spending considerable amounts of time figuring out errors and later fixing them in code. But then, code that doesn't handle situations where it fails to handle the expected (or unexpected) errors can't be considered good code!

It is important to establish proper exception or error handling. This can be ensured by using Julia's built-in exception handling methods, which we will be discussing in this portion of the chapter.

Let's first see the basic difference between an **error** and an **exception**:

```julia
julia> println('hello world!')
ERROR: syntax: invalid character literal


# To get the following, press CTRL+C during the execution of the loop.
julia> for i in 1:100
           println(i)
       end
1
2
3
4
ERROR: InterruptException:
 in process_events(::Bool) at ./libuv.jl:84
 in wait() at ./event.jl:188
 in stream_wait(::Task) at ./stream.jl:44
```

```
    in uv_write(::Base.TTY, ::Ptr{UInt8}, ::UInt64) at ./stream.jl:820
    in unsafe_write(::Base.TTY, ::Ptr{UInt8}, ::UInt64) at ./stream.jl:830
    in unsafe_write(::Base.TTY, ::Base.RefValue{UInt8}, ::Int64) at
./io.jl:155
    in write(::Base.TTY, ::Char) at ./io.jl:194
    in print(::Base.TTY, ::Char) at ./char.jl:45
    in print(::Base.TTY, ::Char) at
/Applications/Julia-0.5.app/Contents/Resources/julia/lib/julia/sys.dylib:?
    in print(::Base.TTY, ::Int128, ::Char, ::Vararg{Char,N}) at
./strings/io.jl:19
    in macro expansion; at ./REPL[5]:2 [inlined]
    in anonymous at ./<missing>:?
```

An error is something that indicates a problem and should be avoided, and hence the code should not be catching it. By catch, we mean to say that it should not be expecting it. On the other hand, an exception is something the code might be expecting, and there may be conditions in which the developer wants to catch the exceptions.

Julia provides many types of errors:

- `ArgumentError`: The argument passed to a function does not resemble the argument the function was expecting originally.
- `AssertionError`: This is the result when there is a wrong assertion statement written and it evaluates to `false`.
- `BoundsError`: Trying to access an out-of-bounds element while indexing an array.
- `DivideError`: This is the result when a number is divided by 0.
- `DomainError`: Arguments outside a valid domain.
- `EOFError`: This means that you have reached the end of the file, and hence there is nothing more to be read from it.
- `InexactError`: Failure in trying to do exact type conversion.
- `KeyError`: An attempt was made to access an element that isn't a key element - that is, non-existent.
- `LoadError`: An error occurred while loading a file.
- `MethodError`: There was an error while trying to use a signature of a function that isn't supported. In other words, the user tried to use a method that wasn't listed in the list of `methods(function)`.
- `OutOfMemoryError`: The computation requires more memory than allocated.
- `ReadOnlyMemoryError`: Trying to write in read-only memory.

- `OverflowError`: This happens when the result of an operation is too large.
- `ParseError`: Problem in parsing the given expression.
- `StackOverflowError`: This happens when a function call goes beyond the call stack.
- `SystemError`: An error due to the failure of a system call.
- `TypeError`: An assertion failed for type checking. This happens most commonly when the wrong type of argument is passed to a function.
- `UndefRefError`: Unknown reference made.
- `UndefVarError`: Unknown reference made to a variable that doesn't exist.
- `InitError`: This error occurs when there is a problem calling the module's __init__ method.

There are many types of exception as well:

- `ErrorException`: An error occurred
- `InterruptException`: An external interruption occurred in the computation
- `NullException`: Trying to access a `Null` value
- `ProcessExitedException`: The process ended, hence further attempts to access this process will result in errors

Interestingly, `Exception` is itself a `DataType` that is available by default in Julia. This would mean that we can write our own custom exceptions by inheriting the type:

```julia
julia> typeof(Exception)
DataType

julia> type CustomException <: Exception
       end

julia> typeof(CustomException)
DataType

julia> supertype(CustomException)
Exception
```

Let's now discuss some more useful functions one by one, which will come in handy while exception handling.

The throw() function

The `throw()` function does not throw an exception *as soon as it encounters one*. It **immediately** throws an error when called. Looking over the official documentation, this is what it says:

```
throw(e)

    Throw an object as an exception.
```

Here, `e` is any object. `throw` will convert it into an exception.

```
julia> throw("")
ERROR: ""

julia> throw(3+3)
ERROR: 6

julia> throw("some error message")
ERROR: "some error message"

julia> throw(ErrorException("an ErrorException has occurred"))
ERROR: an ErrorException has occurred
```

To correctly throw a `TypeError`, you must actually throw an instance of the object. An instance can be created using type `TypeError` constructor.:

```
julia> function say_hi(name)
           if typeof(name) != String
               throw(TypeError)
           else
               println("hi $name")
           end
       end
say_hi (generic function with 1 method)

julia> say_hi('n')
ERROR: TypeError
Stacktrace:
[1] say_hi(::Char) at ./REPL[155]:3

julia> try
           say_hi('n')
       catch e
           println(typeof(e))
       end
DataType
```

Notice that the `typeof(e)` call returns DataType. To correct this, create an instance of a TypeError.

```
julia> function say_hi(name)
           if typeof(name) != String
               throw(TypeError(:say_hi, "printing name", String, name))
           else
               println("hi $name")
           end
       end
say_hi (generic function with 1 method)

julia> say_hi('n')
ERROR: TypeError: say_hi: in printing name, expected String, got Char
Stacktrace:
[1] say_hi(::Char) at ./REPL[158]:3

julia> try
           say_hi('n')
       catch e
           println(typeof(e))
       end
TypeError
```

Here, we have a function named `say_hi`, which takes in a name and prints out a message, `hi $name`, where the name is to be provided externally. When we provide "`jack`" as the name, the function works; but then, if the name provided is not of the `String` type, then it's coded to throw a `TypeError`, which it does when 1 is passed as the argument.

Although the example is just meant to provide an understanding of how `throw` works, the preceding situation could have easily been avoided without using `throw` at all, if we were to use multiple dispatch as shown in the following code:

```
julia> workspace()

julia> function say_hi(name :: String)
           if typeof(name) != String
               throw(TypeError)
           else
               println("hi $name")
           end
       end
say_hi (generic function with 1 method)

# MethodError will be thrown instead of TypeError
julia> say_hi(1)
```

```
ERROR: MethodError: no method matching say_hi(::Int64)
Closest candidates are:
  say_hi(::String) at REPL[15]:2
```

So a more useful example would be to check whether the length of the given name matches a specific number. Here is the modified code:

```
julia> workspace()

julia> function say_hi(name :: String)
           if length(name) < 5
               throw(ArgumentError)
           else
               println("hi $name")
           end
       end

say_hi (generic function with 2 methods)

julia> say_hi("joe")
ERROR: ArgumentError
 in say_hi(::String) at ./REPL[21]:3

julia> say_hi("david")
hi david
```

The error() function

This function can be used to raise an `ErrorException` of a custom type, which the developer wants to show the end user.

It should be noted that the use of this function is generally discouraged outside of debugging and logging. It is almost always better to use a more specific or custom exception.

Taking the example of the previous `throw()` function, we have:

```
julia> function say_hi(name :: String)
           if length(name) < 5
               error("Name less than 5!!!")
           else
               println("hi $name")
           end
       end
say_hi (generic function with 1 method)
```

```
julia> say_hi("joe")
ERROR: Name less than 5!!!
 in say_hi(::String) at ./REPL[33]:3
```

Here, we have used a custom message of our own, `Name less than 5!!!`, which gets printed on the screen if the length is less than 5.

We also have two more slightly less-used functions compared to `throw()` and `error()`, namely `info()` and `warn()`. These two basically resemble log levels, when we want to tell the end user about the level of problems in the code:

```
julia> info("I am an information to the end user")
INFO: I am an information to the end user

julia> warn(" I am a warning issues to the end user")
WARNING:  I am a warning issues to the end user
```

The try/catch/finally blocks

The most important part of exception handling is to take care using these statements. They not only provide effective safety from unknown errors, but also increase control over the code from the developer's perspective. In other words, all well-written code, if possible, must include `try`/`catch` blocks:

```
julia> try
          exponent("alpha")
       catch(e)
          println(e)
       end
MethodError(exponent, ("alpha",), 0x00000000000055aa)
```

We already know that `exponent` doesn't work over String-type values; however, in this example, we tried to evaluate it firsthand inside the `try` block, and failing that, `catch` will catch and hold the exception as `e`.

In the end, we can see that there was an `MethodError` exception raised by the code, which was then later on reported by the `catch` block.

The `finally` block is used when we need to do a cleanup once the code execution is done. You can think of this in terms of closing a database connection once the entry in the database table has been made. The syntax for that would be:

```
try
        . . .
        . . .
finally
        db_connection.close()
end
```

This wraps up our discussion of exception handling. Next, we will be looking at how tasks are made in Julia.

Tasks in Julia

Tasks are a feature similar to coroutines in other languages. They help us to suspend an operation and resume when required.

In normal sequential code, when we call a function, let's say `f1`, and then call function `f2`, it's understood that `f2` will start when the `f1` function ends. But, in this whole operation, we do not have any control over the function once it has started to execute itself. A task in Julia is different, as it allows itself to be interrupted while getting executed!

Julia provides a function named `task()` to create any function as a task (also known as a **coroutine**). This makes the function behave differently from usual. However, the whole process is very different from a function call. There are two main reasons for this:

- At the time when we want to interrupt and resume a task, there is no space taken at all by this operation, so there is no excess load on the call stack.
- There is no specific order in which the tasks can be switched!

Let's see an example, to see how we can use the tasks:

```
julia> function add_one()
           a = 1
           produce(a)
           while true
               a += 1
               produce(a)
           end
       end
add_one (generic function with 1 method)
```

```
julia> generator = Task(add_one)
Task (runnable) @0x00000001149e9210

julia> consume(generator)
1

julia> consume(generator)
2

julia> consume(generator)
3

julia> consume(generator)
4

julia> consume(generator)
5
```

Let's start to look at the problem by focusing on what this program does. It includes a function named add_one, which simply adds 1 to the variable named a, while this is done inside a while loop, which seems to run infinitely (if called). But here in the catch block, the function add_one will be passed on as an argument to what we call a Task, by using the task() function.

However, there is one more function, by the name of produce(), which is a function similar to a yield in Python. In other words, it remembers the state of the variable. Once we have declared the task, we need to call it.

This is done by another function called consume(). The work of this function is to take the latest (or next) value passed to a task. So when we call consumer(generator) the complete operation could be broken down as:

- For the first run, a = 1, produce(a) results in 1, and this gets passed to the consume function, which returns 1.

- For the second run, a = 1+1. That is 2, produce(a) results in 2, which then gets returned on calling the consume function, and so on.

Here is another simple example of `task` in Julia. The function computes the squares of numbers from 1 to 3, and stops when the limit is reached:

```
# valid for julia v0.5
julia> function sample_task()
            for i in 1:3
                produce(i^2)
            end
        produce("END")
        end
sample_task (generic function with 1 method)

julia> result = Task(sample_task)
Task (runnable) @0x0000000113bfc6d0

julia> consume(result)
1

julia> consume(result)
4

julia> consume(result)
9

julia> consume(result)
"END"

julia> consume(result)
()
```

Summary

We have now successfully completed this chapter, which was all about flow control in Julia. We saw how conditional and repeated evaluation works in Julia using keywords and various constructs such as `if`, `while`, and `for`, as well as discussing how to write good code that handles exceptions with constructs, such as `try/catch`. To conclude, we took a look at how to create tasks or coroutines in Julia using the special `Task` function.

In the next chapter, we shall move our focus towards learning metaprogramming in Julia, and understanding the various aspects of interoperability in the language.

6
Interoperability and Metaprogramming

In this chapter, we will be focusing on finding out how Julia interacts with the outside world, by using different ways of making system calls to the **operating system** (**OS**), or using code from other languages such as C and Python. Later on, we will explore another great aspect of Julia in the form of metaprogramming. We'll also study various types of macros provided by default in Julia, and how to create one, if and when required. To conclude, we will try to understand the different reflection properties of Julia.

Here is the list of topics we will be covering in this chapter:

- Interacting with operating systems
- Calling C and Python
- Expressions and macros
- Built-in macros
- Type introspection and reflection capabilities

Interacting with operating systems

One of the best features of Julia is its great REPL, which provides users with a lot of flexibility while calling OS-specific commands. For this book, I have been using a Linux-based operating system, and hence, going forward, all the commands used will be purely Linux-based. For users using Windows, the system commands would be different and native to the underlying OS.

To call any operating system command from inside the Julia REPL, we just have to press a ";" key and the prompt immediately changes:

```
julia >;    # As soon as you press this ";"

shell >
```

The change in the prompt is immediate, and on the same line. To start with, Julia provides a command named `pwd()`, which is synonymous with the one we used in a Linux operating system to discover a user's current directory:

```
shell> pwd
/home/myuser

julia> pwd()
"/home/myuser"
```

Notice closely, for the first command, we have used a ";" and then called the `pwd` command in shell mode. While for the next one, we have used the `pwd()` function inside the Julia prompt. We will now be discussing some of the major functions used for performing filesystem operations as well as I/O operations.

Filesystem operations

Accessing files and doing operations over them is one of the most basic operations, and one can achieve the desired results by having the right knowledge about functions that interact with the filesystem. Given here are some of the most useful functions, along with some examples.

- `homedir()` and `joinpath()` functions: Julia is platform independent. This means that it runs on any platform without any hiccups and you can easily make a script which is cross-platform and can be used by everyone:

  That being said, how to handle the different conventions while using directories and paths across different operating systems? This question is easily addressed by the two functions `homedir` and `joinpath`. Have a look at the following example:

  ```
  # check the home directory
  julia> homedir()
  "/Users/myuser"

  # can be used to create paths which can be used further
  julia> joinpath(homedir(), "Documents")
  ```

```
"/Users/myuser/Documents"
```

We will now be moving on to other commands, which can make use of these 2 functions and work seamlessly across any platform.

- `cd()`: Lets the user change the current directory to the desired one. The usage is simple. To see the effects of the directory change, we will be using `pwd()` function, which we studied earlier. Here is an example:

```
julia> pwd()
"/Users/myuser"

julia> cd("../")

julia> pwd()
"/Users/"
```

- `readdir` function: This function is used for reading the contents of any specific directory. One example is as follows:

```
# homedir() is cross platform
julia> d = homedir()

julia> readdir(d)
45-element Array{String,1}:
 ".CFUserTextEncoding"
 ".DS_Store"
 ".Trash"
 ".anaconda"
 ".atom"
 ...
 "dosbox"
 "dottest.dot"
 "dottest.png"
 "test"
 "transformations.jl"
```

Here, we have passed the `"d"` directory (which we initialized with `home` directory) as an argument to the function, which then shows all the contents of this directory as an array.

- `mkdir` function: This is used to create an empty directory, along with the permissions to create it. Here is an example of the function used:

```
# cross-platform
julia> d = joinpath(homedir(), "LearningJulia")
```

```
julia> mkdir(d)

julia> cd("LearningJulia")

julia> pwd()
"/Users/julians/LearningJulia"
```

The function `mkdir()` can also take a second argument that has to be an unsigned integer, wherein the permissions can be passed. The permissions are calculated as (r,w,x), and more on file permissions can be read at `https:/` `/en.wikipedia.org/wiki/File_system_permissions`.

- `stat` function: This function is very useful, if you want to have a lot of information about a specific file. To show what this function is capable of, let's create an empty file with the name `sample.jl`, and run this function over the file:

```
julia> stat("sample.jl")
StatStruct(mode=100644, size=0)

julia> stat("sample.jl").ctime
1.502545241e9

julia> stat("sample.jl").mtime
1.502545241e9

julia> stat("sample.jl").size
0

julia> stat("sample.jl").uid
0x000000006d16c610

julia> stat("sample.jl").gid
0x0000000064cbf778

julia> stat("sample.jl").rdev
0x0000000000000000

julia> stat("sample.jl").blksize
4096

julia> stat("sample.jl").blocks
0

julia> stat("sample.jl").device
0x0000000001000004
```

```
julia> stat("sample.jl").mode
0x00000000000081a4

julia> stat("sample.jl").inode
0x00000000002f538d
```

- `cp` and `mv` functions: These two functions mimic the two basic functionalities of copying and moving a file from a source to a destination. The following simple example shows their usage:

```
julia> cp(".viminfo", "new_viminfo")

julia> isfile("new_viminfo")
true

julia> mv("new_viminfo","viminfo.bkp")

julia> isfile("viminfo.bkp")
true
```

In the first command, the `cp` function copies `.viminfo` to a new location, which is `new_viminfo`; however, on the other hand, `mv` moves this new `new_viminfo` file to another file called `viminfo.bkp` (or basically renames it).

- `isdir`, `homedir`, `basename`, `dirname`, and `splitdir`: These are very useful functions while getting to know more about the directories. Given here is a set of examples that clearly help in understanding the differences between these commands, and where they can be used:

```
# to check whether the given path is a directory or not.
julia> isdir(joinpath(homedir(),"Documents"))
true

julia> isdir("sample.txt")
false

# To know your home directory.
julia> homedir()
"/Users/myuser"

# to know the exact name of the directory you are in, without
the full path.
julia> basename(homedir())
"myuser"
```

```
# To know about the directory which has the directory you are
looking for.
julia> dirname(homedir())
"/Users"

# To split the directory path and split them into a tuple
julia> splitdir(homedir())
("/Users","myuser")
```

- `mkpath`, `ispath`, `abspath`, and `joinpath`: Sometimes, while working with files and directories, you may want to know if you are in the right path, or whether the file that you are trying to access is in the right path or not. To resolve such issues and to make sure they don't occur, keeping a check on the current path is important. Given here are the four most important path-specific commands, along with their examples:

```
# To check whether the path exists or not
julia> ispath(homedir())
true

julia> ispath(joinpath(homedir(),"random"))
false

# To know the absolute path of a directory
julia> abspath("Documents")
"/Users/rahullakhanpal/Documents"

# To make a path and subsequent directories in it
julia> mkpath(joinpath("Users","adm"))

#To make sure the path was created in real!
julia> for (root, dirs, files) in walkdir("Users")
           println("Directories in $root")
       end
Directories in Users
Directories in Users/adm
=#
```

I/O operations

After having read about some filesystem operations, let's move on to I/O and network-related tasks. Here, we will be going through a list of some of the most used functions, while performing the operations mentioned earlier.

The STDOUT, STDERR, and STDIN are the three global variables inside Julia for denoting a standard output, error, and input stream respectively.

- open() function: This function is used to open up a file for the purpose of reading or writing a file. A very simple use case would be to create a file named sample.txt in your current directory, and open Julia REPL:

```
julia> file = open("sample.txt")
IOStream(<file sample.txt>)

julia> file
IOStream(<file sample.txt>)
```

  Now, since the file is opened, what do we do with it? We probably will go ahead and read the contents of it. Let's suppose we had hello world!! written inside the sample.txt file; what happens when we try to read its contents now? Take a look at the following code:

```
julia> lines = readlines(file)
1-element Array{String,1}:
"hello world!!\n"
```

  The function readlines() will specifically be used to read all the contents of this file. The result comes out as an Array of String. However, there is more than one way of opening a file in Julia, and that depends upon the mode in which we open the file. The common ones are r, w, and r+, where r+ stands for read as well as write.

- write and read function: This function, as the name suggests, is used to write and read contents to and from a file, respectively. A quick example shown here will help you gain a basic understanding of both these functions:

```
# open up a file named "sample.txt" and write the message
julia> write("sample.txt", "hi how are you doing?")
21

julia> read("sample.txt")
21-element Array{UInt8,1}:
 0x68
 0x69
 0x20
 0x68
 0x6f
 0x77
 0x20
```

```
0x61
0x72
0x65
0x20
0x79
0x6f
0x75
0x20
0x64
0x6f
0x69
0x6e
0x67
0x3f
```

```
# to actually read the contents
julia> readline("sample.txt")
"hi how are you doing?"
```

Here, first, we have called the write function to open up a file sample.txt, and write the contents "hi how are you doing?". Next up, we now use the read function to open up the same file and try to read the contents. But the result is not what we expected!

Instead, we get an Array{UInt8,1} type of array, which shows that we are trying to access a stream of unsigned integers. A close look at the methods for this function further clears the confusion:

```
julia> methods(read)
# 37 methods for generic function "read":
read(::Base.DevNullStream, ::Type{UInt8}) at coreio.jl:13
read(s::IOStream) at iostream.jl:236
read(s::IOStream, ::Type{UInt8}) at iostream.jl:151
read(s::IOStream,
T::Union{Type{Int16},Type{Int32},Type{Int64},Type{UInt16},Type{
UInt32},Type{UInt64}}) at iostream.jl:160
read(s::IOStream, ::Type{Char}) at iostream.jl:180
read(s::IOStream, nb::Integer; all) at iostream.jl:260
...
..
.
```

To close the file after reading, we have a function named `close()` that takes in the name of the file as its parameter:

```
julia> close("sample.txt")
```

Example

Now that we have read about filesystem and I/O operations, we can now give a fully fledged example of how a simple Julia script can be created to read and write data into a file.

Here, we have a file named `sample.jl`, which we have created in the following manner:

```
# Arguments
in_file = ARGS[1]
out_file = ARGS[2]

# Keeping track using a counter
counter = 0
for line in eachline(in_file)
    for word in split(line)
        if word == "Julia"
            counter += 1
        end
    end
end

# write the contents to the output file
write(out_file, "the count for julia is $counter")

# read the contents fom the o/p file for user's help
for line in readlines(out_file)
    println(line)
end
```

This script basically takes in two inputs:

- `in_file`, which is a TXT file from which we will be reading the data
- `out_file`, to which we will be writing the result

The `in_file` that we are going to supply has the name `readme.txt`, and contains the following information (the following text has been taken from the official Julia website):

```
mylinux-machine:home myuser$ cat readme.txt
```

Julia is a high-level, high-performance dynamic programming language for numerical computing. It provides a sophisticated compiler, distributed parallel execution, numerical accuracy, and an extensive mathematical function library. Julia's Base library, largely written in Julia itself, also integrates mature, best-of-breed open source C and Fortran libraries for linear algebra, random number generation, signal processing, and string processing. In addition, the Julia developer community is contributing a number of external packages through Julia's built-in package manager at a rapid pace. IJulia, a collaboration between the Jupyter and Julia communities, provides a powerful browser-based graphical notebook interface to Julia.

While the `out_file` will be the file we write to, in this case, we have `result.out`. Now we go ahead and call the script in the following manner from the Command Prompt:

```
mylinux-machine:home myuser$ julia sample.jl readme.txt result.out
the count for julia is 4
```

If you examine the script `sample.jl` closely, we are just reading in a file that we have passed as an argument (in this example, `readme.txt`), and computing the number of times the exact word *Julia* appears in the text. Finally, the total number of words are written into the file `result.out`:

```
mylinux-machine:home myuser$ cat result.out
the count for julia is 4
```

Calling C and Python!

Julia, as we know it from our very first introduction, takes the best from both worlds. It matches Python in terms of ease of code and maintenance, while it targets to achieve the speeds of C.

But what if we really need to make outside calls to code or functions written in these two languages? We then require the ability to import the code directly into Julia, and be able to make use of it. Let's see, one by one, how Julia manages to make external calls to these two programming languages.

Calling C from Julia

C can be called as the mother of modern-day programming languages, and most of the languages today use C somewhere in their source codes to either make their code run quicker or just to add a wrapper over an existing C function or library.

Julia also makes use of C in some of its libraries, although most of the core libs are written in
Julia itself. There are some things that make Julia stand apart from the crowd when it comes to calling C. They are as follows:

- Make calls to C without any hassle
- Absolutely no overhead
- No further processing or compilation needed before calling the C function, hence it
  can be used directly

Now before we move on to actually start calling C from Julia, let's take a look at what a compiler (like LLVM) needs to know before it makes a call to any C function.

- Name of the library
- Name of the function itself
- Number and types of the arguments (also called Arity)
- Return type of the function
- Values of the arguments passed

The function which does this all in Julia is called `ccall()`. It's syntax can be written as the following:

```
ccall((:name,"lib"), return_type, (arg1_type, arg2_type...), arg1, arg2)
```

The following is a simple example of how to make a call to a C function using `ccall`. Here we are calling the `clock` function from the standard C library itself, and it will return a value which will be an `Int64` type value:

```
julia> ccall((:clock, :libc), Int64, ())
1437953
```

Here we can also do something like this:

```
julia> ccall((:clock, :libc), Cint, ())
1467922
```

Notice that we were able to replace Int64 with `Cint`. But what is `Cint`? `Cint` here is actually the C equivalent of signed `int` c-type, if you open up the REPL:

```julia
julia> Int32 == Cint
true
```

Is that surprising? No! The reason is that Julia makes use of these aliases for C-based types. There are more of them defined such as `Cint`, `Cuint`, `Clong`, `Culong`, and `Cchar`. Let's try another example, but a complex one:

```julia
julia> syspath = ccall( (:getenv, :libc), Ptr{Cchar}, (Ptr{Cchar},),
"SHELL")
Ptr{Int8} @0x00007fff5ca5bbe0

julia> unsafe_string(syspath)
"/bin/bash"
```

Here we are making `ccall` to the standard C library to make use of the `getenv` function and getting the SHELL value from it, which in itself is a Julia string.

However, here we are passing an argument of type `Ptr{Cchar}` and the expected argument type of the result is also `Ptr{Cchar}`, both of which represent a Julia type (pointer to a character). So the overall result we are trying to get here is the value of the SHELL parameter from the environment variables.

But how does this execution happen? Before even `ccall` is called, there is a call to convert function internally, which converts SHELL (which is a Julia string) to a `Ptr{Cchar}` type.

After this the actual call happens that returns a `Ptr{Int8}` @0x00007fff5ca5bbe0 value, wherein there is a Pointer to an `Int8` along with the buffer address. To make this more readable, we make use of a function by the name `unsafe_string` that converts it to a Julia String type.

The reason why this function is prefixed with unsafe is because it will crash if the the value of the pointer is not a valid memory address. This is popularly called a segmentation fault. However, here it works as usual as `Ptr{Int8}` @0x00007fff5ca5bbe0 is a valid memory address.

The reason why we are able to get the value as a Julia type is because there are lots of conversions defined as standard while doing calls to C-based Strings and Integers. Even C structs can be replicated to Julia using composite types.

Calling Python from Julia

Using another language inside Julia may not be the best of ideas as far as speed and efficiency is concerned. But, there may be situations when you would be required to do so. Here, we talk about a package named `PyCall`, which is used to import Python code in Julia.

Here is how `PyCall` can be downloaded from inside a Julia shell:

```
julia> Pkg.add("PyCall")
```

Once it is installed, we can start using Python commands right away. Given here are some code snippets that let you quickly understand how easy it is to invoke and use in Julia right away:

```
# Invoke PyCall
julia> using PyCall

# Starting with a simple hello world
julia> py"""
       print 'hello world'
       """
hello world

# Some random operations
julia> py"len('julia')"
5
julia> py"str(5)"
"5"
```

As you can see, we have been using the syntax; `py"""` to invoke and run common Python functions. But what if we need to invoke third-party libraries such as Numpy? We then make use of the `@pyimport` macro, which lets us use them. Here is one such quick example:

```
julia> @pyimport numpy as np

julia> np.sin(120)
0.5806111842123143
```

It should be noted that the syntax of Python code we are using should be according to the Python path set in the environment variable. This can easily be rechecked as:

```
julia> ENV["PATH"]
"/Applications/Julia-0.6.app/Contents/Resources/julia/bin:/Library/Framewor
ks/Python.framework/Versions/3.6/bin:/usr/bin:/bin:/usr/sbin:/sbin:/Applica
tions/Julia-0.6.app/Contents/Resources/julia/bin/:/usr/local/go/bin:/usr/lo
cal/mysql/bin"
```

Now, what if we want to use Python's built-in data types, such as `dict`? The `PyCall` has a solution for that too, in the form of `pybuiltin`. Let's see a detailed example:

```
# Using pybuiltin, directy create a python dict object
julia> pybuiltin(:dict)(a=1,b=2)
Dict{Any,Any} with 2 entries:
  "b" => 2
  "a" => 1

julia> pycall(pybuiltin("dict"), Any, a=1, b=2)
PyObject {'a': 1, 'b': 2}

julia> d = pycall(pybuiltin("dict"), Any, a=1, b=2)
PyObject {'a': 1, 'b': 2}

# making sure of the type, still a python object
julia> typeof(d)
PyCall.PyObject

# using pyDict to convert python's object to a juia dict object
julia> julia_dictionary = PyDict{Symbol, Int64}(pycall(pybuiltin("dict"),
Any, a=1, b=2))
PyCall.PyDict{Symbol,Int64,true} with 2 entries:
  :a => 1
  :b => 2

# as we see, its now a julia dict object
julia> typeof(julia_dictionary)
PyCall.PyDict{Symbol,Int64,true}

# accessing dictionary elements
julia> julia_dictionary[:a]
1

# accessing dictionary elements
julia> julia_dictionary[:b]
2

# a function that takes kw arguments
julia> f(; a=0, b=0) = [10a, b]
f (generic function with 1 method)

julia> f(;julia_dictionary...)
2-element Array{Int64,1}:
 10
  2
```

Expressions and macros

Metaprogramming is fun, and Julia definitely has one of the best metaprogramming features compared with some of its rivals. The initial cues and inspiration have been taken from Lisp, and similarly to Lisp, Julia is written in Julia itself—or in other words, Julia is homoiconic.

To explain how Julia interprets a code, here is a small code snippet:

```
julia> code = "println(\"hello world \")"
"println(\"hello world \")"

julia> expression = parse(code)
:(println("hello world "))

julia> typeof(expression)
Expr
```

Here, we have simply passed a normal Julia code `println("hello world")` as a string to the function parse. This function, in turn, takes this piece of string and converts it into a data type called `Expr`, which is evident from the preceding code.

To see what's inside this `Expr` type of data closely, we can dig deeper:

```
julia> fieldnames(expression)
3-element Array{Symbol,1}:
 :head
 :args
 :typ

julia> expression.args
2-element Array{Any,1}:
 :println
 "hello world "

julia> expression.head
:call

julia> expression.typ
Any
```

Any `Expr`-type object has three parts:

- Symbols, which, in this case, are `:call` and `:println`
- A series of arguments, which, in this case, are `:println` and `"hello world "`
- Finally, a result type, which, here, is `Any`

Julia also provides another function called `dump`, which helps to provide detailed information about the expression-type objects:

```
julia> dump(expression)
Expr
  head: Symbol call
  args: Array{Any}((2,))
    1: Symbol println
    2: String "hello world "
  type: Any
```

But, we know what arguments and return types are. The one thing we don't have a good understanding of is a symbol!

Symbols in Julia are the same as in Lisp, Scheme or Ruby. When a language can represent its own code, it needs a way to represent things like assignments, function calls, things that can be written as literal values. It also needs a way to represent its own variables. That is, you need a way to represent it as data.

Let's take the example:

```
julia> foo == "foo"
```

The difference between a symbol and a string is the difference between `foo` on the left hand side of that comparison and `"foo"` on the right hand side. On the left, `foo` is an identifier and it evaluates to the value bound to the variable `foo` in the current scope. On the right, `"foo"` is a string literal and it evaluates to the string value `"foo"`. A symbol in both Lisp and Julia is how you represent a variable as data. A string just represents itself.

There is one more way to create an expression, which is by using an `Expr` constructor. Given here is a most basic type of expression that one can create:

```
julia> sample_expr = Expr(:call, +, 10, 20)
:((+)(10,20))

julia> eval(sample_expr)
30
```

So, what is happening here? We have created a custom expression wherein we are passing `:call` as the first argument, which symbolized the head of the expression. Next, we supply `+`, `10`, and `20` as the arguments to this expression. To evaluate this expression finally at runtime, we use a function named `eval`:

```
julia> sample_expr.args
3-element Array{Any,1}:
   +
```

```
10
20

julia> eval(sample_expr)
30
```

Please take note that `eval` takes an `Expr` -type value as input, which is why the data type of `sample_expr` is `Expr`.

Now, suppose we wanted to evaluate this expression instead:

```
julia> sample_expr = Expr(:call, +, x, y)
ERROR: UndefVarError: x not defined
```

This throws an error, saying x is not defined, which indeed is the case too. But how do we go about it? How do we replace these values with the one we want to pass? Or, in other words, how do we interpolate these variables?

One way is to inject the values of x and y directly in the expression we are trying to create and later evaluate:

```
julia> x = 10
10

julia> y = 10
10

julia> sample_expr = Expr(:call, +, :x, :y)
:((+)(10,10))

# or even this works
julia> sample_expr = Expr(:call, +, x, y)
:((+)(10,10))

julia> eval(sample_expr)
20
```

Another way to achieve the same results is to use $, but, in this case, we won't be interpolating the values at runtime; rather, we will be doing it at the time of parsing the expression. See the following example:

```
julia> x = 10
10

julia> y = 10
10
```

```
julia> e = :($x + $y)
:(10 + 10)

julia> eval(e)
20
```

Hence, overall there are two ways by which interpolation can be done with `Expr` objects:

- Using quotes (:) at runtime
- Using dollar ($) at parse time

Another way of expressing the expression is by using the `quote` keyword. For the most part, using a quoted expression is synonymous with the one we have been using so far—for example, expression preceded by a ":" key:

```
julia> quote
          30 * 100
          end
quote  # REPL[12], line 2:
    30 * 100
end

julia> eval(ans)
3000

julia> :(30 * 100)
:(30 * 100)

julia> eval(ans)
3000
```

As you may have noticed, there is no difference between the two! But then, why is `quote` available separately to the end user? The main reason, as the official Julia documentation states, is because when using `quote`, this form introduces `QuoteNodes` elements to the expression tree, which must be considered while manipulating the tree.

In other words, using `quote`, you can splice what is implemented better.

Macros

Macros in Julia are a very powerful tool for code evaluation, and in some of the previous chapters, we have been using them regularly (for instance, using `@time` to know the overall compute time of a program).

Macros are similar to functions, but where functions take in normal variables as arguments, macros, on the other hand, take expressions and return modified expressions.

 Functions are evaluated at runtime. Macros are evaluated at parse time. This means that macros can manipulate functions (and other code) before they are ever executed.

The syntax of a macro could be defined as follows:

```
macro NAME
        # some custom code
        # return modified expression
end
```

At the time of calling a macro, the @ symbol is used, which is used to denote a macro in Julia. This symbol is, however, similar to the ones used in other languages, such as decorators in Python:

```
julia> macro HELLO(name)
           :( println("Hello! ", $name))
       end
@HELLO (macro with 1 method)
julia> @HELLO("Raaaul")
Hello! Raaaul
```

To see what's going on inside a macro and to help debug them better, we can use the Julia function with the name macroexpand:

```
julia> macroexpand(:(@HELLO("rahul")))
:(println("Hello!","rahul"))
```

But why metaprogramming?

To understand why metaprogramming is used, have a look at this scenario. You have a function similar to the one given here, which takes a number and prints it the given number of times:

```
julia> function foo(n::Int64)
           for i=1:n
               println("foo")
           end
       end
foo (generic function with 1 method)
```

```
julia> foo(2)
foo
foo
```

Simple? Yes. But now suppose, in some different module in your code, you are doing the same kind of operation, but with some other name:

```
julia> function bar(n::Int64)
            for i=1:n
                println("bar")
            end
        end
bar (generic function with 1 method)

julia> bar(2)
bar
bar

julia> function baz(n::Int64)
            for i=1:n
                println("baz")
            end
        end
baz (generic function with 1 method)

julia> baz(2)
baz
baz
```

A lot of code repetition, right? You certainly want to avoid this problem, and here is where metaprogramming comes to the rescue. With metaprogramming, you can essentially generate code on the fly, which can cut down your time as a developer.

So, to make sure we don't repeat ourselves, let's see what we can do instead:

```
julia> for sym in [:foo, :bar, :baz]
            @eval function $(Symbol(string(sym)))(n::Int64)
                for i in 1:n
                    println("$sym")
                end
            end
        end

julia> foo(1)
foo

julia> bar(1)
bar
```

```
julia> baz(1)
baz
```

So as you can see, we were able to do the same with the help of metaprograms! In the next section, we will be talking about some very important built-in macros available in Julia!

Built-in macros

Given here is a list of available macros in Julia:

```
@MIME_str         @code_typed       @fetch          @less           @schedule     @timed
@__FILE__         @code_warntype    @fetchfrom      @linux          @show         @timev
@allocated        @deprecate        @functionloc    @linux_only     @simd
@uint128_str
@assert           @doc              @generated      @noinline       @spawn        @unix
@async            @doc_str          @gensym         @osx            @spawnat
@unix_only
@b_str            @edit             @goto           @osx_only       @sprintf      @v_str
@big_str          @elapsed          @html_str       @parallel       @static
@vectorize_1arg
@boundscheck      @enum             @inbounds       @polly          @sync
@vectorize_2arg
@cmd              @eval             @inline         @printf         @task         @view
@code_llvm        @evalpoly         @int128_str     @profile        @text_str     @which
@code_lowered     @everywhere       @ip_str         @r_str          @threadcall
@windows
@code_native      @fastmath         @label          @s_str          @time
@windows_only
```

We will be focusing on discussing some of the most used ones out of these. Let's start exploring them:

- @time: This one is a useful macro to find out the total time taken by a program to complete. In other words, we can use it to keep track of our program's execution speed. Its usage, along with a small example, is given here:

```
# simple function to find recursive sum
julia> function recursive_sum(n)
if n == 0
return 0
else
return n + recursive_sum(n-1)
end
end
recursive_sum (generic function with 1 method)
```

```
# A bit slow to run for the 1st Time, as the function gets
compiled.
julia> @time recursive_sum(10000)
0.003905 seconds (450 allocations: 25.816 KiB)
50005000

# Much much faster in the second run!
julia> @time recursive_sum(10000)
0.000071 seconds (5 allocations: 176 bytes)
50005000
```

Julia is good at scientific calculations, and @time comes in handy when understanding the time taken by the program to run.

- @elapsed: Closely resembling the @time macro is the @elapsed macro, which discards the result and just displays the time taken by the program to run. Reapplying @elapsed to the previous average function:

```
julia> @elapsed average(10000000, 1000000000)
2.144e-6

julia> typeof(@elapsed average(10000000, 1000000000))
Float64
```

The result of @elapsed is always represented in floating point numbers.

- @show: This macro, when used along with any piece of code, will return an expression as well as compute the result of it. The sample given here will be helpful in using @show:

```
julia> @show(println("hello world"))
hello world
println("hello world") = nothing

julia> @show(:(println("hello world")))
$(Expr(:quote, :(println("hello world")))) = :(println("hello
world"))
:(println("hello world"))

julia> @show(:(3*2))
$(Expr(:quote, :(3 * 2))) = :(3 * 2)
:(3 * 2)

julia> @show(3*2)
3 * 2 = 6
6
julia> @show(Int64)
```

```
Int64 = Int64
Int64
```

- @which: This macro is quite useful when you have multiple methods for a single function and you want to inspect or know about the method that would be called when a specific set of arguments will be supplied.
  Because Julia relies heavily on multiple dispatch, the @which macro comes in handy at a lot of places. The following is a example which showcases its usage.

```
# create a function that tripples an Integer
julia> function tripple(n::Int64)
           3n
       end
tripple (generic function with 1 method)

# redefine the same function to accept Float
julia> function tripple(n::Float64)
           3n
       end
tripple (generic function with 2 methods)

# check the methods available for this function
julia> methods(tripple)
# 2 methods for generic function "tripple":
tripple(n::Float64) in Main at REPL[22]:2
tripple(n::Int64) in Main at REPL[21]:2

# Get the correct method , when 'n' is an Int64
julia> @which tripple(10)
tripple(n::Int64) in Main at REPL[21]:2

# Get the correct method , when 'n' is Float64
julia> @which tripple(10.0)
tripple(n::Float64) in Main at REPL[22]:2
```

So, as you can see, for given a set of arguments, @which was able to tell the correct method for a function.

- `@task`: A task in Julia is similar to a coroutine. This macro can be used to return a task without running it, and hence it can be run later on. We will now try to create a very simple task and show how `@task` can be used to run it at a later time:

```
julia> say_hello() = println("hello world")
say_hello (generic function with 1 method)

julia> say_hello_task = @task say_hello()
Task (runnable) @0x000000010dcdfa90

julia> istaskstarted(say_hello_task)
false

julia> schedule(say_hello_task)
hello world
Task (queued) @0x000000010dcdfa90

julia> yield()

julia> istaskdone(say_hello_task)
true
```

- `@code_llvm`, `@code_lowered`, `@code_typed`,`@code_native`, and `@code_warntype`: These macros are all related to the way the code gets represented in Julia, as well as how it interacts with the layer beneath it. It basically digs down an extra layer and helps you to debug and know what's going on behind the scenes. Let's take up a simple example of a `fibonacci` sequence:

```
julia> function fibonacci(n::Int64)
            if n < 2
                n
            else
                fibonacci(n-1) + fibonacci(n-2)
            end
        end
fibonacci (generic function with 1 method)

# OR, can also define it this way
julia> fibonacci(n::Int64) = n < 2 ? n : fibonacci(n-1) +
fibonacci(n-2)
fibonacci (generic function with 1 method)

julia> fibonacci(10)
55
```

Now let's try each of these macros on this piece of code one by one:

The @code_lowered displays code in a format that is intended for further execution by the compiler. This format is largely internal and isn't intended for human usage. The code is transformed into a single static assignment, in which each variable is assigned only once, and every variable is defined before it is used:

```
julia> @code_lowered fibonacci(10)
CodeInfo(:(begin
    nothing
    unless n < 2 goto 4
    return n
    4:
    return (Main.fibonacci)(n - 1) + (Main.fibonacci)(n - 2)
    end))
```

The @code_typed represents a method implementation for a particular set of argument types after type inference and inning:

```
julia> @code_typed fibonacci(10)
CodeInfo(:(begin
        unless (Base.slt_int)(n, 2)::Bool goto 3
        return n
        3:
        SSAValue(1) = $(Expr(:invoke, MethodInstance for
fibonacci(::Int64), :(Main.fibonacci), :((Base.sub_int)(n,
1)::Int64)))
        SSAValue(0) = $(Expr(:invoke, MethodInstance for
fibonacci(::Int64), :(Main.fibonacci), :((Base.sub_int)(n,
2)::Int64)))
        return (Base.add_int)(SSAValue(1), SSAValue(0))::Int64
    end))=>Int64

julia> @code_warntype fibonacci(10)
Variables:
  #self#::#fibonacci
  n::Int64

Body:
  begin
      unless (Base.slt_int)(n::Int64, 2)::Bool goto 3
      return n::Int64
      3:
      SSAValue(1) = $(Expr(:invoke, MethodInstance for
fibonacci(::Int64), :(Main.fibonacci), :((Base.sub_int)(n,
1)::Int64)))
```

```
        SSAValue(0) = $(Expr(:invoke, MethodInstance for
fibonacci(::Int64), :(Main.fibonacci), :((Base.sub_int)(n,
2)::Int64)))
        return (Base.add_int)(SSAValue(1), SSAValue(0))::Int64
    end::Int64
```

Julia uses the LLVM compiler framework to generate machine code. It uses the LLVM's C++ API to construct this LLVM intermediate representation. So when we do @code_llvm, the code that it generates is just the intermediate representation along with some high-level optimizations:

```
julia> @code_llvm fibonacci(10)

define i64 @julia_fibonacci_61143.2(i64) #0 !dbg !5 {
top:
  %1 = icmp sgt i64 %0, 1
  br i1 %1, label %L3, label %if

if:                                              ; preds =
%top
  ret i64 %0

L3:                                              ; preds =
%top
  %2 = add i64 %0, -1
  %3 = call i64 @julia_fibonacci_61143(i64 %2)
  %4 = add i64 %0, -2
  %5 = call i64 @julia_fibonacci_61143(i64 %4)
  %6 = add i64 %5, %3
  ret i64 %6
}
```

Julia uses and executes native code. The @code_native represents exactly that, and it's just a binary code in memory. This one resembles the assembly language closely enough, which represents instructions:

```
julia> @code_native fibonacci(10)
        .section          __TEXT,__text,regular,pure_instructions
Filename: REPL[50]
        pushq    %rbp
        movq     %rsp, %rbp
        pushq    %r15
        pushq    %r14
        pushq    %rbx
        pushq    %rax
        movq     %rdi, %rbx
Source line: 1
```

```
            cmpq     $1, %rbx
            jle      L63
            leaq     -1(%rbx), %rdi
            movabsq  $fibonacci, %r15
            callq    *%r15
            movq     %rax, %r14
            addq     $-2, %rbx
            movq     %rbx, %rdi
            callq    *%r15
            addq     %r14, %rax
            addq     $8, %rsp
            popq     %rbx
            popq     %r14
            popq     %r15
            popq     %rbp
            retq
L63:
            movq     %rbx, %rax
            addq     $8, %rsp
            popq     %rbx
            popq     %r14
            popq     %r15
            popq     %rbp
            retq
            nopl     (%rax)
```

Type introspection and reflection capabilities

Type introspection and reflection capabilities form a very useful part of any modern-day programming language. Their need arises due to the fact that many a time while coding, we come across a situation where we need to understand the types of objects or data that we are dealing with. Sometimes, we may need to find the type of an object, and other times we may end up coding some logic based on that object's types and properties.

Type introspection

As we know from the starting chapters that Julia supports multiple dispatch and we can create a new data type from any abstract data type, let's define a new type, named `Student`, and then create two sample objects for this type:

```julia
julia> type Student
           name::String
           age::Int64
       end

julia> alpha = Student("alpha",24)
Student("alpha", 24)

julia> beta = Student("beta",25)
Student("beta", 25)
```

Pretty simple! Now that we have two of these students, with the names `alpha` and `beta`, how can I be sure of which type they are? You should definitely be thinking of a function that we studied earlier, remember? If not, then let's look at the following example for the answer:

```julia
julia> typeof(alpha)
Student

julia> typeof(beta)
Student
```

Ah, the `typeof` function was the one. But what if we wanted to check whether an object is of a given type using a single function? Let's take a look at the following code:

```julia
# similar to isinstance in python
julia> isa(alpha, Student)
true

# even this is possible!
julia> alpha isa Student
true
```

If you look at the second implementation, that is, `alpha` is a `Student`, you can see an inline syntax being used. How easy is that for the end user to read and understand? It is for this and many reasons that Julia is such a nice language to read.

Reflection capabilities

Reflection actually provides you with the ability to manipulate the attributes of an object at runtime. So whenever we create a function in Julia, we can ask some basic things about it, such as how many arguments does that function have, or more likely, what are the methods of that function available in the current scope, and so on.

To understand better, have a look at this code snippet, which creates a function and then tries to ask some questions about its properties:

```
# the first method tries to take in all integer values
julia> function calculate_quad(a::Int64,b::Int64,c::Int64,x::Int64)
           return a*x^2 + b*x + c
       end
calculate_quad (generic function with 2 methods)

julia> calculate_quad(1,2,3,4)
27

# the second method takes all but x as integer values
julia> function calculate_quad(a::Int64,b::Int64,c::Int64,x::Float64)
           return a*x^2 + b*x + c
       end
calculate_quad (generic function with 3 methods)

julia> calculate_quad(1,2,3,4.75)
35.0625

# to know what all methods does the function supports
# which as we can see that there are 2 currently
julia> methods(calculate_quad)
# 3 methods for generic function "calculate_quad":
calculate_quad(a::Int64, b::Int64, c::Int64, x::Float64) in Main at
REPL[31]:2
calculate_quad(a::Int64, b::Int64, c::Int64, x::Int64) in Main at
REPL[29]:2
calculate_quad(a, b, c, x) in Main at REPL[27]:2
```

This was a demonstration of how method signatures can be known for a function. Next is how to know what all the fields are inside a type. For that, we use a function called `fieldnames`, which gives all the names of the fields declared inside of the type:

```
# from the already declared Student class
julia> fieldnames(Student)
2-element Array{Symbol,1}:
 :name
 :age
```

On the other hand, if you want to know the individual field types of all the fields inside a type, you may be prompted to use the `types` property of a type, which results in a `SimpleVector` holding all the data types:

```julia
julia> Student.types
svec(String, Int64)

julia> typeof(Student.types)
SimpleVector
```

Reflection is widely used in metaprogramming, and Julia, being homoiconic, uses this property to its advantage. In the previous topic, when we covered built-in macros, we talked a great deal about how Julia reads its own code, and how some macros (`@code_llvm`, `@code_lowered`, `@code_native`, `@code_typed`, and `@code_warntype`) break down the code into different readable formats. We strongly urge you to go back to the previous topic and try them out for yourselves.

Summary

In this chapter, we learned how we can run C as well as Python codes in Julia. We also went on to study how one interacts with the operating system internals, including the filesystem and I/O-related tasks. We then moved forward to learn and explore the world of metaprogramming, where we read in detail about what expressions are, and how one can create macros, as well as use the already provided built-in macros.

In the next chapter, we will be using all the knowledge gained so far to apply our learning of the Julia language, and we'll work together to make the most of it for mathematical as well as for statistical purposes.

7
Numerical and Scientific Computation with Julia

When we talk about the scientific community and its work, we always take into account the heavy mathematical and statistical operations being performed on raw and processed data to achieve desired results. In order to work with this huge data and the complexity it holds, the tools that are to be used to evaluate the data itself should be perfectly suited both in terms of speed of execution and ease of use.

Julia provides an excellent combination of both. The one area in which this language completely outshines its counterparts is its standings in the numerical computation and statistical operations. In this chapter, we will be throwing light on how Julia helps us achieve great results. Furthermore, we have divided this chapter into several subsections, which will make it easier for the reader to follow along:

- Working with data
- Linear algebra and differential calculus
- Statistics
- Optimization

Working with data

There are various ways and sources from which we can get data. We can get data directly from the user through the Terminal or using a script or from a source file (which can either be a binary file or structured files like CSV or XML files). To see how Julia accepts data from the user from any of these resources, let's dive right into these ways one by one.

When starting to play with data for the very first time, it's obvious to use the Julia REPL or a notebook environment such as the `IJulia` notebook. Now, Julia understands every incoming bit of data in a byte stream. So if we try to use the regular built-in functions such as `read()` and `write()`, they will basically be oriented toward a binary I/O. Let's see a simple example of a `read()` operation in action:

```
# usage of read with Char
julia> read(STDIN, Char)
j
'j': ASCII/Unicode U+006a (category Ll: Letter, lowercase)

# usage of read with Bool
julia> read(STDIN, Bool)
true
true

# usage of read with Int8
julia> read(STDIN, Int8)
23
50

# method signature for Bool Type
julia> @which read(STDIN,Bool)
read(s::IO, ::Type{Bool}) in Base at io.jl:370

# method signature for Char Type
julia> @which read(STDIN,Char)
read(s::IO, ::Type{Char}) in Base at io.jl:403

# method signature for Int8 Type
julia> @which read(STDIN,Int8)
read(s::IO, ::Type{Int8}) in Base at io.jl:365

# Or Alternatively
julia> for val in [:Bool, :Char, :Int8]
          @eval println(@which read(STDIN, $val))
       end
read(s::IO, ::Type{Bool}) in Base at io.jl:370
read(s::IO, ::Type{Char}) in Base at io.jl:403
read(s::IO, ::Type{Int8}) in Base at io.jl:365
```

So as we can see, `read` basically expects an I/O stream along with the type of data to be expected. However, we do not use `read()` often; rather we use a more generalized function by the name `readline()`, which helps us take the user input in the string format (along with a newline character in the end). Take a look at the following command:

```
julia> statement = readline()
julia is fast!
"julia is fast!"

julia> readline(chomp = false)
julia
"julia\n"

julia> methods(readline)
# 4 methods for generic function "readline":
readline(s::IOStream; chomp) in Base at iostream.jl:234
readline() in Base at io.jl:190
readline(filename::AbstractString; chomp) in Base at io.jl:184
readline(s::IO; chomp) in Base at io.jl:190
```

So as you see, the `readline()` function (similar to the `input()` function of Python 3) returns the value in a `String` type. To be able to take in integer data from the user, we then have to use the `parse()` function:

```
julia> number = parse(Int64, readline())
23

julia> println(number)
23
```

But wait, wasn't `parse()` the same function that takes in a String as an input and converts it into an Expr? The answer is yes, it's the same function, but it is also used to convert a string value to an integer value! So you see, the power of multiple dispatch in Julia certainly changes things for the better.

However, what if you wanted to take a list of integers as an input from the user? This is a bit trickier, but still easy:

```
# take input from user
julia> numbers = readline()
23 45 67 89
"23 45 67 89"

# use the split function to convert string to array
julia> split(numbers)
4-element Array{SubString{String},1}:
```

```
"23"
"45"
"67"
"89"

# the easy way
julia> for item in split(numbers)
           println(parse(Int64, item))
       end
23
45
67
89

# the array comprehension way
julia> [parse(Int64, item) for item in split(numbers)]
4-element Array{Int64,1}:
 23
 45
 67
 89
```

We took a string of four numbers from the user and then converted the entire string into an array using the `split` function. For converting the individual elements to integers, we used the `parse` function again.

Working with text files

We now know how to read data from the user. But how about if we had a text file that was supposed to be read? We may then have to take the help of the `open` function, which helps us read files from the system.

On a closer look at the `open` function, we can see it has multiple ways of being invoked:

```
julia> methods(open)
# 8 methods for generic function "open":
open(fname::AbstractString) in Base at iostream.jl:113
open(fname::AbstractString, rd::Bool, wr::Bool, cr::Bool, tr::Bool,
ff::Bool) in Base at iostream.jl:103
open(fname::AbstractString, mode::AbstractString) in Base at
iostream.jl:132
open(f::Function, cmds::Base.AbstractCmd, args...) in Base at
process.jl:599
open(f::Function, args...) in Base at iostream.jl:150
open(cmds::Base.AbstractCmd) in Base at process.jl:575
open(cmds::Base.AbstractCmd, mode::AbstractString) in Base at
```

```
process.jl:575
open(cmds::Base.AbstractCmd, mode::AbstractString,
other::Union{Base.FileRedirect, IO, RawFD}) in Base at process.jl:575
```

The simplest of forms in which open is used is with a filename passed as the argument. However, for the file to be opened and worked upon, an access mode must be chosen. The modes can be summed up as follows:

```
Mode Description
____ _____
r    read
r+   read, write
w    write, create, truncate
w+   read, write, create, truncate
a    write, create, append
a+   read, write, create, append
```

For a detailed example, let's take an example of a file stored at a location on my desktop, and try reading it in Julia. For the sake of simplicity, I have created a file by the name of sample.txt, which has the underlying five lines about Julia:

```
shell> cat sample.txt
Julia is a great and powerful language
It is homoiconic.
It supports static as well as dynamic typing.
Julia walks like python runs like C.
Julia uses multiple dispatch.
```

Let's open this file inside Julia:

```
# read file from the device folder in the current path
julia> file = open("sample.txt")
IOStream(<file sample.txt>)

# read the contents of file
julia> file_data = readlines(file)
5-element Array{String,1}:
 "Julia is a great and powerful language"
 "It is homoiconic."
 "It supports static as well as dynamic typing."
 "Julia walks like python runs like C."
 "Julia uses multiple dispatch."
```

So far, we have successfully opened up the file and read its content. Also, we have been able to convert the contents of the file in to the array format, which will later help us do some quick operations. This is where the fun part starts!

```julia
# running an enumerate over the file provides us with a counter too!
julia> enumerate(file_data)
Enumerate{Array{String,1}}(String["Julia is a great and powerful language",
"It is homoiconic.", "It supports static as well as dynamic typing.",
"Julia walks like python runs like C.", "Julia uses multiple dispatch."])

# using enumerate to our advantage to get the length of each line
julia> for lines in enumerate(file_data)
           println(lines[1],"-> ", lines[2])
       end
1-> Julia is a great and powerful language
2-> It is homoiconic.
3-> It supports static as well as dynamic typing.
4-> Julia walks like python runs like C.
5-> Julia uses multiple dispatch.

# convert everything to uppercase
julia> for line in file_data
           println(uppercase(line))
       end
JULIA IS A GREAT AND POWERFUL LANGUAGE
IT IS HOMOICONIC.
IT SUPPORTS STATIC AS WELL AS DYNAMIC TYPING.
JULIA WALKS LIKE PYTHON RUNS LIKE C.
JULIA USES MULTIPLE DISPATCH.

# reverse each line!!
julia> for line in file_data
           println(reverse(line))
       end
egaugnal lufrewop dna taerg a si ailuJ
.cinociomoh si tI
.gnipyt cimanyd sa llew sa citats stroppus tI
.C ekil snur nohtyp ekil sklaw ailuJ
.hctapsid elpitlum sesu ailuJ

# to simply count the number of lines in a file
julia> countlines("sample.txt")
5

# print the first line of the file
julia> first(file_data)
"Julia is a great and powerful language"
```

```
# print last line of the file
julia> last(file_data)
"Julia uses multiple dispatch."
```

Cool! Julia has built-in support for many common operations over files. Moving on to more formats in which data can be read inside Julia, we may have data coming in the form of a CSV file or any delimited format. These kind of file formats are very commonly used and almost every language supports functions or packages to read them.

But Julia is special! Why? Because it has given some of the most useful functions provided as built-in into the core Julia module, which eliminates the need for any third-party packages all together. These functions are readcsv and readdlm.

Working with CSV and delimited file formats

Let's say we have a CSV file by the name sample.csv and we want to read its content. This is how we do it in Julia:

```
julia> csvfile = readcsv("sample.csv")
5×3 Array{Any,2}:
 1   "James"        "UK"
 2   "Lora"         "UK"
 3   "Raj"          "India"
 4   "Rangnatham"   "Sri lanka"
 5   "Azhar"        "Bangladesh"
```

So using readcsv, we have converted the CSV file into an array of 5x3 matrix which can now be manipulated using the various array operations, as shown in the following example:

```
# getting only the names of the people
julia> csvfile[:,2]
5-element Array{Any,1}:
 "James"
 "Lora"
 "Raj"
 "Rangnatham"
 "Azhar"

# getting only the top 3 data
julia> csvfile[1:3,:]
3×3 Array{Any,2}:
 1   "James"   "UK"
 2   "Lora"    "UK"
 3   "Raj"     "India"
```

```
# reverse sorting the rows
julia> sortrows(csvfile, rev=true)
5×3 Array{Any,2}:
 5  "Azhar"       "Bangladesh"
 4  "Rangnatham"  "Sri lanka"
 3  "Raj"         "India"
 2  "Lora"        "UK"
 1  "James"       "UK"
```

Apart from the CSV files, which are files delimited by a comma, there can be other formats which may be delimited by a pipe (|) or semicolon (;). For all those formats, we have the `readdlm` function. The following is a sample usage:

```
# A pipe seperated file with the same data as above
shell> cat sample.psv
1|"James"|"UK"
2|"Lora"|"UK"
3|"Raj"|"India"
4|"Rangnatham"|"Sri lanka"
5|"Azhar"|"Bangladesh"

# using '|' as delimiter
julia> readdlm("sample.psv",'|')
5×3 Array{Any,2}:
 1  "James"       "UK"
 2  "Lora"        "UK"
 3  "Raj"         "India"
 4  "Rangnatham"  "Sri lanka"
 5  "Azhar"       "Bangladesh"
```

Working with DataFrames

What are `DataFrames`? They are basically a type of data structure that can hold the metadata about their data and hence they can be easily accessed as well as queried just like a database table does using SQL.

Julia provides a package named `DataFrames.jl`, which provides the necessary data structures for doing the job. It's the recommended source for doing `DataFrame` operations and as it's listed in the `METADATA.jl`. It can easily be downloaded as follows:

```
# install the package
julia> Pkg.add("DataFrames")

# first time load takes times due to precompilation
julia> using DataFrames
```

```
# check the functions provided by DataFrames
julia> names(DataFrames)
254-element Array{Symbol,1}:
 :&
 Symbol("@csv2_str")
 Symbol("@csv_str")
 Symbol("@data")
 Symbol("@formula")
 Symbol("@pdata")
 Symbol("@tsv_str")
 Symbol("@wsv_str")
 Symbol("@~")
 :AIC
 :AICc
 :AbstractContrasts
 :AbstractDataArray
 :AbstractDataFrame
 :AbstractDataMatrix
 :AbstractDataVector
 ...
 :winsor
 :winsor!
 :wmean
 :wmean!
 :wmedian
 :wquantile
 :writetable
 :wsample
 :wsample!
 :wsum
 :wsum!
 :xor
 :zscore
 :zscore!
 :|
```

However, some of the most important data structures provided by the DataFrames packages are:

- NA: This corresponds to a missing value.
- DataArray: This provides extra functionalities in comparison with the default Array type in Julia.
- DataFrame: This is a 2D data structure and it's much like R DataFrames and Pandas DataFrames. It provides a much richer set of functions to manipulate data.

There are two more data structures by the name of `DataMatrix` and `DataVector`, but they are just type aliases of `DataArrays` of different dimensions. This can be simply explained as follows:

```
julia> DataMatrix{Any} == DataArray{Any, 2}
true

julia> DataVector{Any} == DataArray{Any, 1}
true
```

Now we will go in depth to explore the three key data structures provided by `DataFrames.jl`. Let's start with the data type `NA`.

NA

In the real world, every data that we get or apply our manipulations and transformations to can always have missing data. So the immediate question that follows is how do we handle that missing value?

In Julia, when we create an Array, suppose of length 5 with some random values, if we try having any array position as `nothing`, we can get something like:

```
julia> a = [1,2,3,nothing,5,6]
6-element Array{Any,1}:
 1
 2
 3
  nothing
 5
 6

# try to access the element
julia> a[4]

# check the data type
julia> typeof(a[4])
Void
```

But we might not want to have this kind of empty data in our result set. After all, we might need to classify the data as `Not Available` or `NA` to make more sense in the result set. Hence, the `NA` data of the `DataFrames` structure can be used instead:

```
julia> using DataArrays

julia> a = DataArray([1.1, 2.2, 3.3, 4.4, 5.5, 6.6])
```

```
6-element DataArrays.DataArray{Float64,1}:
 1.1
 2.2
 3.3
 4.4
 5.5
 6.6

julia> a[1] = NA
NA

julia> a
6-element DataArrays.DataArray{Float64,1}:
  NA
 2.2
 3.3
 4.4
 5.5
 6.6

julia> typeof(a[1])
DataArrays.NAtype
```

One of the biggest features that are associated with using NA is that it may or may not prevent a function from modifying the values of a given data. In other words, if the data which we might work on does not contain NA, then the result won't be different from what is expected. Take a look at the following block of code for an illustration as to how the DataArray behaves in the presence or absence of NA:

```
julia> true || a
true

julia> true && a
6-element DataArrays.DataArray{Float64,1}:
  NA
 2.2
 3.3
 4.4
 5.5
 6.6

julia> mean(a)
NA

julia> mean(a[2:length(a)])
4.4
```

DataArrays

Let's take a look at what DataArrays in Julia look like:

```julia
# creating a 2D data matrix
julia> data_matrix = DataArray([1 2 3;4 5 6])
2×3 DataArrays.DataArray{Int64,2}:
 1  2  3
 4  5  6

# Creating a 1D vector
julia> data_vector = DataArray([1 2 3 4 5 6 7 8])
1×8 DataArrays.DataArray{Int64,2}:
 1  2  3  4  5  6  7  8

# Creating a column major 1D array
julia> data_vector_column_major = DataArray([1,2,3,4])
4-element DataArrays.DataArray{Int64,1}:
 1
 2
 3
 4

# assigning the first value as NA
julia> data_vector_column_major[1] = NA
NA

# dropping NA values
julia> data_vector_column_major
4-element DataArrays.DataArray{Int64,1}:
  NA
 2
 3
 4
```

As you may have noticed, the NA value can be dropped from DataArray using the dropna function, which is provided by the DataFrames.jl module. A great feature right out of the box!

DataFrames

After discussing NA and DataArrays, now let's come to the most important data structure provided by the DataFrames module--DataFrame. As previously discussed, they contain extra information about the data they hold, or, in other words, the metadata.

This is how `DataFrame` is created:

```
julia> dframe = DataFrame(Names = ["John","Ajay"], Age = [27,28])
2×2 DataFrames.DataFrame
| Row | Names  | Age |
|-----+--------+-----|
| 1   | "John" | 27  |
| 2   | "Ajay" | 28  |
```

Now this dataset cannot be represented in the form of a DataArray. There are many reasons as to why DataFrames are unique in their purpose, including the following :

- They can hold data of different data types. A Matrix, which is just a 2D Array, cannot hold data of different data type, hence it's of no use when it comes to data from the real world. A DataFrame is thus heterogeneous in nature.

- They hold metadata, that is, labels in forms similar to a database table's headings for each column; thus the data inside them can be easily examined.

- Their individual rows are of the type `DataArray` and not vectors. Given here is the code that shows that individual rows and columns of `DataFrame` are `DataArrays`:

```
julia> dframe.columns[1]
2-element DataArrays.DataArray{String,1}:
 "John"
 "Ajay"

julia> typeof(dframe.columns[1])
DataArrays.DataArray{String,1}
```

With this, we wrap us the general introduction to `DataFrames`. However, we will be coming back to it in the upcoming section *Statistics*, where we discuss more on the usage of DataFrames and their importance in statistical and mathematical analysis.

Linear algebra and differential calculus

Julia is targeted toward the scientific community. Starting with this topic, we will see how Julia greatly eases mathematical calculations in the real world. We will start off by explaining how Julia proves to be a great resource for solving problems in linear algebra.

Linear algebra

The syntax used in Julia closely resembles that of **MATLAB**, but there are some important differences. To begin with, look at the matrix of some randomly generated numbers:

```
julia> A = rand(3,3)
3x3 Array{Float64,2}:
 0.821807   0.828687   0.974031
 0.996824   0.805663   0.274284
 0.0341033  0.224237   0.39982
```

The `rand` function takes in parameters asking for the dimensions of the array, and as we have passed here a `(3,3)`, we get an array of size 3x3 of type `Float64`, containing random Gaussian numbers.

Similarly, we have another function named `ones`, which takes in a single parameter and reproduces an array containing `1.0`:

```
julia> ones(5)
5-element Array{Float64,1}:
 1.0
 1.0
 1.0
 1.0
 1.0
```

However, before we move any further, we need to know the difference between a vector and a matrix in Julia, as this could be confusing for those coming from a MATLAB background. So, in Julia, we have the following:

- `Vector{T}` is nothing but an alias for `Array{T, 1}`. This could be clearly seen in the Julia REPL:

    ```
    julia> Vector{Float64} == Array{Float64,1}
    true
    ```

- `Matrix{T}` is nothing but an alias for `Array{T, 2}`, which again could be easily proved in the Julia REPL:

    ```
    julia> Matrix{Float64} == Array{Float64,2}
    true
    ```

Let's now move on to some generic operations that can be done in linear algebra and try to get you at ease with most of these:

- **Multiplication**: Unlike any other language, Julia gives you the freedom to write expressions in the form that you would usually do in your mathematical assignments, that is, without using any * keywords in between! However, you can still use it:

```
# create a random matrix of 3x3 dimension
julia> A
3x3 Array{Float64,2}:
 0.673465  0.880229  0.100458
 0.752117  0.545464  0.0180286
 0.531316  0.221628  0.179626

# Easily, we could do
julia> b = 2 * A
3x3 Array{Float64,2}:
 1.34693  1.76046   0.200917
 1.50423  1.09093   0.0360573
 1.06263  0.443255  0.359252

# Julia's advantage! Omit the '*' while multiplication
julia> b = 2A
3x3 Array{Float64,2}:
 1.34693  1.76046   0.200917
 1.50423  1.09093   0.0360573
 1.06263  0.443255  0.359252
```

- **Matrix transpose**: Again, very easy to follow!

```
julia> transpose_of_A = A'
3x3 Array{Float64,2}:
 0.673465  0.752117   0.531316
 0.880229  0.545464   0.221628
 0.100458  0.0180286  0.179626
```

- **Linear equations**: Code in a way that you would write and solve on a paper! Julia makes it very easy to solve equations:

```
# define the value of x
julia> x = 5
5

# solve the equation
julia> equation = 3x^2 + 4x + 3
98
```

Differential calculus

Differential calculus is a branch of mathematics concerned with the determination, properties, and application of derivatives and differentials. In broader terms, these are concerned with the rate at which quantities change.

We will not go into much detail explaining this topic as it's vast and there are various internet resources for those unfamiliar with it. However, people with a strong math background will find themselves at home while discussing some of the problems.

For working with differential calculus, we will be using the Julia package `Calculus.jl`. Let's install the package and then start exploring its functions:

```julia
julia> Pkg.add("Calculus")
julia> using Calculus

# list of functions supported by Calculus
julia> names(Calculus)
22-element Array{Symbol,1}:
 Symbol("@sexpr")
 :AbstractVariable
 :BasicVariable
 :Calculus
 :SymbolParameter
 :Symbolic
 :SymbolicVariable
 :check_derivative
 :check_gradient
 :check_hessian
 :check_second_derivative
 :deparse
 :derivative
 :differentiate
 :hessian
 :integrate
 :jacobian
 :processExpr
 :second_derivative
 :simplify
 :symbolic_derivative_bessel_list
 :symbolic_derivatives_1arg
```

Most of the differential calculus revolves around differentiation and integration. In the given example, we are using the ' operator to denote the differentiation levels of a function. Hence ' ' ' would mean a third order differentiation:

```
julia> f(x) = sin(x)
f (generic function with 1 method)

julia> f'(1.0) - cos(1.0)
-5.036193684304635e-12

julia> f''(1.0) - (-sin(1.0))
-6.647716624952338e-7

julia> f'''(1.0) - (-cos(1.0))
0.11809095011119602
```

You can also perform symbolic differentiation, as depicted here:

```
julia> differentiate("cos(x) + sin(x) + exp(-x) * cos(x)", :x)
:(-(sin(x)) + cos(x) + (-(exp(-x)) * cos(x) + exp(-x) * -(sin(x))))

julia> differentiate("cos(x) + sin(y) + exp(-x) * cos(y)", [:x, :y])
2-element Array{Any,1}:
 :(-(sin(x)) + -(exp(-x)) * cos(y))
 :(cos(y) + exp(-x) * -(sin(y)))
```

Statistics

One of the strongest points of Julia has been its powerful support for statistical and mathematical functions. The Julia community has been very active in identifying the areas that can be covered using packages made purely in Julia, and hence we have now a group that deals purely in packages of Julia for stats. It's called **JuliaStats**, and can be found on GitHub at https://github.com/JuliaStats.

Some of the notable packages listed on the Julia stats page are as follows:

- PDMats.jl: Uniform interface for positive definite matrices of various structures
- Klara.jl: MCMC inference in Julia
- StatsBase.jl: Basic statistics for Julia
- HypothesisTests.jl: Hypothesis tests for Julia
- ConjugatePriors.jl: A Julia package to support conjugate prior distributions
- PGM.jl: A Julia framework for probabilistic graphical models

- `TimeSeries.jl`: Time series toolkit for Julia
- `StatsModels.jl`: Specifying, fitting, and evaluating statistical models in Julia
- `Distributions.jl`: A Julia package for probability distributions and associated functions

Simple statistics

We will now be exploring the various simple statistical operations that can be performed in Julia, using some default built-in functions:

```
julia> x = [10,20,30,40,50]
5-element Array{Int64,1}:
 10
 20
 30
 40
 50

# computing the mean
julia> mean(x)
30.0

# computing the median
julia> median(x)
30.0

# computing the sum
julia> sum(x)
150

# computing the standard deviation
julia> std(x)
15.811388300841896

# computing the variance
julia> var(x)
250.0
```

As we can see, given an array of elements, we can easily draw out basic statistical inferences from the data. However, Julia does have functions that support some cumulative operations on the data as well! These are as follows:

- cummax(): This function is used to find the cumulative maximum
- cummin(): This function is used to find the cumulative minimum
- cumsum(): This function is used to find the cumulative maximum
- cumprod(): This function is used to find the cumulative product

However, all these are now **deprecated** and the newer implementation is by using accumulate(). Let's see an example showing the usage of both the previous and newer implementations:

```
# old implementations
julia> cummax(x)
5-element Array{Int64,1}:
 10
 20
 30
 40
 50

julia> cummin(x)
5-element Array{Int64,1}:
 10
 10
 10
 10
 10

julia> cumsum(x)
5-element Array{Int64,1}:
  10
  30
  60
 100
 150

julia> cumprod(x)
5-element Array{Int64,1}:
       10
      200
     6000
   240000
 12000000
```

Metaprogramming
As we have already studied metaprogramming in previous chapters, we can use it here, as we can see that the code is repetitive and boring! We could have also tried out the above statements in an underlying manner.

```
julia> for i in [:cummax,:cummin,:cumsum,:cumprod]
            @eval print($i, "->")
            @eval println($i(x))
       end
cummax->[10, 20, 30, 40, 50]
cummin->[10, 10, 10, 10, 10]
cumsum->[10, 30, 60, 100, 150]
cumprod->[10, 200, 6000, 240000, 12000000]
```

Checking out the new accumulate function, we have the following:

```
# using accumulate function
julia> accumulate(+,x)
5-element Array{Int64,1}:
   10
   30
   60
  100
  150

julia> accumulate(*,x)
5-element Array{Int64,1}:
        10
       200
      6000
    240000
  12000000

julia> accumulate(max,x)
5-element Array{Int64,1}:
  10
  20
  30
  40
  50

julia> accumulate(min,x)
5-element Array{Int64,1}:
  10
  10
  10
  10
  10
```

Basic statistics using DataFrames

We have studied what DataFrames are and how they can be created in the previous topics. DataFrames can hold extra information about data and hence they prove to be very efficient while describing a data set:

```
julia> dframe = DataFrame(Subjects = ["Maths","Physics","Chemistry"],Marks
= [90,85,95])
3×2 DataFrames.DataFrame
| Row | Subjects    | Marks |
|-----+-------------+-------+-----------+------------------|
| 1   | "Maths"     | 90    |
| 2   | "Physics"   | 85    |
| 3   | "Chemistry" | 95    |

julia> describe(dframe)
Subjects
Summary Stats:
Length:         3
Type:           String
Number Unique:  3
Number Missing: 0
% Missing:      0.000000

Marks
Summary Stats:
Mean:           90.000000
Minimum:        85.000000
1st Quartile:   87.500000
Median:         90.000000
3rd Quartile:   92.500000
Maximum:        95.000000
Length:         3
Type:           Int64
Number Missing: 0
% Missing:      0.000000
```

As you see here, we have declared a DataFrame dframe, which holds the name of the subjects as well the marks scored by a student out of 100. The describe function when runs upon this DataFrame returns all the possible statistical inferences that can be made from the given data. As rightly noted in the official documentation of Julia for this function:

```
describe(df)

Pretty-print the summary statistics provided by summarystats: the mean,
minimum, 25th percentile, median, 75th
  percentile, and maximum.
```

Using Pandas

For those familiar with data analysis in Python, the package `Pandas` has always played a major role in manipulating data. Similar to `DataFrames.jl`, it provides with its own set of data structures. Because of its widely known abilities and robust performance, the `Pandas` package is available for Julia as well.

To install `Pandas`, you need to have Python running on your system and `Pandas` installed as a package. That can be achieved by running the `sudo pip install pandas` command.

Run the following command inside Julia REPL:

```
julia> Pkg.add("Pandas")
julia> using Pandas
```

Once done, we can revisit the same DataFrame we made earlier, but with a little twist. We need to supply the arguments to `pandasDataFrame` in the form of a hashmap:

```
julia> pandasDataframe = Pandas.DataFrame(Dict(:Subjects =>
["Maths","Physics","Chemistry"],:Marks => [90,85,95]))
    Marks    Subjects
0     90        Maths
1     85      Physics
2     95    Chemistry

julia> Pandas.describe(pandasDataframe)
        Marks
count     3.0
mean     90.0
std       5.0
min      85.0
25%      87.5
50%      90.0
75%      92.5
max      95.0

julia> pandasDataframe[:Subjects]
0         Maths
1       Physics
2     Chemistry
Name: Subjects, dtype: object

julia> pandasDataframe[:Marks]
0     90
1     85
2     95
Name: Marks, dtype: int64
```

```
# simple query operation
julia> query(pandasDataframe,:(Marks>90))
    Marks    Subjects
2     95    Chemistry
```

It is to be noted that, if you are using `Pandas` as well as DataFrame in the same workspace, you need to specify the name of the package first and then use the functions provided by the same. In this case, both `Pandas` and `dataframes.jl` provide the `describe` function, and hence there could be a conflict while trying to run `describe` over `pandasDataFrame`.

Advanced statistics topics

So far we have been seeing very simple statistics operations. Now we will discuss some of the advanced statistical operations in brief, including the Julia packages that help in achieving the results:

- `Distributions.jl`
- `Timeseries.jl`
- `HypothesisTests.jl`

We won't be going into much detail about each and every topic from a mathematical point of view, as there are tonnes of resources already available; rather, we will be focusing on the functions provided by these packages.

Distributions

As per the official documentation of `distributions.jl`, here are the features implemented by this package:

- Moments (for example, mean, variance, skewness, and kurtosis), entropy, and other properties
- Probability density/mass functions (`pdf`) and their logarithms (`logpdf`)
- Moment generating functions and characteristic functions
- Maximum likelihood estimation
- Posterior w.r.t. conjugate prior and **Maximum-A-Posteriori** (**MAP**) estimation

To start working with it, we need to install it using the command:

```
julia> Pkg.add("Distributions")
julia> using Distributions
```

After the installation, we are ready to use it over different distributions, the most common being normal distribution:

```
# setting the seed
julia> srand(123)
MersenneTwister(UInt32[0x0000007b],
Base.dSFMT.DSFMT_state(Int32[1464307935, 1073116007, 222134151, 1073120226,
-290652630, 1072956456, -580276323, 1073476387, 1332671753, 1073438661 ...
138346874, 1073030449, 1049893279, 1073166535, -1999907543, 1597138926,
-775229811, 32947490, 382, 0]), [1.23253, 1.95067, 1.54183, 1.85035,
1.28927, 1.24474, 1.40729, 1.95055, 1.39839, 1.92576 ... 1.79227, 1.83391,
1.89061, 1.74502, 1.57469, 1.24833, 1.69181, 1.48955, 1.40392, 1.75348],
382)

# initialize the distribution
julia> distribution = Normal()
Distributions.Normal{Float64}(μ=0.0, σ=1.0)

# create the random array of 10 element following Normal distribution
julia> x = rand(distribution, 10)
10-element Array{Float64,1}:
  1.19027
  2.04818
  1.14265
  0.459416
 -0.396679
 -0.664713
  0.980968
 -0.0754831
  0.273815
 -0.194229
```

Other than the normal distribution, we also have other distributions, which are as follows:

- Binomial distribution:

  ```
  julia> Binomial()
  Distributions.Binomial{Float64}(n=1, p=0.5)
  ```

- Cauchy distribution:

  ```
  julia> Cauchy()
  Distributions.Cauchy{Float64}(μ=0.0, σ=1.0)
  ```

- Poisson distribution:

  ```
  julia> Poisson()
  Distributions.Poisson{Float64}(λ=1.0)
  ```

TimeSeries

TimeSeries are often used in places where there is financial data and every second holds its own importance. In Julia, we have the package by the name `TimeSeries.jl`, which supports all the `timeseries` operations.

The most significant data structure provided by TimeSeries is the TimeArray data structures, which help in holding the dates as timestamps and not strings.

For understanding it in detail, let's just also install the `TimeSeries` package as well as the `MarketData` package, which will help us study some `TimeSeries` data:

```julia
julia> Pkg.add("TimeSeries")
julia> Pkg.add("MarketData")

julia> using TimeSeries
julia> dates  = collect(Date(2017,8,1):Date(2017,8,5))
5-element Array{Date,1}:
 2017-08-01
 2017-08-02
 2017-08-03
 2017-08-04
 2017-08-05

julia> sample_time = TimeArray(dates, rand(length(dates)))
5x1 TimeSeries.TimeArray{Float64,1,Date,Array{Float64,1}} 2017-08-01 to
2017-08-05

2017-08-01 | 0.7059
2017-08-02 | 0.292
2017-08-03 | 0.2811
2017-08-04 | 0.7929
2017-08-05 | 0.2092
```

So here, we make use of the `Date` function to effectively represent the date August 1, 2017 and August 5, 2017. Now from this array of dates, we try to create a `TimeArray` data.

If we closely look at this `TimeArray` object `sample_time`, we can see that it has four fields. Out of these four, the `timestamp` field holds the dates array while `values` holds data from the time series, and its row count must match the length of the timestamp array. The `meta` defaults to hold nothing while `colnames` contains the names of the columns:

```julia
julia> fieldnames(sample_time)
4-element Array{Symbol,1}:
 :timestamp
 :values
```

```
    :colnames
    :meta

julia> sample_time.timestamp
5-element Array{Date,1}:
 2017-08-01
 2017-08-02
 2017-08-03
 2017-08-04
 2017-08-05

julia> sample_time.values
5-element Array{Float64,1}:
 0.70586
 0.291978
 0.281066
 0.792931
 0.20923

julia> sample_time.colnames
1-element Array{String,1}:
 " "

julia> sample_time.meta

# retrieve the first element
julia> head(sample_time)
1x1 TimeSeries.TimeArray{Float64,2,Date,Array{Float64,2}} 2017-08-01 to
2017-08-01
2017-08-01 | 0.7179

# retrieve the last element
julia> tail(sample_time)
1x1 TimeSeries.TimeArray{Float64,2,Date,Array{Float64,2}} 2017-08-05 to
2017-08-05
2017-08-05 | 0.4142
```

Hypothesis testing

A hypothesis test is a testing mechanism that is used to determine whether the sample data had enough evidence that a given condition is true for the entire population of data.

There are two kinds of opposing hypothesis examined for a population (that is, the entire data set,) namely:

- Null hypothesis: This is the statement being tested
- Alternative hypothesis: This is the statement that you will be able to conclude as true

In Julia, the hypothesis testing can be achieved using the HypothesisTests.jl package. The package can be installed and used just like the packages discussed so far in this chapter (the reason being that METADATA.jl has the entry for these packages):

```
julia> Pkg.add("HypothesisTests")
julia> using HypothesisTests
```

Once the package is installed, we can start testing. For the sake of simplicity, I will be discussing a simple example to demonstrate how the package can be used:

```
julia> using Distributions

julia> srand(123)
MersenneTwister(UInt32[0x0000007b],
Base.dSFMT.DSFMT_state(Int32[1464307935, 1073116007, 222134151, 1073120226,
-290652630, 1072956456, -580276323, 1073476387, 1332671753, 1073438661  …
138346874, 1073030449, 1049893279, 1073166535, -1999907543, 1597138926,
-775229811, 32947490, 382, 0]), [1.04643, 1.18883, 1.92848, 1.52435,
1.80384, 1.20354, 1.40414, 1.04937, 1.25594, 1.66531  …  1.86043, 1.53826,
1.54179, 1.83724, 1.85687, 1.14965, 1.14176, 1.03677, 1.17827, 1.21738],
382)

julia> sampleOne = rand(Normal(), 10)
10-element Array{Float64,1}:
   1.19027
   2.04818
   1.14265
   0.459416
  -0.396679
  -0.664713
   0.980968
  -0.0754831
   0.273815
  -0.194229

julia> testOne = OneSampleTTest(sampleOne)
One sample t-test
------------------
Population details:
```

```
    parameter of interest:   Mean
    value under h_0:         0
    point estimate:          0.47641935520300993
    95% confidence interval: (-0.13332094295432084, 1.0861596533603408)

Test summary:
    outcome with 95% confidence: fail to reject h_0
    two-sided p-value:           0.11093746407653728

Details:
    number of observations:   10
    t-statistic:              1.7675319478229796
    degrees of freedom:       9
    empirical standard error: 0.2695393176852065
```

Here, we used the `OneSampleTTest` function, which, if we see, implements the method for the preceding example as follows:

```
julia> @which OneSampleTTest(sampleOne)
HypothesisTests.OneSampleTTest(v::AbstractArray{T,1}) where T<:Real
```

We can also retrieve the p-values for the preceding tests using `pvalue()`:

```
julia> pvalue(testOne)
0.11093746407653728


# the most significant
julia> pvalue(testOne, tail=:right)
0.05546873203826864


# the least significant
julia> pvalue(testOne, tail=:left)
0.9445312679617314
```

Similarly, we can do one test for a Binomial distribution too! This can be achieved using the `BinomialTest` function. We'll check whether 25 successes from 1000 samples is inconsistent with a 50% success rate:

```
julia> BinomialTest(25, 1000, 0.50)
Binomial test
-------------
Population details:
    parameter of interest:   Probability of success
    value under h_0:         0.5
    point estimate:          0.025
    95% confidence interval: (0.01624253569688223, 0.036684823051923)

Test summary:
```

```
outcome with 95% confidence: reject h_0
two-sided p-value:            9.125992175283306e-252
```

```
Details:
    number of observations: 1000
    number of successes:    25
```

Optimization

In mathematics and computer science, an optimization problem is a problem of finding the best solution from all the feasible solutions. They can broadly be divided into two categories depending upon the variables:

- Continuous (continuous optimization problem)
- Discrete (combinatorial optimization problem)

Some of the problems that can be categorized as optimization problems are given here:

- Shortest path
- Maximum flow through a network
- Vehicle routing

Julia, in particular, provides a number of optimization packages, the group of which is collectively called as JuliaOpt. The two most notable packages used are:

- **JuMP (Julia for Mathematical Programming)**
- `Convex.jl`

Both of these are **Algebraic modeling languages** (**AMLs**), which sit over `MathProgBase.jl`.

JuMP

JuMP is an AML implemented in Julia. Readers coming from a Python background may be familiar with PuLP. It currently supports several open source solvers for a wide variety of problem cases. Some of its features include:

- User friendliness
- Speed
- Solver independence

- Access to advanced algorithmic techniques
- Ease of embedding

Installing and getting started with JuMP is easy. However, we also need to install a solver alongside, which in this case will be Clp:

```julia
julia> Pkg.add("JuMP")
julia> Pkg.add("Clp")

julia> using JuMP
julia> using Clp

# creating a model without a solver
julia> m = JuMP.Model()
Feasibility problem with:
 * 0 linear constraints
 * 0 variables
Solver is default solver

# but we want to use Clp as solver, we have
julia> m = JuMP.Model(solver = Clp.ClpSolver())
Feasibility problem with:
 * 0 linear constraints
 * 0 variables
Solver is ClpMathProg
```

Moving on, let's now have a look at a full-fledged example. Let's save the underlying code snippet in a file named optimiser.jl:

```julia
using JuMP
using Clp

m = Model(solver = ClpSolver())
@variable(m, 0 <= a <= 2 )
@variable(m, 0 <= b <= 10 )

@objective(m, Max, 5a + 3*b )
@constraint(m, 1a + 5b <= 3.0 )

print(m)

status = solve(m)

println("Objective value: ", getobjectivevalue(m))
println("a = ", getvalue(a))
println("b = ", getvalue(b))
```

On trying to run this file from the shell, we have the following output:

```
mymachine:user$ julia optimiser.jl
Max 5 a + 3 b
Subject to
 a + 5 b ≤ 3
 0 ≤ a ≤ 2
 0 ≤ b ≤ 10
Objective value: 10.6
a = 2.0
b = 0.2
```

Convex.jl

`Convex.jl` is a Julia package for disciplined convex programming. To use `Convex`, we also need a solver, which in this case will be SCS:

```
julia> Pkg.add("Convex")
julia> Pkg.add("SCS")
```

The following is a simple example of how to use `Convex.jl`. More can be found out at the official documentation of `Convex.jl` listed at http://nbviewer.jupyter.org/github/JuliaOpt/Convex.jl/tree/master/examples/:

```
julia> using Convex
julia> X = Variable(2, 2)
Variable of
size: (2, 2)
sign: Convex.NoSign()
vexity: Convex.AffineVexity()

julia> y = Variable()
Variable of
size: (1, 1)
sign: Convex.NoSign()
vexity: Convex.AffineVexity()

julia> p = minimize(vecnorm(X) + y, 2 * X <= 1, X' + y >= 1, X >= 0, y >= 0)
Problem:
minimize AbstractExpr with
head: +
size: (1, 1)
sign: Convex.NoSign()
vexity: Convex.ConvexVexity()
```

```
subject to
Constraint:
<= constraint
lhs: AbstractExpr with
head: *
size: (2, 2)
sign: Convex.NoSign()
vexity: Convex.AffineVexity()

rhs: 1
vexity: Convex.AffineVexity()
                Constraint:
>= constraint
lhs: AbstractExpr with
head: +
size: (2, 2)
sign: Convex.NoSign()
vexity: Convex.AffineVexity()

rhs: 1
vexity: Convex.AffineVexity()
                Constraint:
>= constraint
lhs: Variable of
size: (2, 2)
sign: Convex.NoSign()
vexity: Convex.AffineVexity()
rhs: 0
vexity: Convex.AffineVexity()
                Constraint:
>= constraint
lhs: Variable of
size: (1, 1)
sign: Convex.NoSign()
vexity: Convex.AffineVexity()
rhs: 0
vexity: Convex.AffineVexity()
current status: not yet solved

julia> println(round(X.value, 2))
[0.0 0.0; 0.0 0.0]

julia> println(y.value)
1.0000106473513

julia> p.optval
1.0000111259613518
```

Here is the screenshot of `solve!(p)` in Julia 0.6:

```
julia> solve!(p)

            SCS v1.2.6 - Splitting Conic Solver
            (c) Brendan O'Donoghue, Stanford University, 2012-2016
--------------------------------------------------------------------------
Lin-sys: sparse-direct, nnz in A = 25
eps = 1.00e-04, alpha = 1.80, max_iters = 20000, normalize = 1, scale = 5.00
Variables n = 7, constraints m = 19
Cones:  primal zero / dual free vars: 1
        linear vars: 13
        soc vars: 5, soc blks: 1
Setup time: 8.20e-05s
--------------------------------------------------------------------------
 Iter | pri res | dua res | rel gap | pri obj | dua obj | kap/tau | time (s)
--------------------------------------------------------------------------
    0|     inf      inf      nan      inf      inf      inf  2.39e-05
   60| 6.94e-06 8.04e-05 4.05e-05 1.00e+00 1.00e+00 2.20e-16 1.56e-04
--------------------------------------------------------------------------
Status: Solved
Timing: Solve time: 1.61e-04s
        Lin-sys: nnz in L factor: 51, avg solve time: 5.90e-07s
        Cones: avg projection time: 8.73e-08s
--------------------------------------------------------------------------
Error metrics:
dist(s, K) = 5.8351e-19, dist(y, K*) = 0.0000e+00, s'y/|s||y| = 3.3410e-18
|Ax + s - b|_2 / (1 + |b|_2) = 6.9388e-06
|A'y + c|_2 / (1 + |c|_2) = 8.0432e-05
|c'x + b'y| / (1 + |c'x| + |b'y|) = 4.0465e-05
--------------------------------------------------------------------------
c'x = 1.0000, -b'y = 0.9999
--------------------------------------------------------------------------
```

Summary

In this chapter, we saw how Julia proves its mettle in the field of numerical and statistical computations. We saw how data from various sources can be read and written using Julia's built-in features as well as how to use `DataFrames` for our own advantage. Next, we saw how linear algebra and differential equations can be solved using some of the most advanced mathematical packages. Later on, Statistics proved to be an area of deep interest for Julia developers, as we saw how easy it is for someone coming from a traditional language background to easily pick up stats in Julia. Lastly, we talked about some optimization problems and how they can be solved in Julia.

Coming up, in the next chapter, we will see how to make more sense out of data using graphs and what packages in Julia can be used to complete the job.

8
Data Visualization and Graphics

Data visualization is the representation of some sample (or complete) data in a graphical format. It forms a very important part of scientific decision-making, as data visualization not only enables us to understand the data in a more appealing and convenient way, but also proves to be a strong tool for reaching wider audiences when it comes to evaluating business decisions.

In this chapter, we will be breaking down all the components of how data visualization can be done in Julia. The following listed items are topics which we shall be covering during the course of the chapter:

- Basic plots
- Vega
- Gadfly

Basic plots

In this chapter, we will be focusing on creating some of the very simple and easily used graphs and plots. The library of choice which we will be using to create such plots will be `PyPlot`, which is based on Python's `matplotlib.pyplot` module.

The installation of the library is easy if you have `matplotlib` already installed on your system. If not, you need to install it manually by running the following command:

```
python -m pip install matplotlib
```

Once this is done, we will open the Julia REPL and run `Pkg.add("PyPlot")`.

PyPlot is a large and rich library. Here is a very simple example of a line plot:

```
x = 1:100
y = rand(100)
p = plot(x,y)
xlabel("X")
ylabel("Y")
title("Basic plot")
grid("on")
```

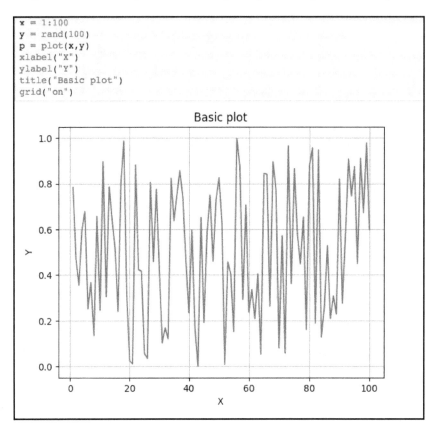

Let's explain how this works quickly:

- We have an *x*-coordinate, which is simply a range of numbers from 1 to 100 as given in the code. The label for this axis has been set to **X** using the function xlabel.
- Similarly, we have the *y*-coordinate, which is a randomly generated range of 100 numbers. The label for *y*-axis is set to **Y** by using a ylabel function.
- Our graph has been labeled, but we still don't have any title for it. This can be achieved using the function title, which takes in a string value.
- Finally, the plot function is the one that actually generates the graph.

Here is yet another line graph, which makes use of the `sin` and `cos` functions:

```
using PyPlot
x = linspace(0, 4pi, 1000);xlabel("X-axis")
y = cos(pi + sin.(x));ylabel("Y-axis")
plot(x, y, color="red", linewidth=2.0, linestyle="--");
title("Using sin and cos functions");
```

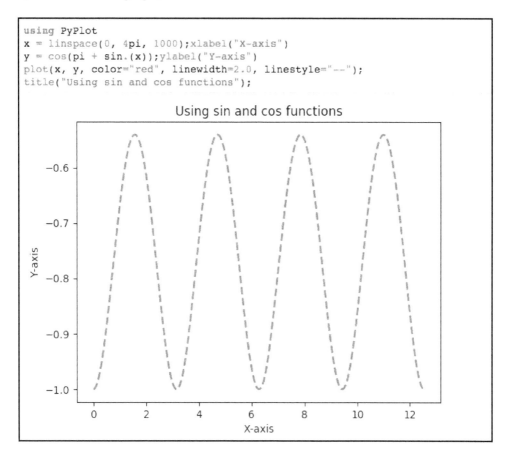

One final example is an **XKCD** graph, which is just a casual-style, handwritten graph mode:

```
x = [1:1:10;];y = ones(10)
for i=1:1:10 y[i] = pi + i*i end
xkcd();xlabel("X-axis");ylabel("Y-axis")
title("XKCD Comic hand drawing");plot(x,y)
```

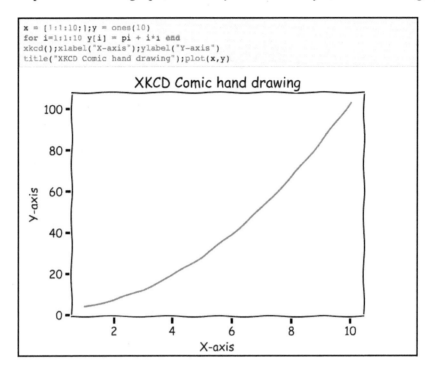

We will now see how various different types of plots can be drawn in Julia using
`PyPlot.jl`.

Bar graphs

A bar chart or bar graph is a chart or graph that presents categorical data with rectangular bars, with heights or lengths proportional to the values that they represent. The bars can be plotted vertically or horizontally. We will now see how to create a bar graph in Julia using the very simple `bar` function:

```
x = [10,20,30,40,50];y = [2,4,6,8,10]
xlabel("Values of X");ylabel("Values of Y")
title("Vertical Bar Graph")
bar x,y,color = "red"
```

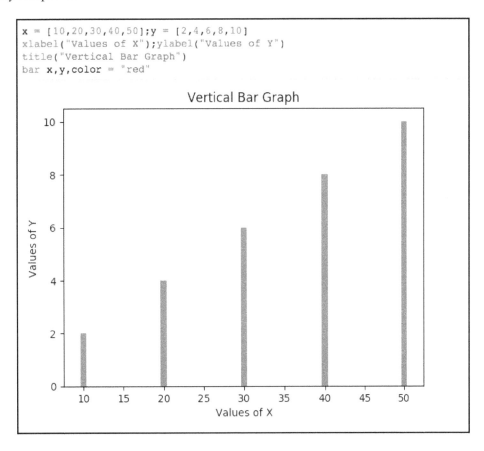

This is a simple vertical bar graph. What if we wanted to have a horizontal bar graph in its place? For this we have the `barh` function, which does exactly that:

```
x = [10,20,30,40,50];y = [2,4,6,8,10]
xlabel("Values of X");ylabel("Values of Y")
title("Horizontal Bar Graph")
barh(x,y,color = "red")
```

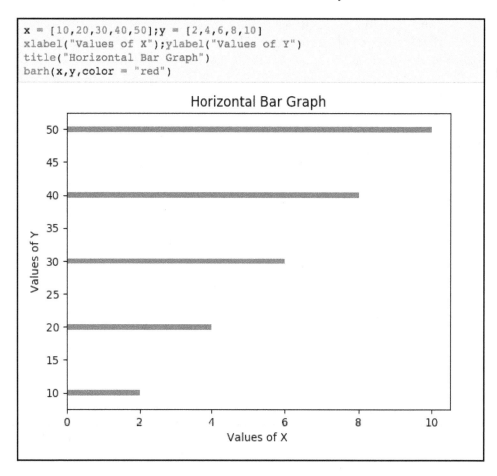

Histograms

`PyPlot` provides a function named `hist2D`, which helps to create a histogram. It takes in three parameters, which are generally *x*-axis parameters, *y*-axis parameters, and bins. The following figure shows how `hist2D` creates the graphical representation of the data:

```
x = rand(1000);xlabel("Values of X");
y = rand(1000);ylabel("Values of Y");
title("2-D Histogram")
hist2D(x,y,bins = 50)
```

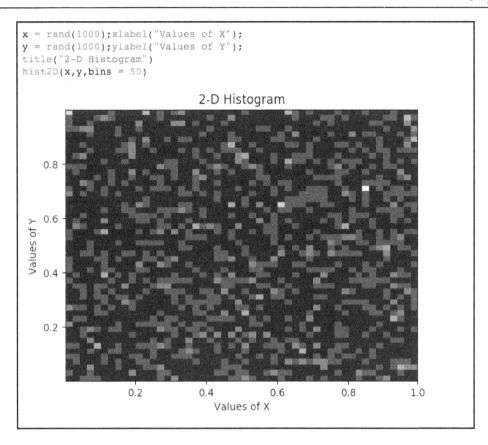

Pie charts

A pie chart is a graphical representation of data that displays all possible numerical proportions. The length of the arc in pie charts is directly proportional to the quantity it represents.

PyPlot, has a function named `pie`, which helps to do exactly the same. Given here is a simple diet layout (fictional) for a person who eats just three things:

```
labels = ["Fruits";"Vegetables";"Wheat"]
colors = ["orange";"blue";"red"]
sizes = [25; 40; 35]
explode = zeros(length(sizes))
fig = figure("pyplot_piechart",figsize=(10,10))
p = pie(sizes,labels=labels,shadow=true,
    startangle=90,colors=colors,
    autopct="%1.1f%%")
title("pie chart")
```

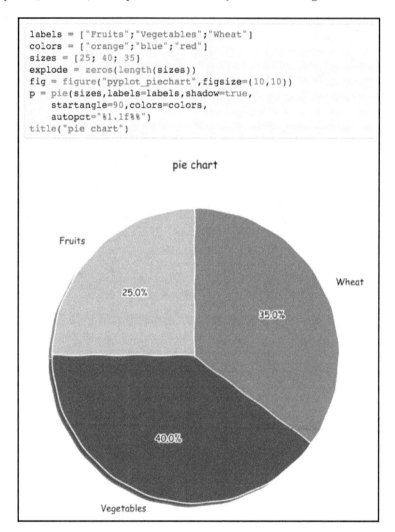

Scatter plots

Scatter plots help us to identify the correlation between the two variables. Or, in other words, they help us understand the relationships between data.

Here is an example of a scatter plot implemented using the PyPlot library:

```
using PyPlot
fig = figure("scatterplot",figsize=(10,10))
x = rand(50)
y = rand(50)
areas = 1000*rand(50);
scatter(x,y,s=areas,alpha=0.5)
title("Scatter Plot")
xlabel("X")
ylabel("Y")
grid("on")
```

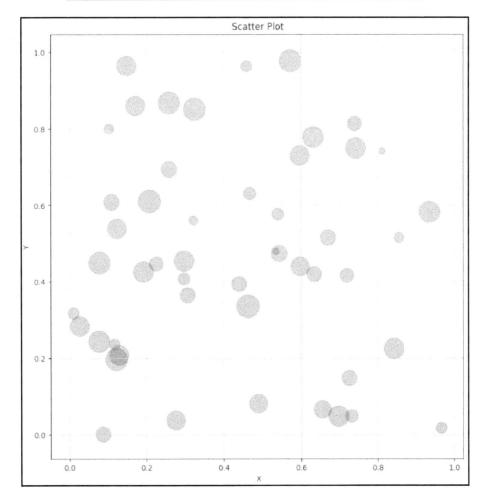

3-D surface plots

After creating lots of 2-D plots, we now move on to try making a simple 3-D plot. In
`PyPlot`, we have a function named `surf`, which provides the functionality of creating
three-dimensional plots. As per the docs, here are the usages and parameters used by the
function `surf`.

The usage for this function is `surf(x,y,z,facecolors=colors)`:

```
Argument      Description
========      ====================================================
X,Y,Z         Data values as 2D arrays
rstride       Array row stride (step size)
cstride       Array column stride (step size)
rcount        Use at most this many rows, defaults to 50
ccount        Use at most this many columns, defaults to 50
color         Color of the surface patches
cmap          A colormap for the surface patches.
facecolors    Face colors for the individual patches
norm          An instance of Normalize to map values to colors
vmin          Minimum value to map
vmax          Maximum value to map
shade         Whether to shade the facecolors
```

The following is a simple example showing the use of a 3-D plot:

```
using PyPlot
a = linspace(0.0,2pi,500);b = linspace(0.0,2pi,500)
len_of_a = length(a);len_of_b = length(b)
x = ones(len_of_a,len_of_b)
y = ones(len_of_a,len_of_b)
z = ones(len_of_a,len_of_b)

for i=1:len_of_a
    for j=1:len_of_b
        x[i,j]= sin(a[i])
        y[i,j]= cos a[i]
        z[i,j]= sin(b[j])
    end
end
colors = rand(len_of_a,len_of_b,3);
fig = figure()
surf(x,y,z,facecolors=colors)
fig[:canvas][:draw]()
```

Now, after seeing lots of basic plots and graphs, let's move on to a very powerful library called `Vega.jl`:

Vega

`Vega` is a data visualization library that provides a Julia wrapper around the Vega Visualization Grammar from Trifacta. It was created and developed by **Randy Zwitch** as an open source project.

Installing `Vega` is pretty simple to do, as listed in the `METADATA.jl`:

```
julia> Pkg.add("Vega")
julia> using Vega
```

However, `Vega` requires an internet connection to render all graphs because it does not store local copies of the JavaScript libraries. However, efforts are made to actually include all the JavaScript libraries as part of the package so that it does not require any internet connection in the future.

`Vega` provides a series of composite types, which are literally just the translation of `Vega` grammar in Julia. They help the end user to build visualizations in native Julia syntax. The following are all the primitives defined in Julia:

- `VegaVisualization`
- `VegaData`
- `VegaScale`
- `VegaAxis`
- `VegaLegend`
- `VegaMark`

Apart from these visualizations, `Vega` also provides interactivity to the graphs by providing some very interesting functions collectively called, **Visualization Mutating Functions**. They all are listed as follows:

- `colorscheme!`: This is used to change or alter the color scheme of the graph. Here is an example:

  ```
  colorscheme!(v::Vega.VegaVisualization; palette,
  reversePalette)
  ```

- General visualization properties:
    - height `height::Int`
    - width `width::Int`
    - background `background::AbstractString`, as of Julia 0.5
    - padding `padding::Union(VegaPadding, Number, String)`
    - viewport `viewport::Vector{Int}`

- `hline!`/`vline!`: These functions help in drawing horizontal or vertical lines on the graph. Their usage syntaxes are `hline!(v::Vega.VegaVisualization; value, strokeDash, strokeWidth, stroke)` and `vline!(v::Vega.VegaVisualization; value, strokeDash, strokeWidth, stroke)`.

- `hover!`: Those familiar with JavaScript or jQuery must know the use for hover. It basically alters the property of the element inside a graph if hovered over using a mouse:

  ```
  hover!(v::Vega.VegaVisualization; opacity, color)
  ```

  Here, opacity can range from 0 to 1, while colors can be set to any hex code or as names of the original RGB colors, which the graph will change to once hovered over.

- `jitter!`: This is used as `jitter!(v::Vega.VegaVisualization; pctXrange, pctYrange)`. Jitter adds a random amount of noise to data as a means of remedying *overplotting*.The pctXrange/pctYrange arguments are the percentages of the data series range allowable (+/-) to add to the data.

- `legend!`: This is used as `legend!(v::Vega.VegaVisualization; title, show)`. It helps in changing or altering the visualization's title.

- `stroke!`: This is used as `stroke!(v::Vega.VegaVisualization; color, width, opacity, visible)`. This function helps by adding borders around VegaMarks and changes their visualization.

- `text!`: This is used as `text!(v::Vega.VegaVisualization; title, y, fill, fontSize, align, baseline, fontWeight, font, x)`. This function changes the visualization by adding text annotations. It's just an alias of `title!` with some default values.

- `title!`: This is used as `title!(v::Vega.VegaVisualization; title, y, fill, fontSize, align, baseline, fontWeight, font, x)`. As the name suggests, it modifies the title of the graph.
- `xlab!`/`ylab!`: This is used as `xlab!(v::Vega.VegaVisualization; title, grid, ticks, format, formatType, layer, properties, tickSize, tickSizeMajor, tickSizeMinor, tickSizeEnd)` or `ylab!(v::Vega.VegaVisualization; title, grid, ticks, format, formatType, layer, properties, tickSize, tickSizeMajor, tickSizeMinor, tickSizeEnd)`. It just helps in modifying the *x*-axis/*y*-axis.
- `xlim!`/`ylim!`: This is used as `xlim!(v::Vega.VegaVisualization; min, max, reverse, round, _type, exponent)` or `ylim!(v::Vega.VegaVisualization; min, max, reverse, round, _type, exponent)`.

Now, we will discuss some of the predefined visualizations provided out of the box by `Vega`. Some of them you will already know about, and some of them are really exciting and new. Let's explore them one by one.

Area plots

An area chart or area graph displays graphically quantitative data. It is based on a line chart. The area between an axis and a line are commonly emphasized with colors, textures, and hatchings. Commonly, we compare two or more quantities with an area chart.

`Vega` provides a function named `areaplot`. The following is a sample code depicting the usage of `areaplot`:

```
using Vega, KernelDensity, Distributions

x = rand(Beta(3.0, 2.0), 10)
k = kde(x)

areaplot(x = k.x, y = k.density)
```

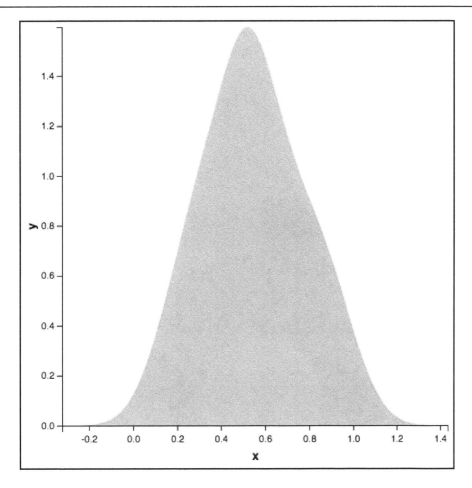

Aster plots

An aster plot displays pie slices as lengths extending outward to the edge (0 at the inner edge to 100 at the outer). The widths of the pie slices represent the weight of each pie, which is used to arrive at a weighted mean of the length scores in the center.

Aster plots in `Vega` are recreations of `d3.js` aster plots. Apart from producing simple plots, you can actually add a bit of interactivity, too, using functions like `hover!`:

```
score = [59, 24, 98]
id = ["FIS", "MAR","AO"]
weight = [0.5, 0.5, 1]

v = asterplot(x = id, y = score, weight = weight, holesize = 75)
colorscheme!(v, palette = ["red", "green", "blue"])
hover!(v, opacity = 0.5)
```

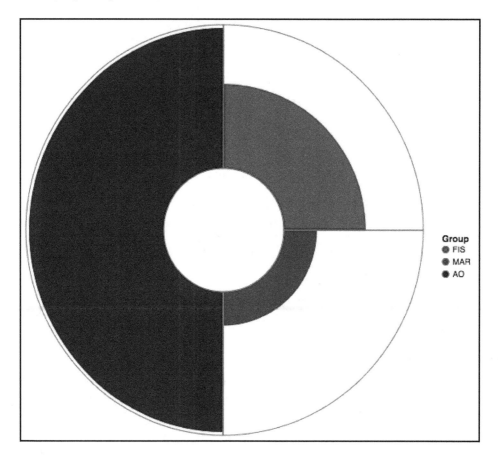

Choropleth map

A choropleth map is a thematic map. It provides an easy way to visualize how a measurement varies across a geographic area, or it shows the level of variability within a region.

The following is a simple choropleth map of the US:

```
x = 1:60
y = rand(Float64, 60)

a = choropleth(x = x, y = y, entity = :usstates)
```

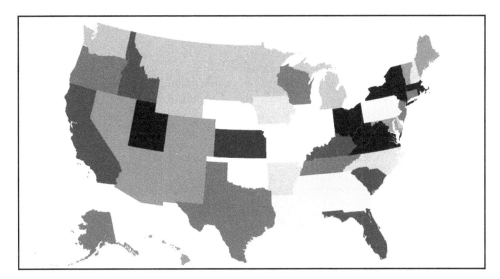

Heatmaps

A heat map (or heatmap) is a graphical representation of data where the individual values contained in a matrix are represented as colors. In Vega, we have a function named heatmap that does exactly this.

Here is a sample heatmap in action:

```
heatmap(x = rand(1:10,100), y = rand(1:10,100), color=rand(100))
```

Here, *x* and *y* are in the range of 100 random numbers between 1 and 10, while the color is an array of 100 random color boxes:

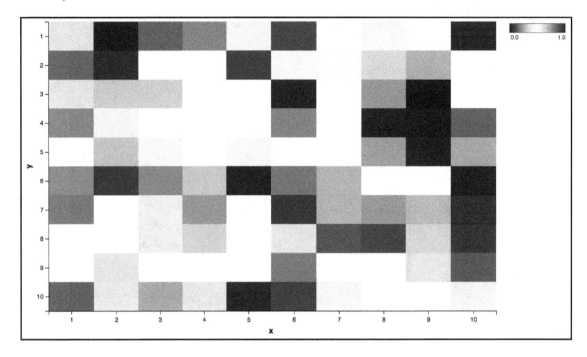

Ribbon plots

Ribbon plots are made by drawing two path plots of *N* points each, and connecting the two paths by a sheet made of *N* triangles, Just to add, a ribbon does not have to be of a constant width.

In Vega, we have a function named `ribbonplot`, which helps us create ribbon plots. A simple example of this is illustrated as follows:

```
x = [0,1,2,3,4,5,6,7,8,9,0,1,2,3,4,5,6,7,8,9]
y = rand(1:100,20)
g = [0,0,0,0,0,0,0,0,0,0,1,1,1,1,1,1,1,1,1,1]
a = ribbonplot(x = x, ylow = 0.9y, yhigh=1.1y, group = g)
```

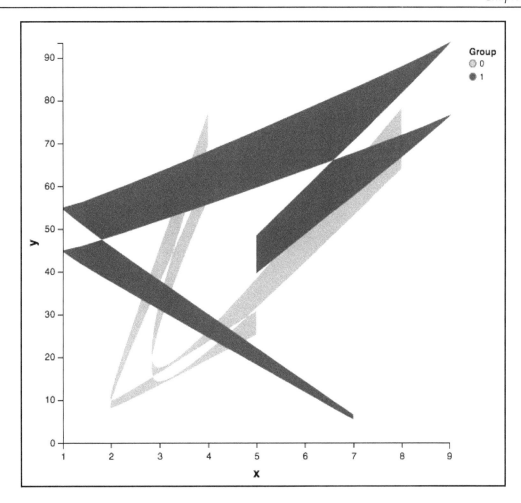

Wordcloud

A wordcloud plot can be a great tool when you want to showcase the most used or most prominent word from a given collection of words or sentences. This can be very helpful when analyzing on Twitter posts or even blog posts.

First, we create a `corpus` for the wordcloud to operate on. The following sentences are taken from Wikipedia:

```
corpus = [
    "Julia is a high-level, high-performance dynamic programming
language for technical computing, with syntax that is familiar to users of
other technical computing environments. It provides a sophisticated
compiler, distributed parallel execution, numerical accuracy, and an
extensive mathematical function library. Julia's Base library, largely
written in Julia itself, also integrates mature, best-of-breed open source
C and Fortran libraries for linear algebra, random number generation,
signal processing, and string processing. In addition, the Julia developer
community is contributing a number of external packages through Julia's
built-in package manager at a rapid pace. IJulia, a collaboration between
the IPython and Julia communities, provides a powerful browser-based
graphical notebook interface to Julia.",
    "Julia programs are organized around multiple dispatch; by defining
functions and overloading them for different combinations of argument
types, which can also be user-defined. For a more in-depth discussion of
the rationale and advantages of Julia over other systems, see the following
highlights or read the introduction in the online manual."
    ]
wc = wordcloud(x = corpus)
colorscheme!(wc, palette = ("Spectral", 11))
```

Here is the result that we get from the text:

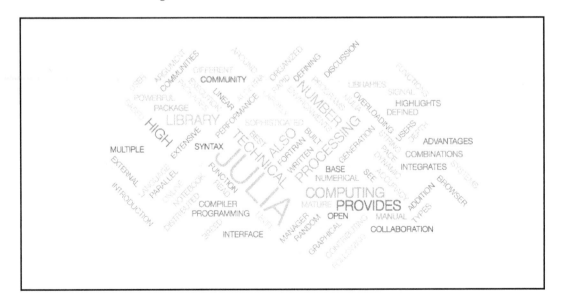

Scatter plots

We have previously seen what scatter plots are when we were working with the PyPlot library. Here too, we will see how to create a scatter plot in Vega using a function named scatterplot.

Here is a simple example of a scatter plot:

```
using Vega, Distributions

d1 = MultivariateNormal([0.0, 0.0], [1.0 0.9; 0.9 1.0])
d2 = MultivariateNormal([10.0, 10.0], [4.0 0.5; 0.5 4.0])
points = vcat(rand(d1, 1000)', rand(d2, 1000)')

x = points[:, 1]
y = points[:, 2]
group = vcat(ones(Int, 1000), ones(Int, 1000) + 1)

scatterplot(x = x, y = y, group = group)
```

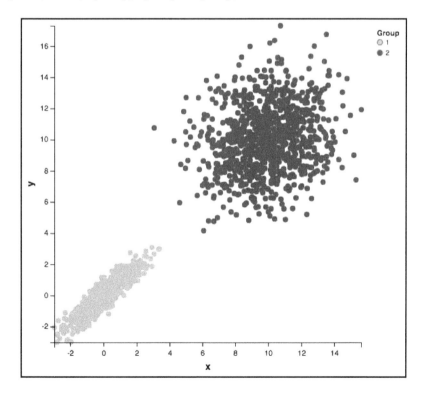

With this, we will wrap up our discussion on one of the most amazing data visualizing libraries in Julia. We will now move to a more advanced and newer library called `Gadfly`.

Gadfly

`Gadfly` is an exhaustive plotting and data visualization package written in Julia by Daniel Jones. It is based on the book, *The Grammar of Graphics*, by Leland Wilkinson. It is largely inspired by `ggplot2` for R, which is another amazing package for plotting and visualizations.

Some of the great features of `Gadfly` that set it apart from all other libraries are listed here:

- It renders publication quality graphics to SVG, PNG, PostScript, and PDF
- It has an intuitive and consistent plotting interface
- It works with **IJulia** out of the box
- It offers tight integration with `DataFrames.jl`
- It provides interactivity, like panning, zooming, and toggling, powered by `snap.svg`
- It supports a large number of common plot types

Installing `Gadfly` is pretty easy and similar to `Vega`. The entry for this package can be found in `METADATA.jl`. There are, however, some dependencies, which will also be automatically installed by the package itself:

```
julia> Pkg.add("Gadfly")
julia> using Gadly
```

Interacting with Gadfly using the plot function

The `plot` function is used to interact with the `Gadfly` package and create the desired visualizations. Aesthetics are mapped to the plot geometry and are used to specify how the `plot` function would work. They are specially named variables. The `plot` elements can be scales, coordinates, guides, and geometries. It is defined in the grammar of graphics to avoid special cases, and aesthetics help this by approaching the problem with well-defined inputs and outputs, which produces desired results.

A plot can operate on the following data sources:

- Functions and expressions
- Arrays and collections
- DataFrames

Here is a simple example of a graph made using the `plot` function. We will be using `IJulia` to draw all our plots:

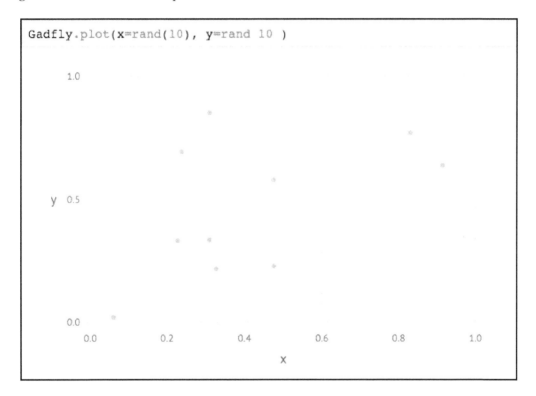

We can also add more elements to have a slightly different output. For example, to have both line and point geometries on the same dataset, we can make a layered plot using the following:

- `Geom.line`: Line plot
- `Geom.point`: Point plot

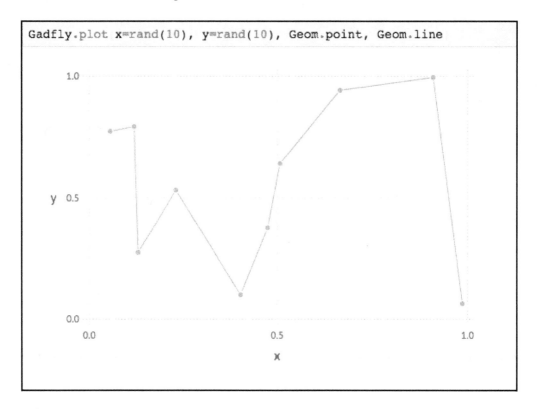

```
Gadfly.plot x=rand(10), y=rand(10), Geom.point, Geom.line
```

This generates a layered plot that has both lines and points. A complex plot can be generated by combining various elements:

1. `Scale`: Use this to scale any desired axis of the plot up or down.

2. `Guide`: Using `xlabel` and `ylabel`, `guide` can be used to give the necessary labels to the plot that we use. `Title` is used to provide a title for the plot.

Let's create a similar plot that includes these elements. We will add the x and y labels, add a title to the plot, and scale the plot:

```
Gadfly.plot(x=1:10, y=10.^rand(10),
     Scale.y_sqrt, Geom.point, Geom.smooth,
     Guide.xlabel("X"), Guide.ylabel("Y"), Guide.title("Graph with Labels"))
```

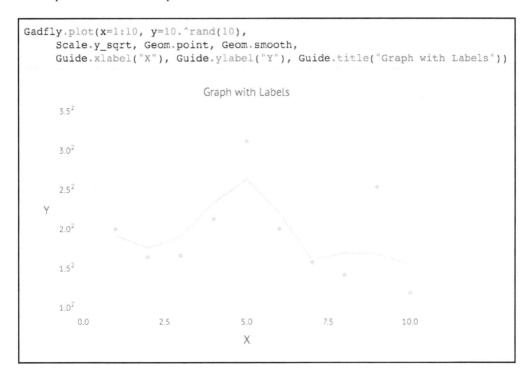

Plotting DataFrames with Gadfly

The capability provided by `Gadfly` to work with DataFrames out of the box is really useful. We studied the capability of the DataFrame in previous chapters.

It is a powerful data structure used to represent and manipulate data. Using `Gadfly`, we can generate complex plots easily. DataFrame is passed to the plot function as the first argument.

The columns in the DataFrame are used by the `plot` function in the aesthetics by name or index. We will use `RDatasets` to create the DataFrame for the `plot` function. To install `RDatasets`, just follow the underlying method similar to how we did it in `Gadfly`:

```
julia> Pkg.add("RDatasets")
julis> using RDatasets
```

The RDatasets provides us with some real-life datasets, from which we can make some visualizations to understand the capabilities of the Gadfly package:

```
Gadfly.plot dataset("datasets", "iris"),
    x="SepalLength",
    y="SepalWidth",
    Geom.line
```

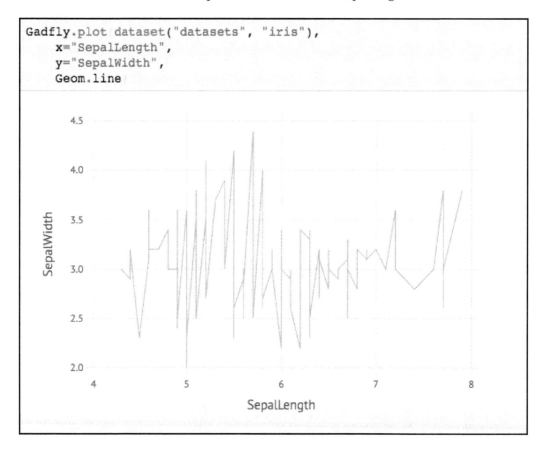

Now, here is the same plot, using the point plotting:

```
using Gadfly, RDatasets
Gadfly.plot(dataset("datasets", "iris"),
    x="SepalLength",
    y="SepalWidth",
    Geom.point)
```

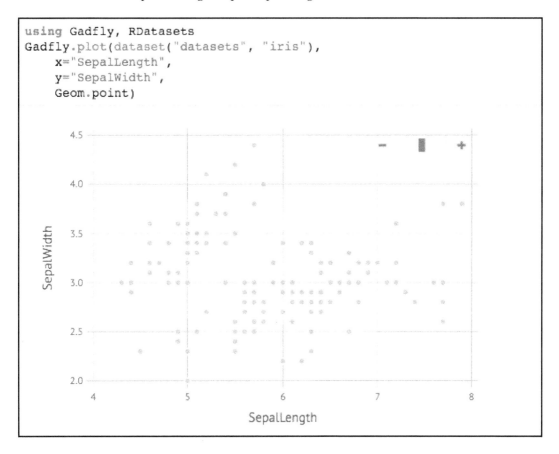

The following is a point plot that uses the Iris dataset provided by the RDatasets package. We are trying to plot a graph between SepalLength and SepalWidth:

```julia
using RDatasets, Gadfly
Gadfly.plot(dataset("datasets","iris"),
        x=:SepalLength,
        y=:SepalWidth,
        color=:Species, shape=:Species, Geom.point,
        Theme(point_size=3pt))
```

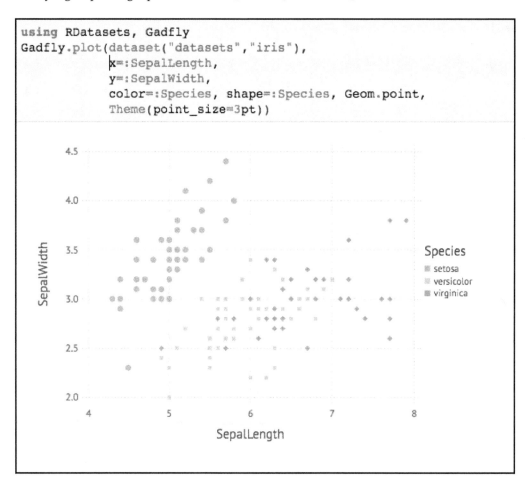

Now, let's create a histogram using a random number generator. We will pass the array, which we will create using a random number generator, and then we will create the histogram:

```
using Gadfly
Gadfly.plot(x = randn(4000), Geom.histogram(bincount = 100))
```

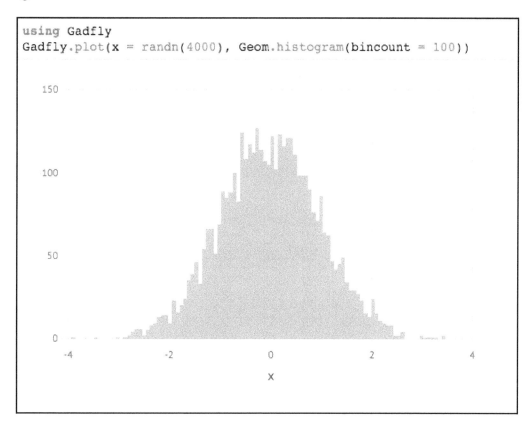

However, the preceding showcased histogram was a fairly simple example. We now move on to a complex example wherein we will be using a dataset provided by the RDatasets package:

```
using Gadfly, RDatasets
Gadfly.plot dataset("mlmRev","Gcsemv"),
    x = "Course", color="Gender", Geom.histogram
```

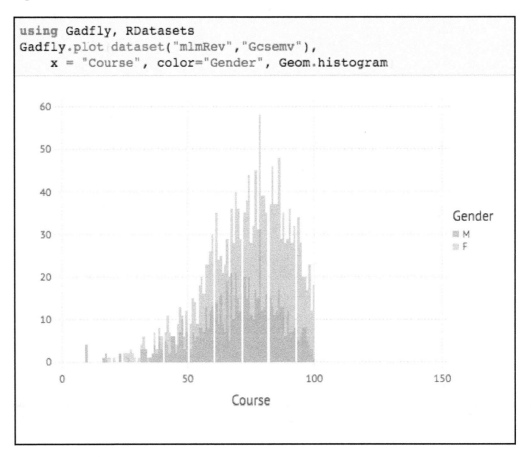

There is much much, more than what we have discussed for Gadfly in this chapter. For more information on various other kinds of operations that are possible with Gadfly, do check out the official documentation.

Summary

In this chapter, we saw how Julia provides a set of very advanced and feature-rich libraries to accomplish the mammoth task of effectively doing data visualization. In the starting section, we got to know how PyPlots work and how we can make simple graphical plotting using the package. However, in the later sections of the chapter, we went into detail about the two most popular libraries in Julia, namely `Vega.jl` and `Gadfly.jl`.

We will now be shifting our focus, and in the next chapter, we will discuss how to use a database in Julia and what packages, as well as database bindings, are available to help us accomplish the task.

9
Connecting with Databases

Databases are one of the most important and almost inseparable parts of any modern application architecture. They help us store data in a meaningful format so that they can later be queried by the application or end user to fetch results on demand.

In this chapter, we will see how Julia interacts with various databases, be it a **Relational Database Management Systems** (RDBMSs) or NoSQL database. We will cover the following topics in this chapter:

- How to connect with databases?
- Relational databases
- NoSQL databases
- Introduction to REST

How to connect with databases?

Connecting with databases requires us to have a middle layer (that is, a database driver) that can help us establish a connection between a database and an application system. The choice of driver will depend on these two underlying factors:

- Language (in which the application is coded)
- Database

A database connection is the means by which a database server and its client software communicate with each other. This interaction usually takes place using a query language such as SQL, wherein the user writes his commands in the form of a query and the database fetches the result based upon that. However, the interaction can only take place once a database connection has been established. This is achieved by using a database string, which is the standard way of connecting using a driver's connection API.

In today's modern world, we have the following two broader kinds of databases available for us to make use of:

- Relational DBMS
- Non-Relational DBMS

Given these two categories, the community of Julia developers has come up with a group of Database drivers that are helpful in connecting with some of the most popular databases in the world. In fact, the community is active on GitHub and their contributions keep coming in even at the time of writing this book; they are as follows:

- `ODBC.jl`: This is an ODBC interface for the Julia programming language
- `SQLite.jl`: This is a Julia interface to the SQLite library
- `MySQL.jl`: This is used to access MySQL from Julia
- `PostgreSQL.jl`: PostgreSQL DBI driver
- `JDBC.jl`: Julia interface to Java database drivers
- `Hive.jl`: Hive, Spark SQL, Impala client. Based on Thrift and HiveServer2 protocol
- `DBDSQLite.jl`: DBI-compliant driver for SQLite3

We will now focus on how Julia interacts with both relational and non-relational databases in the following sections. First, we will start off with relational, or the more traditional, database management systems.

Relational databases

A relational database is a kind of database that is based on the relational model of data, that is, the kind of model that organizes data into tables of rows and columns along with a unique key identifying each row.

To access the data organized in such a format, we make use of **Structured Query Language** (**SQL**) that enables us to fetch data from a database in a fairly easy manner. Here is an example of an SQL query in MySQL that helps by fetching the records from a table inside a database:

```
mysql> select * from employee
    -> ;
+----+--------+--------+---------+---------------+
| id | name   | salary | retired | department_id |
+----+--------+--------+---------+---------------+
|  1 | alpha  |  72000 |       0 |             0 |
|  2 | beta   |  12000 |       0 |             0 |
|  3 | gamma  |  60000 |       0 |             0 |
|  4 | kappa  |  92000 |       0 |             0 |
+----+--------+--------+---------+---------------+
4 rows in set (0.00 sec)
```

Here, `employee` is the name of the table from which we are trying to get the data, while `select` and `from` are reserved SQL keywords. The `*` sign is a wildcard character used to denote all the records.

However, we do not want to fetch the data using Julia rather than running SQL queries inside the SQL query editor or shell. For this, we need database drivers for the database written for Julia. We will now discuss some RDBMS in order to understand how to interact with them using Julia.

SQLite

SQLite is a lightweight database majorly used for study and testing purposes. This is what the official SQLite website has to say about it:

> *SQLite is a self-contained, high-reliability, embedded, full-featured, public-domain, SQL database engine. SQLite is the most used database engine in the world.*

You may install the database from `https://www.sqlite.org/download.html`. Once you are done with the database installation, it's time we now move on to installing SQLite's Julia database driver.

We will be making use of the package named SQLite, and since its entry is made available inside the `METADATA.jl`, you will be installing it easily using this:

```
julia> Pkg.add("SQLite")
```

MySQL

MySQL is one of the most popular databases and it's currently supported and maintained by Oracle. Although it's free and open source, it has an enterprise version too.

To install MySQL on any of the operating systems, visit `https://www.mysql.com/downloads/`. Once installed on your system, just check out whether it is installed correctly or not by opening up the shell:

```
my-machine:~ user$ mysql --version
mysql  Ver 14.14 Distrib 5.6.36, for macos10.12 (x86_64) using  EditLine
wrapper

my-machine:~ user$ mysql
Welcome to the MySQL monitor.  Commands end with ; or \g.
Your MySQL connection id is 3
Server version: 5.6.36 MySQL Community Server (GPL)
Copyright (c) 2000, 2017, Oracle and/or its affiliates. All rights
reserved.

Oracle is a registered trademark of Oracle Corporation and/or its
affiliates. Other names may be trademarks of their respective
owners.
Type 'help;' or '\h' for help. Type '\c' to clear the current input
statement.
```

This is of course on macOS; the shell will probably be very similar to Linux and Windows systems as well. Now, we move on to installing MySQL's database driver for Julia:

```
julia> Pkg.add("MySQL")
julia> using MySQL
```

Again, similar to SQLite, the installation is fairly simple. Let's try out creating a database connection and explore more with it:

```
using MySQL
con = mysql_connect("localhost", "username", "password", "db_name")
command = """CREATE TABLE Employee
                (
                    ID INT NOT NULL AUTO_INCREMENT,
                    Name VARCHAR(255),
                    Salary FLOAT,
                    JoinDate DATE,
                    PRIMARY KEY (ID)
                );"""
mysql_execute(con, command)
```

```
# Insert some values
mysql_execute(con, "INSERT INTO Employee (Name, Salary, JoinDate) values
('Alpha', 25000.00, '2015-12-12'), ('Beta', 35000.00, '2012-18-17'),
('Gamma', 50000.00, '2013-12-14');")

# Get SELECT results
command = "SELECT * FROM Employee;"
dframe = mysql_execute(con, command)

# Close connection
mysql_disconnect(con)
```

Now as we have seen how to work with SQL databases using Julia, we shift our focus towards using Julia with NoSQL databases.

NoSQL databases

We all know that in a traditional setting a database implements a relational model of data organized in row and columns. We call it popularly as RDBMS as studied earlier in this chapter. However, NoSQL databases are very different from this traditional setting.

A NoSQL database is a kind of database that doesn't store data in a row-column format or in other words tabular format. The most common approach used is to store data in the form of JSON document. JSON, which is a very popular format for data exchange can actually be used to organize data in key-value pairs. There is actually a wide classification under which NoSQL databases can be broadly classified. They are as follows:

- Key-value stores
- Document databases
- Wide-column stores
- Graph stores

Now, the question arises, why NoSQL? This is a very important question to be asked to big enterprises with the huge user bases that are expanding with the growing demand. The following are some features of NoSQL which makes it the default choice for such large-scale systems:

- Non-relational databases are schema-less. This will translate roughly into saying that they provide and offer much more flexibility when it comes to making changes in the way data is stored and organized.

- NoSQL databases are cost-effective and open sourced. This means that they are both nicely customizable by the enterprise wanting to use them and also come at a fraction of the cost of the traditional SQL giants.
- NoSQL databases is highly scalable. This is by far their USP when it comes to comparison with SQL databases, as in the age of cloud computing and on-demand scalability in no time, NoSQL data stores scale quickly and can be spread out of 100s of VM's at once. They also function nicely on low-cost hardware that means that they are even effective when the system configurations are not that great.

However, like every other thing, they also have some fare share of disadvantages as compared to RDBMS, which is listing as follows:

- Not that great when it comes to transactional systems. They are very badly in comparison to their SQL counterparts.
- Lack of standardization, when it comes to querying the data. In the case of RDBMS, there is SQL which is almost the same (given some changes here and there) for all the major vendors. NoSQL vendors still implement their own querying commands which becomes a pain while trying to do migrations and move from one database to another kind of database.

Now that we had seen a good introduction into what NoSQL databases are, let's get a bit deeper into starting to know how they can interact with Julia. However, before we see how that is done, let's take a look at how MongoDB works and how we can query it.

MongoDB

MongoDB is the most famous and widely used NoSQL database in the world as of now. The latest version is version 3.6; however, we will be using version 3.4 on the macOS operating system.

To install MongoDB on your system, you just need to go to the website `https://docs.mongodb.com/getting-started/shell/tutorial/install-mongodb-on-os-x/` and follow the instructions given there.

Once installed, you can open up two Terminals. In one of them, just type `mongod` to start the MongoDB daemon; while in the second Terminal, just type `mongo` and the shell will start. The following is a sample of how the mongo shell looks:

```
rahuls-MBP:book-learningJulia rahullakhanpal$ mongo
MongoDB shell version v3.4.10
connecting to: mongodb://127.0.0.1:27017
MongoDB server version: 3.4.10
Server has startup warnings:
2017-11-07T18:24:31.312+0530 I CONTROL   [initandlisten]
2017-11-07T18:24:31.312+0530 I CONTROL   [initandlisten] ** WARNING: Access
control is not enabled for the database.
2017-11-07T18:24:31.313+0530 I CONTROL   [initandlisten] **            Read
and write access to data and configuration is unrestricted.
2017-11-07T18:24:31.313+0530 I CONTROL   [initandlisten]
2017-11-07T18:24:31.313+0530 I CONTROL   [initandlisten]
2017-11-07T18:24:31.313+0530 I CONTROL   [initandlisten] ** WARNING: soft
rlimits too low. Number of files is 256, should be at least 1000
>
```

Once you are inside the shell, you are ready to play with it. Just like the Julia REPL, mongo shell too gives you the flexibility of autocomplete. The following are some commands that are very easy to run and can get you a good feel of how a document-based database looks and runs:

```
# to show all databases
> show databases;
admin                   0.000GB
local                   0.000GB
test                    0.000GB
>

# to change database
> use test;
switched to db test

# to insert a document
> db.test.insertOne({"name":"rahul","book":"learning julia"})
{
        "acknowledged" : true,
        "insertedId" : ObjectId("5a118b098368a9901c9da4ff")
}

# to find all the documents
> db.test.find().forEach(printjson)
{
        "_id" : ObjectId("5a118b098368a9901c9da4ff"),
```

```
        "name" : "rahul",
        "book" : "learning julia"
}

# to find a document fulfilling a condition
> db.test.findOne({"name":"rahul"})
{
        "_id" : ObjectId("5a118b098368a9901c9da4ff"),
        "name" : "rahul",
        "book" : "learning julia"
}
>
```

For connecting and using MongoDB with Julia, we will use a package named Mongo.jl, which is available on GitHub (https://github.com/pzion/Mongo.jl).

Before installing the package, you need to have the latest version of the MongoDB binaries for C language. The following is how you can install and use this package:

```
julia> using Mongo, LibBSON

# Create a client connection
julia> client = MongoClient()

# Get a handle to collection named "test" in database "test".
# Client object, database name, and collection name are stored as
variables.
julia> test = MongoCollection(client, "test", "test")

# Insert a document
julia> document = insert(test, Dict("name" => "rahul", "book" => "learning
julia"))
```

As you can see, it's fairly easy to use and run MongoDB with Julia. For more detailed examples, you need to visit the GitHub link as given earlier and follow JuliaDB (http://juliadb.org/latest/) for the latest announcements and drivers.

Moving to the next topic, we will look at how to work with REST and see what Julia has to offer in terms of web frameworks.

Introduction to REST

REST is the underlying architecture that powers the most modern web application running on the internet. It offers a simpler form of architecture as compared to the traditional SOAP and WSDL-based ones.

Representational State Transfer (**REST**) is a simple way of sending and receiving data between the client and server, which is majorly done using HTTP and the data is transported or exchanged using a JSON format for the most part. It's a truly lightweight alternative to the **Simple Object Access Protocol** (**SOAP**)-based web applications.

REST uses HTTP methods such as GET, POST, PUT, and DELETE, for updating resources on the server. It provides the simplicity of a uniform interface as well as the scalability to support a large number of components.

The following are some architectural constraints that define a RESTful system as per Wikipedia. If a state is found violating any of these constraints, then the whole system may *not* be termed as RESTful:

- **Client-server architecture**: The main idea behind client-server constraints is the separation of concerns. Separating the UI from the data storage greatly improves the portability as well as scalability across multiple platforms.

- **Statelessness**: Each request from the client should be complete in itself in the sense that it should hold all the necessary information to make it possible for the server to handle and respond to the client's request.

- **Cacheability**: As on the World Wide Web, clients and intermediaries can cache responses. Responses must, therefore, implicitly or explicitly, define themselves as cacheable or not to prevent clients from reusing stale or inappropriate data in response to further requests.

- **Layered system**: A client cannot ordinarily tell whether it is connected directly to the end server or to an intermediary along the way. Intermediary servers may improve system scalability by enabling load balancing and by providing shared caches.

- **Code on demand**: Servers can temporarily extend or customize the functionality of a client by transferring executable code. Examples of this may include compiled components such as Java applets and client-side scripts such as JavaScript.

- **Uniform interface**: The uniform interface constraint is fundamental to the design of any REST service. It simplifies and decouples the architecture, which enables each part to evolve independently. The four constraints for this uniform interface are:

  - Resource identification in requests
  - Resource manipulation through representations
  - Self-descriptive messages
  - Hypermedia as the engine of application state

Having gone through the properties and features of RESTful architecture, let's try out exploring how we can use it with Julia. But before that, we need to refresh our knowledge about JSON as a medium of data transfer.

What is JSON?

JSON, short for **JavaScript Object Notation**, is like the gold standard of data transfer between client and server inside a RESTful web application. The following is an example of what a JSON object looks like:

```
{
        "name":"rahul",
        "subjects_with_scores":{
                "maths":80,
                "science":90,
                "computers":100
                },
        "country":"india",


}
```

As you can see, we have a very simple JSON object represented here. It uses a format which uses `key:value` pairs to store data. These can also have nested structures inside them. For more information, you can look up to the official JSON website, `http://www.json.org`.

One of the flaws that JSON has is its inability to have comments on it. However, there is a version of JSON in the JSON5 format, which is very similar to JSON but can hold comments along with some minor improvements that can increase the overall readability for the user. A small example of a JSON5 object is as follows:

```
{
    foo: 'bar',
    while: true,
```

```
      this: 'is a \
  multi-line string',

      // this is an inline comment
      here: 'is another', // inline comment

      /* this is a block comment
         that continues on another line */

      hex: 0xDEADbeef,
      half: .5,
      delta: +10,
      to: Infinity,    // and beyond!

      finally: 'a trailing comma',
      oh: [
          "we shouldn't forget",
          'arrays can have',
          'trailing commas too',
      ],
  }
```

Because of its differences with JSON, it has altogether a different format by the name `.json5`. For more information on the same, you may check out or visit the website `http://www.json5.org`.

However, in this section, we will focus on using JSON with Julia and as to how we can create a small REST-based service. Starting with a very simple example, let's use the website `http://httpbin.org` to actually make some calls and see if we can get a response from the server.

For running it, I will be using JuliaBox's online Julia notebook, which is available for free at `https://www.juliabox.com`. People familiar with Jupyter notebook would face no issues using it; however, for people not used to it, you may jump to the article at `https://lectures.quantecon.org/jl/getting_started.html#jupyter`.

Now let's take a look at the following code:

```
julia> using Requests
julia> using JSON

julia> result = Requests.get("http://httpbin.org/get")
Response(200 OK, 14 headers, 281 bytes in body)

julia> typeof(result)
HttpCommon.Response
```

```julia
julia> fieldnames(result)
8-element Array{Symbol,1}:
 :status
 :headers
 :cookies
 :data
 :request
 :history
 :finished
 :requests

julia> println(result.data)
UInt8[0x7b, 0x0a, 0x20, 0x20, 0x22, 0x61, 0x72, 0x67, 0x73, 0x22, 0x3a,
0x20, 0x7b, 0x7d, 0x2c, 0x20, 0x0a, 0x20, 0x20, 0x22, 0x68, 0x65, 0x61,
0x64, 0x65, 0x72, 0x73, 0x22, 0x3a, 0x20, 0x7b, 0x0a, 0x20, 0x20, 0x20,
0x20, 0x22, 0x41, 0x63, 0x63, 0x65, 0x70, 0x74, 0x22, 0x3a, 0x20, 0x22,
0x74, 0x65, 0x78, 0x74, 0x2f, 0x68, 0x74, 0x6d, 0x6c, 0x2c, 0x61, 0x70,
0x70, 0x6c, 0x69, 0x63, 0x61, 0x74, 0x69, 0x6f, 0x6e, 0x2f, 0x78, 0x68,
0x74, 0x6d, 0x6c, 0x2b, 0x78, 0x6d, 0x6c, 0x2c, 0x61, 0x70, 0x70, 0x6c,
0x69, 0x63, 0x61, 0x74, 0x69, 0x6f, 0x6e, 0x2f, 0x78, 0x6d, 0x6c, 0x3b,
0x71, 0x3d, 0x30, 0x2e, 0x39, 0x2c, 0x2a, 0x2f, 0x2a, 0x3b, 0x71, 0x3d,
0x30, 0x2e, 0x38, 0x22, 0x2c, 0x20, 0x0a, 0x20, 0x20, 0x20, 0x20, 0x22,
0x43, 0x6f, 0x6e, 0x6e, 0x65, 0x63, 0x74, 0x69, 0x6f, 0x6e, 0x22, 0x3a,
0x20, 0x22, 0x63, 0x6c, 0x6f, 0x73, 0x65, 0x22, 0x2c, 0x20, 0x0a, 0x20,
0x20, 0x20, 0x20, 0x22, 0x48, 0x6f, 0x73, 0x74, 0x22, 0x3a, 0x20, 0x22,
0x68, 0x74, 0x74, 0x70, 0x62, 0x69, 0x6e, 0x2e, 0x6f, 0x72, 0x67, 0x22,
0x2c, 0x20, 0x0a, 0x20, 0x20, 0x20, 0x20, 0x22, 0x55, 0x73, 0x65, 0x72,
0x2d, 0x41, 0x67, 0x65, 0x6e, 0x74, 0x22, 0x3a, 0x20, 0x22, 0x52, 0x65,
0x71, 0x75, 0x65, 0x73, 0x74, 0x73, 0x2e, 0x6a, 0x6c, 0x2f, 0x30, 0x2e,
0x30, 0x2e, 0x30, 0x22, 0x0a, 0x20, 0x20, 0x7d, 0x2c, 0x20, 0x0a, 0x20,
0x20, 0x22, 0x6f, 0x72, 0x69, 0x67, 0x69, 0x6e, 0x22, 0x3a, 0x20, 0x22,
0x33, 0x35, 0x2e, 0x31, 0x38, 0x38, 0x2e, 0x31, 0x34, 0x32, 0x2e, 0x31,
0x36, 0x32, 0x22, 0x2c, 0x20, 0x0a, 0x20, 0x20, 0x22, 0x75, 0x72, 0x6c,
0x22, 0x3a, 0x20, 0x22, 0x68, 0x74, 0x74, 0x70, 0x3a, 0x2f, 0x2f, 0x68,
0x74, 0x74, 0x70, 0x62, 0x69, 0x6e, 0x2e, 0x6f, 0x72, 0x67, 0x2f, 0x67,
0x65, 0x74, 0x22, 0x0a, 0x7d, 0x0a]

julia> typeof(result.data)
Array{UInt8,1}

julia> output = JSON.parse(convert(String, result.data))
Dict{String,Any} with 4 entries:
  "headers" => Dict{String,Any}(Pair{String,Any}("Connection",
"close"),Pair{St...
  "args"    => Dict{String,Any}()
  "url"     => "http://httpbin.org/get"
  "origin"  => "35.188.142.162"
```

```
julia> output["headers"]
Dict{String,Any} with 4 entries:
  "Connection" => "close"
  "Host"       => "httpbin.org"
  "Accept"     =>
"text/html,application/xhtml+xml,application/xml;q=0.9,*/*;q=...
  "User-Agent" => "Requests.jl/0.0.0"
```

As you can clearly notice, we have used the packages JSON and Requests (Julia port of the famous requests Python library by Kenneth Reitz). In the first step, we make a GET request to the website http://www.httpbin.org/get, which fetches us resources from the server.

However, if we see the result which we created, we will see that it is of the type HttpCommon.Response. This means that we have got a response object back from the server.

Moving further, the value Response(200 OK, 14 headers, 281 bytes in body) reveals that it was a success in making a request as well as it has around 281 bytes in the contents. We can check out more using the fieldnames function in Julia, which is very handy when it comes to exploring fields inside an object.

However, when we print the data, we get to see that it's in the UInt8 format, which isn't human readable. Hence to make out some sense from the data, we need to convert the same into a string by using the function convert, which does its job well.

Similarly, we can also POST data to the server by using the Requests.post function:

```
julia> result = Requests.post("http://httpbin.org/post"; data = "this is
julia")
Response(200 OK, 14 headers, 436 bytes in body)

julia> JSON.parse(convert(String, result.data))
Dict{String,Any} with 8 entries:
  "headers" => Dict{String,Any}(Pair{String,Any}("Connection",
"close"),Pair{St...
  "json"    => nothing
  "files"   => Dict{String,Any}()
  "args"    => Dict{String,Any}()
  "data"    => "this is julia"
  "url"     => "http://httpbin.org/post"
  "form"    => Dict{String,Any}()
  "origin"  => "35.188.142.162"
```

Web frameworks

The active community of Julia is playing a great role when it comes to making web-based packages. In fact, there is a complete community group that takes care of all the web-based packages and is named JuliaWeb while their work can be found at https://github.com/JuliaWeb.

However, coming to web frameworks, there is a very competent framework named Genie, which, as per its official site, is a full-stack MVC web framework that provides a streamlined and efficient workflow for developing modern web applications. It builds on Julia's strengths (high level, high performance, dynamic, and JIT compiled), exposing a rich API and a powerful toolset for productive web development.

Let's begin by installing the package and creating a small functional web-based app. The package is easy to install and can be done using Julia's default package manager Pkg:

```
julia> Pkg.clone("https://github.com/essenciary/Genie.jl")
```

Once installed, which might take a minute or two, you can then process forward to start using the package:

```
julia> using Genie
julia> Genie.REPL.new_app("sample_julia_app")
2017-11-19T14:58:40.316 - info: Done! New app created at
/Users/rahullakhanpal/sample_julia_app


2017-11-19T14:58:40.331 - info: Looking for dependencies


2017-11-19T14:58:40.331 - info: Checking for Flax rendering engine support

2017-11-19T14:58:41.436 - info: Cloning Flax from
https://github.com/essenciary/Flax.jl
2017-11-19T14:58:45.018 - info: Computing changes...
2017-11-19T14:58:52.142 - info: No packages to install, update or remove

2017-11-19T14:58:52.142 - info: Finished adding dependencies


2017-11-19T14:58:52.142 - info: Starting your brand new Genie app - hang
tight!



 _____    _    _ _____
|    _|__   __|_|__
```

```
|  |  | -_|   | | -_|
|____|__|_|_|_|__|
```

```
Starting Genie in >> DEV << mode using 1 worker(s)
```

```
genie>
```

Note that the shell, in the end, changes itself to Genie. The app gets created in your home directory and is automatically loaded into the shell.

To see the overall default structure of the app, here is the output of tree sample_julia_app:

```
rahuls-MBP:~ rahullakhanpal$ tree sample_julia_app/
sample_julia_app/
├──── LICENSE.md
├──── README.md
├──── REQUIRE
├──── app
│     ├──── assets
│     │     ├──── css
│     │     │     └──── application.css
│     │     ├──── fonts
│     │     └──── js
│     │           ├──── application.js
│     │           └──── channels.js
│     ├──── helpers
│     │     ├──── ControllerHelper.jl
│     │     ├──── ValidationHelper.jl
│     │     └──── ViewHelper.jl
│     ├──── layouts
│     │     └──── app.flax.html
│     └──── resources
├──── bin
│     ├──── repl
│     └──── server
├──── cache
├──── config
│     ├──── app.jl
│     ├──── database.yml
│     ├──── env
│     │     ├──── dev.jl
│     │     ├──── prod.jl
│     │     └──── test.jl
│     ├──── initializers
│     │     ├──── converters.jl
│     │     └──── dependencies.jl
│     ├──── loggers.jl
```

```
│   ├──── plugins.jl
│   ├──── routes.jl
│   └──── secrets.jl
├──── db
│   ├──── migrations
│   └──── seeds
├──── docs
│   ├──── make.jl
│   ├──── mkdocs.yml
│   └──── src
│       └──── index.md
├──── env.jl
├──── genie.jl
├──── lib
├──── log
│   └──── dev.log
├──── package.json
├──── public
│   ├──── css
│   │   ├──── bootstrap-theme.css
│   │   ├──── bootstrap-theme.min.css
│   │   ├──── bootstrap.css
│   │   ├──── bootstrap.min.css
│   │   ├──── dosis-font.css
│   │   ├──── prism.css
│   │   ├──── style.css
│   │   └──── themify-icons.css
│   ├──── error-404.html
│   ├──── error-500.html
│   ├──── favicon.ico
│   ├──── favicon.png
│   ├──── fonts
│   │   ├──── dosis
│   │   │   ├──── 3isE9muMMOq1K7TQ7HkKvIDGDUGfDkXyfkzVDelzfFk.woff2
│   │   │   ├──── O6SOu9hYsPHTU43R17NS5XYhjbSpvc47ee6xR_80Hnw.woff2
│   │   │   ├──── RPKDmaFi75RJkvjWaDDb0nYhjbSpvc47ee6xR_80Hnw.woff2
│   │   │   ├──── VK-RlLrn4NFhRGqPkj6IwBkAz4rYn47Zy2rvigWQf6w.woff2
│   │   │   └──── oaBFj7Fz9Y9_eW3k9Jd9X6CWcynf_cDxXwCLxiixG1c.woff2
│   │   ├──── glyphicons-halflings-regular.eot
│   │   ├──── glyphicons-halflings-regular.svg
│   │   ├──── glyphicons-halflings-regular.ttf
│   │   ├──── glyphicons-halflings-regular.woff
│   │   ├──── glyphicons-halflings-regular.woff2
│   │   ├──── themify.eot
│   │   ├──── themify.svg
│   │   ├──── themify.ttf
│   │   └──── themify.woff
│   ├──── img
```

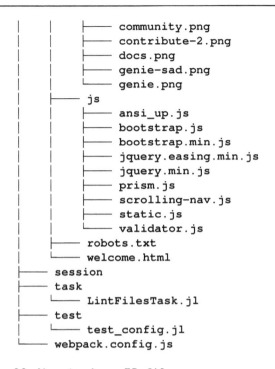

```
        |   |       ├──── community.png
        |   |       ├──── contribute-2.png
        |   |       ├──── docs.png
        |   |       ├──── genie-sad.png
        |   |       └──── genie.png
        |   ├──── js
        |   |       ├──── ansi_up.js
        |   |       ├──── bootstrap.js
        |   |       ├──── bootstrap.min.js
        |   |       ├──── jquery.easing.min.js
        |   |       ├──── jquery.min.js
        |   |       ├──── prism.js
        |   |       ├──── scrolling-nav.js
        |   |       ├──── static.js
        |   |       └──── validator.js
        |   ├──── robots.txt
        |   └──── welcome.html
        ├──── session
        ├──── task
        |       └──── LintFilesTask.jl
        ├──── test
        |       └──── test_config.jl
        └──── webpack.config.js

29 directories, 75 files
```

To configure the app, go to the path $HOME/sample_julia_app/config/, open the
file routes.jl, and append the following to it:

```
using Router

route("/julia") do
  "My first julia web app"
end
```

Once done, save the file and navigate back to the Genie shell in REPL:

```
genie> AppServer.startup()
Listening on 0.0.0.0:8000...
```

Open up the browser and go to the link, http://0.0.0.0:8000/julia, which will give
you My first julia web app as the response on the page:

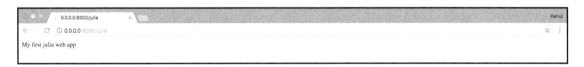

If you navigate to any other URL by chance, you will be greeted by the error page as shown in the following screenshot:

Summary

In this chapter, we went through various topics, including an introduction to databases like RDBMS and NoSQL, along with how to use them with Julia. We explored how to connect to a database using Julia. In the last part of this chapter, we went on to know the ideas behind REST-based systems and how to create a RESTful service along with a web app using Genie.jl in Julia.

In the next chapter, we will go a level deeper into understanding what goes under Julia and how things work the way they do. We will also get to know some performance tips while coding in Julia.

10
Julia's Internals

After covering a ton of new and useful information on Julia and its ecosystem, we now have finally arrived at the final and very important chapter of this book, which talks about Julia's internals and how things are closely knitted around its very rich ecosystem. We will cover the following topics in this chapter:

- Under the hood
- Performance enhancements
- Parallel computing
- TCP sockets and servers
- Creating packages

Under the hood

Julia is a great programming language. So far, we have talked about various reasons for this and given a number of examples to showcase how fast and easy it is to code and execute with Julia. But, how did Julia end up being this good? Sure, there must be different reasons for the positive argument, but in this part of the chapter, we will see all that goes on inside Julia to give it the edge it currently has.

Femtolisp

Femtolisp was started by Jeff Bezanson as a GitHub side project. According to him, the aim was to write the fastest `lisp` interpreter that could be written in under 1,000 lines of C code. This was the initial idea, which later grew bigger and gained attention. Femtolisp is simple and built using scheme.

To open up the `lisp` interpreter, you just need to type in `julia --lisp`:

The Julia Core API

Checking out the code of Julia, as available on GitHub, we can clearly distinguish that around 70% of the code for Julia is written in Julia. This is great for any language. However, the core parts for Julia are mostly in C and C++, which makes up around 25% of the overall codebase when combined.

The link to the Julia GitHub repository is `https://github.com/JuliaLang/julia`. Most of the core components can be found in the src folder where there are lots of C and C++ files as well as header files, which are used by other dependent modules. The core of the system sits on `libjulia`, which also includes `femtolisp` as well as a support library called `libsupport`.

Coming on to the source code again, we can see a header file named `julia.h`. This file contains the `jl_init()` routine, which initializes Julia. Hence to be able to run a C code which can interact with Julia functions, the `julia.h` header file is needed. There is also a lot of code in the base folder of the source code, which is more prominently Julia code.

Performance enhancements

This can be a very crucial topic to discuss when it comes to first-time coders in Julia. As we already know, Julia is quick and fast, but its speed can easily be hampered if the underlying code is badly written or it's inspired by paradigms of some other language like Python.

As per the official website, there can be a number of things we can do as a Julia programmer to enhance the performance of the overall code. We will now discuss them one by one.

Global variables

The use of global variables in a wrong way can certainly put brakes on the performance. A global variable has a value and a data type associated with it, which can change over time, thus making it difficult for the compiler to actually optimize the code. As good practice, the contents should always be declared in the following manner:

```
julia> const A_CONSTANT = 10
10
```

Whenever possible, variables should be passed as arguments to functions in the code.

Type declarations

In Julia, the compiler generally knows the types of all function arguments, local variables, and expressions. Hence, just adding type declarations won't make the code run faster. We will now discuss some points to be checked out in this regard.

Fields with abstract types

Imagine you are creating your own type with some random field `num` in it. You can easily fall into doing this:

```
julia> struct SampleType
                         num
        end
```

This will allow `num` to take any type, and mark the beginning of some unwanted type mismatch errors too! However, from the compiler's perspective, this is bad as it will not be possible to extract more information from the object itself, which results in poor code performance:

```julia
julia> α = SampleType("stringvalue")
SampleType("stringvalue")

julia> β = SampleType(10)
SampleType(10)

julia> γ = SampleType(10.0)
SampleType(10.0)
```

What do you see? Well here, all the three variables are valid and make sense to the compiler, but which one would you choose (if you wrote the code targeted for a specific type!) and could that field hold values of different types? These are the sorts of questions a fellow programmer may ask.

Also, one thing that takes the compiler time is figuring out the exact data type for that field. For instance, when the value is 10, it's an Int64 that takes some specific space, while if the value is 10.0, then its a Float64, which takes different (read more) space than Int64. In that scenario, the running time for both of these will be slightly different.

So, how do we deal with it? Simple—by putting in the exact data type in places where we want to, or we can have it declared initially in the type declaration. Take a look at this:

```julia
julia> type SampleType{T<:AbstractFloat}
           num :: T
       end

julia> α = SampleType(10.0)
SampleType{Float64}(10.0)

julia>
```

Great! We have improved the readability, as well as the code performance by a good margin, as the compiler doesn't have to infer the type by itself. Also, if we try to include a different value, we are greeted with an error:

```julia
julia> α = SampleType(10)
ERROR: MethodError: Cannot `convert` an object of type Int64 to an object
of type SampleType{T<:AbstractFloat}
```

Container fields with abstract type

This is similar to the issue we just discussed in the previous point, but with a distinction that the field in question is a container, such as an array or hashmap. Let's look at a quick example for that too:

```julia
julia> type SampleDataType
           a
       end

julia> alpha = SampleDataType([10,15,20])
SampleDataType([10,15,20])
```

As usual, the code given here is not efficient. However, the following code includes enhancements similar to the one discussed in the first point:

```julia
julia> type SampleDataType{T<:AbstractVector}
           a :: T
       end

julia> alpha = SampleDataType([10,20])
SampleDataType{Array{Int64,1}}([10,20])

julia>
```

Declaring type for keyword arguments

Functions with keyword arguments have near-zero overheads for call sites that pass only positional arguments:

```julia
julia> function testme(a; b::Int64 = 10)
           a, b
       end
testme (generic function with 1 method)
```

Miscellaneous performance tweaks

Let's discuss some other tips for performance enhancements in Julia code:

- Always try breaking a big function with multiple definitions (aka compound functions) into smaller functions with a clearer and more modular approach.

- Write functions that must *always* return the value of a given data type, that is, their return type should always be one and shouldn't change with the change in input. A quick example of this can be as follows:

```julia
julia> function check_bigger(x:: Int64, y::Int64)
           if x < y
               return y
           elseif y < x
               return x
           else
               return "Both are equal"
       end
       end
WARNING: Method definition check_bigger(Int64, Int64) in module
Main at REPL[7]:2 overwritten at REPL[15]:2.
check_bigger (generic function with 1 method)

julia> check_bigger(10,20)
20

julia> check_bigger(30,20)
30

julia> check_bigger(20,20)
"Both are equal"
```

The preceding function has a big flaw since when both the numbers are equal, it chooses to return a string instead of an integer value, which so far it has returned in those cases whenever any of the values were smaller or bigger than the other one. Following are some tips while trying to make your code more performant,

- Access arrays in memory order, that is, along with columns. Julia is basically column-majored, and in a multidimensional array, arrays are stacked one column at a time. Hence, while going through loops in a column-major array, the first index changes rapidly which makes looping faster.
- Use views for slices. This may seem a bit odd at first (or for people used to slicing), but it will start making sense if you consider the fact that every time you slice an array, you make a new copy of it. Essentially, this leads to more memory usage. This shouldn't be mistaken with the fact that if the number of operations performed on slices is large, then it definitely is an advantage as you are working with a smaller portion of that big array.
- In the end, always keep an eye on the amount of time it takes to execute your code. this can be done using @timeit macro which is available in the Julia standard library.

Standard library

Julia's standard library is rich. It is vast and offers lots of functions that can ease the daily work of a programmer/data scientists. Along with a very good support for almost all the functionalities provided by other modern day programming languages, it has a great in-built support for mathematical and statistical functions.

This section will briefly describe the standard Julia library along with some examples to make things easier for you. As per the official documentation given on the Julia website `https://docs.julialang.org/en/release-0.6/#Standard-Library-1`, the standard library can be distributed in the following subheadings:

- Essentials
- Collections and data structures
- Mathematics
- Numbers
- Strings
- Arrays
- Tasks and parallel computing
- Linear algebra
- Constants
- Filesystem
- I/O and network
- Punctuation
- Sorting and related functions
- Package manager functions
- Dates and time
- Iteration utilities
- Unit testing
- C Interface
- C standard library
- Dynamic linker
- Profiling
- StackTraces
- SIMD support

Although explaining each and every heading detail can be summed up in a book of its own, we will try to explore some features of the standard library in general so that it becomes quite familiar to you. We'll start with some functions that are useful in working around the language and act as helper functions while doing a given task:

- Functions such as exit, atexit, quiet, less, and clipboard are useful when using or creating a functionality that does not directly concern with using these, but they inherently help the developers to get around the Julia environment

- Next up are some functions that work on objects, such as ===, isa, isequal, isless, and typeof. A small example of all of these is given as follows:

```julia
julia> 3 === 3
true

julia> isequal(3, 3.0)
true

julia> isless(2, 3)
true

julia> typeof(3)
Int64
```

- Julia has functions that help while working with types. These are one of the most important functions when we are concerned determining properties of types. Some of them are supertype, issubtype, <:, >:, typemin, typemax, subtypes, realmin, realmax, sizeof, and so on. The following code shows their usage:

```julia
julia> supertype(Int64)
Signed

julia> subtypes(Int64)
0-element Array{Union{DataType, UnionAll},1}

issubnormal issubset      issubtype
julia> issubtype(Int64, Real)
true
```

- Next up are some system functions that can be used while interacting with the operating system. They are run, spawn, pipeline, success, kill, cmd, and so on. The following is a sample run command:

```
julia> run(`ls -lrt`)
total 16
drwxr-xr-x+  5 rahullakhanpal  staff   170 Nov  3 16:01 Public
drwx------+  3 rahullakhanpal  staff   102 Nov  3 16:01
Pictures
drwx------+  3 rahullakhanpal  staff   102 Nov  3 16:01 Music
drwx------+  3 rahullakhanpal  staff   102 Nov  3 16:01 Movies
```

Then there are set of functions that help to do iterations, complex nesting, and playing around with Julia's data structures:

- Julia has a rich set of functions that can be used while iterating or while doing complex nesting tasks. Some methods are start, next, and done, which perform sequential iterations. A simple example is given as follows:

```
julia> start(1:3)
1

julia> next(1:3, 1)
(1, 2)

julia> next(1:3, 2)
(2, 3)

julia> next(1:3, 3)
(3, 4)

julia> next(1:3, 4)
(4, 5)

julia> done(1:3, 3)
false

julia> done(1:3, 4)
true
```

- Finally, we have some functions that work over collections in general. They are basically used to know more about the collective data type on which they are operating. Examples of these functions are isempty, length, endof, and empty!.

These are functions and libraries that are concerned with mathematical calculations and computations. Apart from the usual +, −, *, and \ functions, there are lots of functions provided in the start library, but we will show just a few of them in the following example:

```
julia> inv(10) * 10
1.0

julia> div(10,2)
5

julia> rem(10,5)
0

julia> mod(10,2)
0

julia> numerator(4//2)
2

julia> denominator(4//2)
1
```

This was just a very small view of what Julia has to offer to the developers when it comes to creating community packages and things around the Julia ecosystem along with developing their own products.

We will now move forward to the next topic in the chapter, which is understanding LLVM and JIT.

LLVM and JIT explained

LLVM, which is short for **Low-Level Virtual Machine**, is a compiler infrastructure project that is a collection of compiler and toolchain technologies. The LLVM is purely written in C++, started in early 2000 at the University of Illinois at Urbana–Champaign by Vikram Adve and Chris Lattner. In the present day, a lot of modern frontend and backend technologies, including Julia, use LLVM as the baseline compiler architecture.

Since its initial days of development, LLVM has grown much more and today we call it an umbrella project, which features a lot of other exciting stuff:

- LLVM IR
- LLVM Debugger
- LLVM C++ Standard Library and more

In Chapter 1, *Understanding Julia's Ecosystem*, we had already gone through an initial level of discussion about LLVM and JIT; however, in this part of the chapter, we will discuss how Julia uses LLVM and JIT to its advantage. So let's start with a very simple Julia code snippet:

```
julia> function fib(n::Int64)
          if n == 1
              return n
          elseif n == 0
              return 0
          else
              return fib(n-1) + fib(n-2)
          end
       end
fib (generic function with 1 method)

julia> fib(10)
55
```

This was a very common example of a Fibonacci series implemented in Julia. However, to know how the LLVM intermediate representation may seem like, you need to use a macro by the name @code_llvm, which we have taken a look at while studying reflection properties of Julia.

Julia uses the LLVM compiler framework to generate machine code. LLVM defines an assembly-like language which it uses as a shared intermediate **representation** (**IR**) between different compiler optimization passes and other tools in the framework. There are three isomorphic forms of LLVM IR:

- A binary representation that is compact and machine readable
- A textual representation that is verbose and somewhat human readable
- An in-memory representation that is generated and consumed by LLVM libraries

Julia uses LLVM's C++ API to construct LLVM IR in memory (from the last point) and then call some LLVM optimization passes on that form. When you do @code_llvm, you see the LLVM IR after generation and some high-level optimizations:

```
julia> @code_llvm(fib(10))

define i64 @julia_fib_62805.2(i64) #0 !dbg !5 {
top:
  %1 = icmp eq i64 %0, 1
  br i1 %1, label %if, label %L4

if:                                               ; preds = %L4, %top
```

```
    %merge = phi i64 [ 1, %top ], [ 0, %L4 ]
    ret i64 %merge

L4:                                           ; preds = %top
    %2 = icmp eq i64 %0, 0
    br i1 %2, label %if, label %L9

L9:                                           ; preds = %L4
    %3 = add i64 %0, -1
    %4 = call i64 @julia_fib_62805(i64 %3)
    %5 = add i64 %0, -2
    %6 = call i64 @julia_fib_62805(i64 %5)
    %7 = add i64 %6, %4
    ret i64 %7
}
```

This is what the textual representation of the in-memory LLVM - IR looks like. However, this representation is not meant to be human readable.

Moving on to the **Just In Time (JIT)** compilation. The JIT compiler converts the program source code into native machine code just before the program is run.

But how does Julia benefits from it?

Well, Julia's implementation is not interpreted; it is JIT compiled. This means that when you call a function, it is transformed to machine code which is executed directly by the native hardware. This process is a bit more complex than the parsing and lowering to bytecode that Python does, but in exchange for that complexity, Julia gets its hallmark speed. (The PyPy JIT for Python is also much more complex than CPython, but it is also typically much faster—increased complexity is a fairly typical cost for speed.) The four levels of *disassembly* for Julia code give you access to the representation of a Julia method implementation for particular argument types at different stages of the transformation from source code to machine code.

To read more on this topic, I encourage that you take a look at this blog post given on the official Julia Computing website, https://juliacomputing.com/blog/2016/02/09/static-julia.html, which tries to give you a different perspective of Julia.

Up next, we will move on to parallel computing features of Julia and explore them in depth.

Parallel computing

Before we start exploring the parallel computing features provided by Julia, it's interesting to understand briefly what parallel computation means. Parallel computing is a type of computation in which many calculations, or the execution of processes, are carried out simultaneously. Here, a typical task is broken down into multiple similar subtasks that are processed independently, but whose results are combined together to give one final result.

Like every other modern-day programming language, Julia also allows for parallel computation of a different set of tasks. However, the way in which Julia performs parallel computing is different. It provides a multiprocessing environment, which is based on message passing (not to be confused with MPI), which allows programmers to run separate processes in separate memory domains at once. It is also important to note that Julia is, by design, distributed.

In accordance with the message passing implementation of Julia, communication actually happens in a one-sided format. Rather than it being a send-and-receive cycle, it's more similar to making calls to some functions.

In Julia, parallel computing is based on two primitives:

- **Remote references**: An object that can be used from any process to refer to an object stored on a particular process
- **Remote calls**: These are requests by one process to call a certain function about certain arguments on another (possibly the same) process

Digging down further into remote references, we broadly have two flavors:

- Future
- RemoteChannel

Let's start by checking out what remotecall is and what it returns.

Run the following command in the Julia REPL:

```
julia> remote_call = remotecall( + , 1, 2, 2)
Future(1,1,4,Nullable{Any}())
```

Here, we have created a very simple `remotecall` using the already available `remotecall` function in Julia. The first argument of this function is a +, which indicates addition while the rest of arguments are just integers. To understand it well, if we see the method signature of the function `remotecall`, we get this.

```
julia> @which remotecall(+, 1, 2, 2)
remotecall(f, id::Integer, args...) at multi.jl:1052
```

Here, + is the function used, 1 is the ID while 2 and 2 are the arguments to the + function.

Once we execute this function, we are immediately provided with a `Future` value; here, `Future(1,1,1,Nullable{Any}())`. Until this point in time, we have not invoked the result of the operation that we passed to `remotecall`. However, we can do so by calling another useful function called `fetch`. Some quick help from Julia REPL helps in understanding fetch more easily:

```
help?> fetch
search: fetch @fetch @fetchfrom remotecall_fetch PollingFileWatcher
unsafe_trunc

  fetch(x)
```

Waits and fetches a value from x depending on the type of x. Does not remove the item fetched:

- `Future`: Wait for and get the value of a Future. The fetched value is cached locally. Further calls to fetch on the same reference return the cached value. If the remote value is an exception, throws a RemoteException which captures the remote exception and backtrace.
- `RemoteChannel`: Wait for and get the value of a remote reference. Exceptions raised are same as for a Future.
- `Channel`: Wait for and get the first available item from the channel.

So now that we have an idea of what `fetch` is, let's run it over our `Future` object:

```
julia> remote_call = remotecall(+, 1, 2, 2)
Future(1,1,1,Nullable{Any}())

julia> fetch(remote_call)
4
```

So as we have it, fetch returns the value of the $+(2,2)$ operation, which equates to 4.

Moving on, let's add more processes to the already opened Julia environment. For this, we need to use the `addproc` command, which takes in an integer argument for the number of processes to be added:

```
# current processes
julia> nprocs()
2

# add 2 more processes
julia> addprocs(2)
2-element Array{Int64,1}:
 3
 4

# check the updated processes again
julia> nprocs()
4
```

Once we are done with adding more processors, let's use the macro `@spawnat`, which is actually very helpful in running an expression over a process asynchronously. Let's have a look at it here:

```
# Create a remotecall
julia> remote_call = remotecall(+, 2, 2, 3)
Future(2,1,5,Nullable{Any}())

julia> interim_res = @spawnat 2 1 + fetch(remote_call)
Future(2,1,6,Nullable{Any}())

julia> fetch(interim_res)
6
```

Here, in the second step, we use `@spawnat 2 1`, which translates to running expression 1 at process id 2 and adding `fetch(remote_call)`. Finally, when we run a fetch over `interim_res`, we get 6.

Once we are done with the solution, we can bring down the number of processes that we added before the operation at any time. We can do so by using `rmprocs`, which takes in an integer depicting the process to be removed.

Focusing on global variables

Consider a function `fib`, which is a very basic function that prints out a Fibonacci number:

```julia
julia> function fib(n)
            if n <= 1
                return 1
            else
                return fib(n-1) + fib(n-2)
        end
        end
fib (generic function with 1 method)

# small test
julia> fib(10)
89
```

Fairly simple! Next up, we check the number of active processes available in our current Julia REPL:

```julia
julia> workers()
2-element Array{Int64,1}:
 3
 4
```

So we see that two processes are available apart from the main process ID (which is `1`). We then try to run the `fib` function over these available processes as well. Wondering how we would do that? Well, again, it's simple. Just use the `@everywhere` macro, which does the job of running an operation over every single process available to us in the current scope:

```julia
julia> @everywhere fib(10)
ERROR: On worker 3:
UndefVarError: fib not defined
 in eval at .\boot.jl:234
 in #5 at .\multi.jl:1957
 in #627 at .\multi.jl:1421
 in run_work_thunk at .\multi.jl:1001
 in macro expansion at .\multi.jl:1421 [inlined]
 in #626 at .\event.jl:68
 in #remotecall_fetch#608(::Array{Any,1}, ::Function, ::Function,
::Base.Worker) at .\multi.jl:1070
 in remotecall_fetch(::Function, ::Base.Worker) at .\multi.jl:1062
 in #remotecall_fetch#611(::Array{Any,1}, ::Function, ::Function, ::Int64)
at .\multi.jl:1080
 in remotecall_fetch(::Function, ::Int64) at .\multi.jl:1080
 in (::##6#8)() at .\multi.jl:1959
```

```
...and 1 other exceptions.

in sync_end() at .\task.jl:311
in macro expansion; at .\multi.jl:1968 [inlined]
in anonymous at .\<missing>:?
```

But, wait! We get an error. Why is that? Wasn't the `@everywhere` macro supposed to give the `fib` function to every single worker available? The answer to the problem is fairly simple.

Looking at the error, the first line says `UndefVarError: fib not defined`, which means that worker 3 (or process 3) doesn't have any clue about what `fib` is. This is because the definition of the `fib` function was created in the local scope of process 1, and hence it's *not* present in the global scope. For the same reason, workers 3 and 4 have no idea what to do with `fib`.

So now that we have seen the issue, let's see how we prevent it. The logical answer is to make every possible worker know about `fib` and make it available for them to execute. We can do this by creating a sample module and defining the `fib` function in it:

```
module sample
export fib

function fib(n)
        if n <= 1
            return 1
        else
            return fib(n-1) + fib(n-2)
        end
end

end
```

Once done, save it and open up the Julia shell. Follow the next steps to run things in parallel. For this, we need to add extra processes using the `addprocs` function, and then use the `@everywhere` macro to make the module sample available to each and every worker:

```
julia> addprocs(2)
2-element Array{Int64,1}:
 2
 3

julia> nprocs()
3

julia> @everywhere include("C:/Users/Rahul/Desktop/sample.jl")
```

```
julia> a = @spawn sample.fib(10)
Future(2,1,6,Nullable{Any}())

julia> b = @spawn sample.fib(20)
Future(3,1,7,Nullable{Any}())

julia> fetch(a) +  fetch(b)
11035
```

Running loops in parallel

Alright, we all know by now that we can run loops in Julia pretty easily using the `for` and `end` blocks. However, the loops are what we run to compute the data sequentially and not asynchronously. To solve this situation, Julia provides a handy macro named `@parallel`, which takes in an expression, which is, in turn, a `for` loop. To see how it works compared with the normal `for` loops, take a look at the following code snippet:

```
# running on a single process, i.e when workers are just 1.

julia> workers()
1-element Array{Int64,1}:
 1

# simple for loop, works perfectly
julia> for i in 1:5
           println(i)
       end
1
2
3
4
5

# parallel for loop running on sigle worker doesn't give a
# synchronised output
julia> @parallel for i in 1:5
           println(i)
       end
1
1-element Array{Future,1}2:
3
4Future(1,1,1,#NULL)
5
```

So as you see, the `@parallel` macro doesn't behave as expected on a single worker machine, as there is no other process to have the tasks distributed. The output is slow, as well as distorted. However, things change when we add more workers to the current environment. This adds the required arsenal to compute the given loop in parallel.

We now add two workers and run the same code. Let's see what result we get:

```julia
julia> addprocs(2)
2-element Array{Int64,1}:
 2
 3

julia> nprocs()
3

julia> workers()
2-element Array{Int64,1}:
 2
 3

julia> result = @parallel for i in 1:5
           println(i)
       end
2-element Array{Future,1}:
 Future(3,1,5,#NULL)
 Future(2,1,6,#NULL)

julia>  From worker 3:   1
        From worker 3:   2
        From worker 3:   3
        From worker 2:   4
        From worker 2:   5
```

Interesting! The loop now runs in parallel over both workers (that is, 2 and 3) and returns the result in the way that it was processed.

Apart from `@parallel` macro, we have one very important function named `pmap`, which is short for **parallel maps**. It works by appling a function `f` to any collection `c`, and transforms it using the available workers. This may be very helpful in cases where the function call does a large amount of work.

The following is a simple example:

```julia
julia> workers()
2-element Array{Int64,1}:
 2
 3
```

```
julia> pmap(sum, [1 2 3 4 5])
5-element Array{Any,1}:
 1
 2
 3
 4
 5
```

TCP sockets and servers

What do we need in order to send data from one machine to another machine connected to the network? We typically use a TCP/IP connection in which TCP is the protocol that controls the flow of packets between the sender and receiver, and at the same time, it's also responsible for rearranging the packets at the destination in order for the data to make sense.

Like all other languages, Julia also provides a good amount of predefined functions, as well as modules, for completing the task. This is fairly easily done and takes fewer lines of code compared with other languages. The following is an example of a TCP/IP connection being set between the sender and the receiver.

Let's look at the code for the sender first. Create a file, sender.jl, and let's put the underlying code in it:

```
# define the PORT
PORT = 7575

# create the server
server = listen(PORT)

# create the connection
connection = accept(server)

# read the input from the user
aline = readline(connection)

# write the following to the receiver's screen
write(connection, "Hey, how are you?")

# close the connection immediatly
close(connection)
```

As you can see from the code snippet, we first created a simple server, which listens to port 7575, which we have already set on the top of the small script. The server created is an instance of the type `Base.TCPServer(active)`, which indicates that the TCP server has been created by default. An alternative way of checking the same would be as follows:

```
julia> isa(server, Base.TCPServer)
true
```

Once the server is created, it listens on the port that we have set for it. Next, we move to create a connection that will enable this server to accept any input sent to it. This is achieved through the function `accept`. As per the official Julia documentation:

```
julia> accept(server[,client])
```

Accepts a connection on the given server and returns a connection to the client. An uninitialized client stream may be provided, in which case it will be used instead of creating a new stream.

At this point in time, the server, though it can take inputs, isn't capable of sending or responding to any kind of data from itself. For this, we just keep a line as the input from the client machine, (it will work if the enter button is pressed, as that's taken as a kind of input from the user). The `readline` function plays its role here. The next step is optional, but if it is not present, the user won't be notified that the server has actually got the request from the client.

Hence, we use the `write` function, which writes a string of data to the connection stream. Once done, we can finally close the connection safely using the close function already made available to us. This makes our server-side script ready and can be executed from the Terminal or CMD prompt:

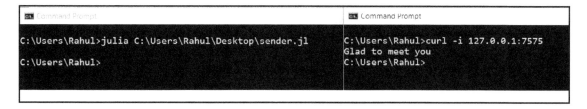

Side by side, open another window from your CMD or terminal (install `curl` if you haven't already installed it). Type the following in the second window:

```
curl -i 127.0.0.1:7575 # HIT Enter
```

Here, we are trying to connect to the already running server in window 1. As soon as we press the enter button, what do we get? unsurprisingly here, we actually are returned the same string that we intended to send to any client trying to connect with us: that is, we get this:

```
C:\Users\Rahul>curl -i 127.0.0.1:7575
Glad to meet you
```

Sockets

Julia supports both types of protocols, namely the UDP as well as TCP. We have already seen the TCP server and how to create a connection with a client in the previous section. However, here we will talk about UDP as well as named pipes, which is yet another functionality that is provided by Julia.

Julia has two very important modules which have most of the code for the sockets and servers:

- `socket.jl`
- `streams.jl`

Coming back to how UDP behaves, **user datagram protocol** (**UDP**). Unlike TCP, it doesn't make sure of the delivery of packets to the destination and hence can allow for some data packets' loss. We can easily make a UDP socket in Julia using the following function:

```
julia> u = UDPSocket()
UDPSocket(init)

julia> bind(u, IPv4(127,0,0,1), 5001)
true

julia> v = UDPSocket()
UDPSocket(init)

julia> bind(v, IPv4(127,0,0,1), 5002)
true
```

Here, we have created two `UDPSockets`, one bound with port `5001` and the other with `5002`. The process of using a `bind` call over a socket is actually part of the process called binding, where a `UDPSocket` is bound or, in other words, attached to a specific IP port.

Once we are done creating `UDPSockets`, let's have a round of sending and receiving signals. Take a look at this code snippet:

```julia
julia> send(v,ip"127.0.0.1",5001,"Hey there!")

julia> msg = recv(u)
10-element Array{UInt8,1}:
 0x48
 0x65
 0x79
 0x20
 0x74
 0x68
 0x65
 0x72
 0x65
 0x21

julia> String(msg)
"Hey there!"

julia> close(u)

julia> close(v)
```

So as we can see, the `send` function takes in `UDPSocket` and helps in sending a message over the socket to `host:port`. In the other socket, we receive the message sent to you by using the `recv` function. As this is a `UInt8` type, we need to convert it to string to get the actual value send, that is, `"Hey There!"`. Once all the communication gets over, the sockets can now be closed successfully.

Creating packages

Every language in the current programming ecosystem comes with a set of built-in packages. Some languages have an extensive list of built-in packages for performing most common operations such as basic IO and HTTP servers, while some prefer to have a bare minimum of built-ins which can be extended later as per their usage.

But, what exactly is a package? In the easiest terms, its a self-contained collection of well-tested code that can be used by other parts of the program or the application. The purpose might be to enhance the already existing functionality, or to create the base for an upcoming new feature, or simply might be a set of utilities, which can be used across the program.

Julia provides an easy way to create a package. But, how should you start creating one from scratch? The first step will obviously be to name the package you want to create. That may sound simple, but the Julia community is very particular about its naming conventions, and hence, following are some directives and guidelines for naming your package correctly.

Guidelines for package naming

Package naming is very important when it comes to making sure that it correctly showcases its abilities and the reason to be used for. Here are some points that needs to be taken care of the following:

- The package naming should be such that it should be easy enough for people coming from various backgrounds (like maths or physics) to understand clearly what the package is all about. Hence, the use of *jargon* should be kept in check.
- The name *Julia* should not be used while naming the package. The biggest reason for this is that it's obvious that the package will be used by the language's users; on the other hand, it might also mislead that the package is somehow related to the language's creators.
- Packages that are usually wrappers around other packages should be named after those. For instance, a package around the GitHub API would be named `github.jl`.

Generating a package

After we are done choosing the right name for our package, we move on to actually creating one. Generating a package is one of the simplest things which can be done if compared to other programming languages.

In Julia version 0.6, to generate a package inside the REPL, you will have to install an additional package named `PkgDev` which can be easily installed and used as given in the following command.

```
julia> Pkg.add("PkgDev")
julia> using PkgDev
```

For the sake of testing, I am going to give my package the name `TestPackage`. Let's begin generating the package now:

```
julia> PkgDev.generate("TestPackage","MIT")
INFO: Initializing TestPackage repo:
/Users/rlakhanpal/.julia/v0.6/TestPackage
```

```
INFO: Generating LICENSE.md
INFO: Generating README.md
INFO: Generating src/TestPackage.jl
INFO: Generating test/runtests.jl
INFO: Generating REQUIRE
INFO: Generating .gitignore
INFO: Generating .travis.yml
INFO: Generating appveyor.yml
INFO: Generating .codecov.yml
INFO: Committing TestPackage generated files
```

As you may have observed, the package PkgDev has a method named generate, which can be used to pass on a package name along with a license. However, there are lots of other optional parameters too that can be passed along with the name and license:

```
julia> methods(PkgDev.generate)
# 1 method for generic function "generate":
generate(pkg::AbstractString, license::AbstractString; force, authors,
config, path, travis, appveyor, coverage)
```

Note: In the versions prior to Julia 0.5, that is, in Julia 0.4 and lower, the PkgDev package isn't available. Instead, you may directly use the following command to accomplish the same results: Pkg.generate("TestPackage","MIT")

Summary

In this chapter, we talked in detail about the things that make Julia stand out as a different language from all other modern-day programming languages, and some features that it derives from the already existing ones. However, during the journey, we got to know about Julia internals and how to improve Julia programming performance. We talked in detail about some of the tips and tricks for hassle-free coding, along with a detailed overview of Julia's standard library. Going further down one level, we explored what the internals of LLVM and JIT were. Toward the end of the chapter, we explained how to achieve parallel programming and create TCP sockets and servers along with creating a package in Julia.

With this, we have come to the end of this book. We have tried our best out to give you a good and detailed explanation of topics that relate closely to Julia and its ecosystem.

Index

www.ingramcontent.com/pod-product-compliance
Lightning Source LLC
LaVergne TN
LVHW081517050326
832903LV00025B/1517